How To
Dotcom

How To Dotcom

Robert McGarvey

Entrepreneur Press
2445 McCabe Way, Irvine, CA 92614

Managing Editor: Marla Markman
Book Design: Sylvia H. Lee
Copy Editor: Julie Flick
Production Editor: Megan Reilly
Cover Design: Mark Kozak
Production Designers: Mia H. Ko, Marlene Natal
Illustrator: Scott Pollack
Indexer: Alta Indexing Service

This publication is designed to provide accurate and authoritative information in regard to the subject matter covered. It is sold with the understanding that the publisher is not engaged in rendering legal, accounting or other professional services. If legal advice or other expert assistance is required, the services of a competent professional person should be sought.

ISBN 1-891984-18-7

Library Of Congress Cataloging-in-Publication Data
McGarvey, Robert.
How to dotcom: a step-by-step guide to e-commerce/by Robert McGarvey.
   p. cm.
Includes index.
ISBN 1-891984-18-7
1. Electronic commerce. I.Title.
HF5548.32 .M3778 2000
658.8'4--dc21

                                                    00-010932
Printed in Canada
09 08 07 06 05 04 03 02 01 00   10 9 8 7 6 5 4 3 2 1

ACKNOWLEDGEMENTS

Thanks for making this book come to be is owed to so many, but high on the list are the editors at *Entrepreneur* magazine who have for many years given me tasty assignments covering the Internet, and big thanks are owed to Rieva, the two Marias, Karen Axelton, Janean, Peggy, Marla, and, for copyediting this manuscript, Julie Flick.

Special thanks are owed Babs S. Harrison for being smart and beautiful.

And gratitude, too, is owed my parents: Robert McGarvey, a career journalist who taught me more about reporting than I ever recognized during his lifetime; and Laura McGarvey, who gave me all I needed to get as intelligent as I could become.

TABLE OF CONTENTS

PREFACE

In 1994, during an interview, Stewart Alsop (then an influential tech editor, now a venture capitalist) told me, "Get on the Web—that's where the excitement is."

Huh? I'd been using e-mail since 1988 when I signed up with General Electric's Genie online service. Mainly I used Genie for checking out prices for airplane tickets (via the incredibly cumbersome Sabre system) or sometimes stock market movements. It was a toy, and not a very interesting one.

A few years later I migrated to CompuServe—same toy, but with somewhat better e-mail capabilities and message boards—then to AOL. Sometime in '94 AOL "discovered" the Internet and began promoting various Net tools to members: FTP (file transfer protocol) and Archie (a file search tool). Boy, was this Internet stuff boring and truly useless! Sure, I could use Archie to find the faculty roster at some irrelevant Virginia college, but so what?

Then Alsop explained what the buzz was about the Web, a graphical Internet that was invented, sort of, by Tim Berners-Lee in 1991 when he posted a little program on the Internet that allowed creation of hyperlinks. The Web languished, though, until 1993, when a group of students working in a University of Illinois computer lab cobbled up Mosaic, the first browser that allowed a truly graphical look at the Web.

Whoosh! The race was on. The Internet, founded in 1969 with a Defense Department-sponsored linking of four university computers but until '93 merely a plaything for super-nerds, was ready to go prime time.

So I did as the man suggested, got a version of Mosaic, and I was hooked. I immediately knew this was going to be big, really big. I had no idea a Priceline loomed before us, but I did know that suddenly we had in our hands a communications tool like no other. "The Web lets everybody be a publisher," Steve Wolff, an Internet pioneer who now works at Cisco Systems, told me. The Web lets us communicate in ways previously unimagined. Not only can everybody be a publisher, but an international audience is within easy reach. Suddenly, the Web emerged as a platform that would forever change how business would be done.

Not that anybody anticipated what was in store when Mosaic hit the streets: "When the Net was invented, nobody envisioned a Yahoo or an eBay, but that's the way technology is," says Barry Leiner, director of the Research Institute for Advanced Computer Science (www.riacs.edu), a NASA-funded laboratory for tinkering with the outer limits of computer science. "Nobody saw that the automobile would spawn shopping malls and suburban sprawl, and with the Internet nobody saw what would happen as information became more accessible."

It's been an incredible few years. Whoever would have thought that a Yahoo—begun as a project by some Stanford graduate school geeks—would eventually have a stock market capitalization of around $100 billion (that's how much all the shares are worth)? And not too long ago, a guy was jawboning with his girlfriend about her mania for collecting Pez dispensers, when poof—eBay arrived on the scene, reaching a market cap north of $20 billion.

Or consider Pete Ellis, a down-and-out car dealer who'd watched his Orange County, California, dealerships go bankrupt. Ellis was in his condo and—with little else to do—was playing with his wife's computer. He signed onto Prodigy, looked around, and a light bulb began to go off. Everybody hates buying cars, thought Ellis, and as a onetime dealer, he also knew many dealers despise the slime that shapes so many of the industry's traditional selling techniques. What if, somehow, buyers could buy new wheels on the Net? What if? Shazam, Autobytel was born (market cap above $200 million), and selling cars has never been the same.

As Miranda gushes near the close of Shakespeare's *The Tempest*, "How beauteous mankind is! O brave new world, that has such people in't!"

Where is your place in this "brave new world?" Nowadays, the answer is entirely yours to write because, in the Internet economy, everything is different. Really. And forever.

Surf's Up: Riding The Web To [Riches]

t's the fast track to money. Dotcom your business and, voila, you're on the road to millions, maybe billions—just look at Yahoo, eBay and Priceline. Except it's not that easy; not easy at all. For every dotcom business that flourishes, hundreds— maybe thousands—go bust. What does it take to build a dotcom that will succeed? Read this book and you'll know because in these pages you'll find recipes for success, roadmaps that pinpoint the hazards, and dozens of interviews with dotcom builders who have cashed in.

What separates the winners from the losers? So many dotcoms are simply stupid. Poor ideas are poorly executed, poorly marketed and poorly funded. Of course they'll fail.

Worse, the bar for succeeding has been raised dramatically higher. In some cases, launching a national, full-scale consumer-oriented site today may require more than $100 million to cover marketing, hardware, software and staffing costs. Gulp! That's a big leap from the graduate school project days that gave rise to Yahoo.

Low-budget Web sites are still launching—and making it to the big-time—but the demands for technical polish and ingenuity keep rising ever higher. Don't think there is no longer a place for low-budget sites. The possibilities of success remain enticing, even when wallets are thin—if your ideas are smart and your execution persistent. But the one inescapable fact is this: It's war on the monitors, and more Web sites will die than will be victors. Which will you be?

The aim of this book is to give you the tools and knowledge you will need to emerge among the victors. In these pages, you'll find the soup to nuts, the A to Z of taking your idea through funding, building partnerships, launch, getting more funding, winning eyeballs, and laughing all the way to the bank. This is not a technical book. It's a book about business, consumer psychology, and even sex (because it's sex sites that first proved people would use credit cards online).

The Web is not about technology; not anymore. The Web is a mass medium. And there can be no denying that fact when AOL (written off as dead just a few years ago because its phone lines were always busy) buys media giant Time Warner—vivid, undeniable proof that the Web has come of age and that the Internet is now about content, service and new ways to communicate. Who knows (or cares) how television works? There is no more reason to know or care how the Web works, or even how Web sites work. Do you have to know how to build a cash register to open a storefront? All you need to know to build a Web site is there for the taking, and it's easy.

We'll tell you what you need and where to get it, and for hard-core do-it-yourselfers, there's even a chapter on building your own Web site. Either way, there's no longer a reason to say "I don't get this Internet stuff." You have to get it, or get out of business.

Some words about how this book is organized: Interspersed among the chapters are "Cheap Tricks," mini-interviews with low-budget Web site builders. Since some time will have passed between when these portraits were assembled and when you have this book in your hand, there will doubtless have been casualties among the low-budget sites, but learn from how these thinly funded site-builders put their online businesses together. The book also features interviews, called "e-Chats," with CEOs of big-budget name-brand sites—among them Drugstore.com, StarMedia Network, OneTravel.com, Autobytel.com, Guru.com and WorldRes.com.

You'll also find tip boxes designed to hammer home key points. Four kinds of tips are featured:

○ *Smart Tip:* bright ideas you want to remember

○ *Beware!:* pitfalls and potholes you want to avoid

○ *Budget Watcher:* money-saving ideas and practices

○ *Opportunity Knocks:* pointers on where to look for online opportunities

Here's the promise of this book: If you need to know it to do business online, you'll find it between these covers. Read on to find out how to make your Internet dreams reality.

How To Be A Millionaire: The Internet [Gold] Rush

This is it—your chance to strike it very rich because suddenly, the Internet has changed all the rules. For a half-century, the big players in business, from IBM to Exxon, dominated the game, leaving little room for newcomers to move to the top of the heap. Then in 1994 a little start-up named Netscape introduced a Web browser, and the race for cash was on. Amazon, eToys, Wine.com, e-Trade, Motley Fool, ChannelPoint, Monster.com—today, these are billion-dollar businesses, but where were they five years ago? Out of nowhere these companies, and hundreds more, have emerged to challenge the gods of commerce. They are succeeding because the new rules favor small companies that are flexible, smart, tough and ultra-quick to react to changing market conditions.

Chew on these numbers: Information technology consulting firm GartnerGroup predicts that sales in business-to-business e-commerce will hit a staggering $2.7 trillion in 2004. By 2005, online sales of consumables (from prescriptions to groceries and wine) will reach $119 billion, according to consulting group Active Media. And in the 1999 Christmas shopping season, consumers spent $7 billion online, with 90 percent of the buyers saying they were largely satisfied with the experience, according to Jupiter Communications, a firm that tracks trends on the Web.

The Internet is for real, and in the 21st century, if you're not on it, you're not in business. That is today's reality byte.

A New Set Of Rules

On the Web, the advantage is yours—it belongs to the entrepreneur. Why? Consider Compaq. It makes fine computers; maybe no better than its competitors, but certainly no worse. So why has it been stumbling while a comparative upstart like Dell has soared into market leadership? Dell long ago made the leap into full-steam Web retailing. It yanked its merchandise out of retail stores and threw the dice, betting the company's future on direct selling (via catalogs and the Web) to corporations and individuals. Compaq, meanwhile, has faltered at every step because it doesn't want to alienate its established retail channels, convinced they would be irked if suddenly the same computers were available for less on the Internet. So Compaq dithers, and in that indecision it loses momentum and leadership while upstarts grab market share.

Think of the Web only as a **new** channel and you miss the **threat** and the promise of the **Internet**.

The Web is both a new distribution channel and a new way of doing business. Don't miss either part of that statement. Think of the Web only as a new channel—a different way of putting products and services in front of customers—and you miss the threat and the promise of the Internet, which is that it will utterly change how you do business.

For one thing, the Web is ruthless in the squeeze it puts on pricing. Fat and waste have to go, and good riddance, because many large companies (and too many small companies) have grown comfortably wealthy by exacting indefensible margins out of the retail process. No more. The Web stomps margins flat, and to make profits, companies have to rethink where their dollars will be earned. Big companies (most of them) have responded to these new rules by shutting their eyes and praying the moment will pass. (Think of the big banks that treat customers terribly, pay laughable interest rates and are forever hiking fees. Most are doomed to be dinosaurs in the 21st century.) All of this is good news for you because it means you've got a wide-open playing field before you.

Better still, the opportunities are unlimited. Would it be wise to go head-to-head against Yahoo or Amazon? Not directly, because these companies are among the few Internet businesses that can legitimately claim to have established major consumer brands. But the Web is so young, possibilities are everywhere. Want proof? Read on for a few amazing stories of Internet success popping up where most people would least expect it.

INSURING SUCCESS

Ken Hollen is chipping away at a number: $54 billion. That's how much is wasted every year by a bureaucratic, bloated, inefficient insurance industry, according to research by investment bank Robertson Stephens Inc. That money is coming out of every pocket in this nation for no good reason, other than that insurance companies just don't get it.

Hollen does get it. As CEO of ChannelPoint (www.channel point.com), a Colorado Springs, Colorado, Internet company, he's created an efficient Web-based marketplace that links insurers with customers and brokers, saving billions of dollars for all of us while pocketing a few billion more for Hollen and his investors. "We have the ability to deliver breakthrough values," says Hollen, whose company has constructed tools that move most insurance transactions onto the Web, where things happen both faster and cheaper than through traditional channels. "We can offer insurance carriers cost reductions of 50 to 90 percent on the administrative side and dramatically improve their customer service. We've already shown we can cut the time involved in case processing from 45 days down to between two and five."

Wow—that's a win-win-win: Insurers win by cutting costs, customers win by reaping some savings and greater efficiency in service, and Hollen wins by earning a profit every time he processes a transaction. And that is exactly what the Internet is about.

ChannelPoint traces its

Smart Tip
Just because a genius shows little interest in your idea, don't quit if you're a believer. Ken Hollen didn't quit, and his ChannelPoint looms as a likely big winner in reinventing the insurance industry.

birth to 1996, when Ken Hollen and his brother, Jim, quit their day jobs to found a little Web start-up, Icon Health, with the mission of making healthcare plan information readily available to members. Within months, Icon Health was snapped up, for an undisclosed amount, by emerging Net giant Healtheon (now Healtheon/WebMD), the brainchild of Net legend Jim Clark, the co-founder of Netscape and, before that, Silicon Graphics. Ken Hollen wasn't enthusiastic about being a part of what was becoming a large company, so he held back rights to insurance company-related software Icon Health had created. Healtheon didn't hesitate to accept that exclusion, and Hollen had the intellectual tools that let him start ChannelPoint.

A Star Is Born

Now, remember just a few lines ago I advised against challenging Yahoo? That only applies to Yahoo's own turf. If you are willing to expand your horizons a little, one entrepreneur discovered, the sky's the limit. Tune into New York City's StarMedia Network (www.starmedia.com), a company co-founded by Fernando Espuelas in 1996 after he quit AT&T because the giant company just wouldn't listen to his idea for building a Web portal aimed at South America. Born in Uruguay, Espuelas knew the Spanish- and Portuguese-speaking world craved Web content in their own languages, but there was little of that to be found anywhere on the Net. Business plan in hand, he marched from venture capitalist to venture capitalist—and always emerged empty-handed. "Many North Americans think '*yo quiero Taco Bell*' is all they need to know about Latin America," he says. "They did not take the idea of an Internet company for Latinos seriously."

With no other funding to be found, Espuelas was forced to use his credit cards, and every month he watched his balance soar higher. Just when it was

> **Beware!**
> Venture capital funding, billions of dollars' worth, is out there—but be prepared for a grilling like you've never had before any check is signed. Never forget that venture capitalists are in business to make money, lots of it, not to speculate on chancy business ideas.

about to be lights out for his dream, Chase Capital Partners (an arm of Chase Manhattan bank) called and said it liked the idea of a Latino portal and wanted to invest $3 million—*if* Espuelas could convince them he was the man to run such an enterprise. "They asked for 60 references," he says. "And they checked them all." Chase liked what it heard and ponied up the cash, and today StarMedia is a leader in a booming South American market as well as a

> If **you** are willing to **expand** your **horizons** a **little**, the sky's the **limit**.

publicly traded company with a market capitalization above $2 billion. Not a bad outcome for a guy on the verge of maxing out his credit cards.

FIGHTING IRISH

Now, what about treading on Amazon territory, a biggie both in books and video? Hop back in time to the Belfast, Northern Ireland, of a few years ago: a war-torn, drab, aging industrial town with no future ahead of it and a past only worth forgetting (its major claim to fame is that the HMS Titanic was built in its shipyards). It's 1998, and three guys, all under age 30, are talking about two things they love—movies and the Net. They wonder, "Why couldn't there be an online store that sold videos?"

You need to keep in mind one technical curiosity: While U.S. VCRs are made to run videotapes in the NTSC format, in the United Kingdom and most of Europe, the prevailing standard is PAL. That's been a nuisance for world travelers (buy a special video in London, and it won't run back home in New Jersey), but for these Belfast boys, it was the key that unlocked a treasure. The big, U.S.-based online video retailers largely ignored PAL tapes, so this was virgin turf.

Still, the lads had virtually no cash and no connections, so what was to be done? They decided to pool a few thousand dollars and build a demo site, just a test to prove what they could do if they had the money. As they cobbled it together, they found themselves liking it more and more. One day, they said, "Why not?" They plugged it in, and BlackStar Videos (www.blackstar.co.uk) was live,

Opportunity Knocks

Always look for niches the Big Boys have neglected—then exploit this opportunity swiftly, before the megacompanies come to their senses. And guess what: There always are such opportunities. Find yours and move fast.

open for business. "We have an impressive degree of arrogance," shrugs Tony Bowden, one of the co-founders.

Then what happened? As customers stumbled in, they loved BlackStar. Word spread. Investment money came in, and, within a year, BlackStar could claim to be the UK's biggest video store. It had beaten Amazon, Virgin, and bunches of others, and now a lucrative IPO (one that doubtless will put tens of millions into the pockets of those Belfast boys) looms as a near certainty.

Incredible stories? You bet, but the Internet is filled with them because—I'll say it again—all the rules are new in the Internet economy. Even the biggest players can be successfully challenged by the upstart who sees an opportunity, then seizes it.

Better yet, the odds are stacked in your favor because you are little. How? When a big company like Toys "R" Us fumbles its e-commerce debut—which it did by disappointing many 1999 holiday season shoppers—it makes headline news. That company has a well-established brand; consumers who shop there, offline or on, come with expectations. When it made hash of its Web storefront, it hurt.

What if you do likewise—dropping a few balls at start-up? Customers don't know you, don't have expectations, and odds are you'll be forgiven. A few years ago, business guru Tom Peters' mantra was that the moment had come for business to practice "Ready, Fire, Aim" because no longer was there latitude to spend months scoping the target. On the Web, too, action counts. Take it—as BlackStar did—and you just may come out way ahead.

SWEET DREAMS

Sometimes even when your dreams aren't so lofty, the Internet can still save the day, as Barbara McCann found out. She and her husband, Jim, own The Chocolate Vault, a hometown

The e-Commerce Quiz Click

Think you're ready to become a "Netpreneur"? Prove it. Before moving onto the next chapter, take this quiz. Answers are "true" or "false."

1. I'm comfortable in a game where tomorrow's rules are invented the day after tomorrow.
2. I see inefficiencies—waste and delay—in many current business practices.
3. I'm willing to delay this year's profits to potentially make more money next year.
4. I know how to size up customers I've never seen or talked with.
5. The Net excites me—I honestly like surfing around and seeing what's new.
6. I can live with thin margins.
7. Customer satisfaction is the most important thing a business can deliver.
8. I'm not afraid of battling titans.
9. I see opportunity where others see risks.
10. I'm willing to work harder and smarter than I ever could have imagined possible.

Scoring: Guess what—"true" is always the right answer for any Netpreneur. But you knew that already because you are ready to compete on this merciless playing field.

store in Tecumseh, Michigan, a village about 60 miles west of Detroit. They'd watched traffic—and customers—veer away from little towns, and they'd watched their cash flow dry to a trickle. "We were on the verge of closing our shop," says McCann. Then she decided to give the Internet a whirl.

On a skimpy budget—a few thousand dollars—she personally built her Web site, www.chocolatevault.com, and then she watched an amazing thing happen. "People from all over the country found us, and they started buying our chocolates!" she says.

She doesn't have the money to buy major advertising space, so she meticulously maintains an e-mail list and regularly sends a newsletter to anyone who signs up. The newsletter is filled with chatty news about chocolate and special product pricing, and its flavor is scrupulously homespun, much like Barbara McCann herself. People read it, and many click into the site to make impulse buys of pecan clusters and other goodies.

> **Budget Watcher**
> Think small, and a Net business's operating costs are nigh unto nil—meaning fast profits can come your way if you've watched your costs going in.

Will The Chocolate Vault rise to the top and challenge the biggies in that space, such as Godiva and others? Never, says Barbara, who knows her budget and her ambition. But the big miracle is that "the Internet has been a lifesaver for us," says McCann. "We would have closed our shop without it."

Set the scale of your Internet ambitions—dream large in the way of Ken Hollen or Fernando Espuelas, or dream on a more diminutive scale like Barbara and Jim McCann—because there is no "right" approach to the Internet. Good, steady money can be earned by strictly local players who open on the Net and find a stream of global business pouring in. Or big bucks may be yours if you invent a new eBay or Monster.com.

CHAPTER 2

The Commandments: [10 Reasons] You Should Be Online

Need convincing that the Web is the place for your business to be? It would be no sweat to list 25 reasons, even 50 to 100, but to get you started, here are 10 reasons why you've got to be online.

1. *It's cheap.* There is no more inexpensive way to open up a business than to mount a Web site. While you could spend up to many millions of dollars to get started, low-budget Web sites (started with as little as $100) remain viable businesses.

2. *You cut your order fulfillment costs.* Handling orders by phone is expensive. Ditto for incoming mail orders. There's no more efficient—cheap, fast, accurate—way to process orders than via a Web site.

3. *Your catalog is always current.* A print catalog can cost big bucks, and nobody wants to order a reprint just to change one price or to correct a few typos. A Web site can be updated in minutes.

4. *High printing and mailing costs are history.* Your customers can download any information you want them to have from your Web site. Sure, you'll still want to print some materials, but lots now can be distributed via the Web.

5. *You cut staffing costs.* A Web site can be a low-manpower operation.

6. *You can stay open 24 hours daily.* And you'll still get your sleep because your site will be open even when your eyes are closed.

7. *You're in front of a global audience.* Ever think what you sell might be a big hit in Scotland or China, but feel clueless about how to penetrate foreign markets? The Web is your answer because it truly is a borderless marketplace. Watch your site log, and you'll see visitors streaming in from Australia, New Zealand, Japan, Malaysia—wherever there are computers and phone lines.

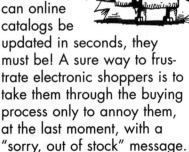

Beware!
Not only can online catalogs be updated in seconds, they must be! A sure way to frustrate electronic shoppers is to take them through the buying process only to annoy them, at the last moment, with a "sorry, out of stock" message. Never do that. If merchandise is out of stock, clearly note that early in the buying process. Customers can accept inventory problems, but they will never accept wasting their time.

8. *There are no city permits and no hassles.* It could change, but in most of the country small Web businesses can be run without permits and with little government involvement. As you expand and add employees, you will start to bump into laws and regulations, but it certainly is nice to be able to kick off a business without first filling out reams of city and state forms.

9. *There are no angry customers in your face.* You cannot ignore unhappy customers in any business; in fact, how well you deliver customer service will go far toward determining how successful you are. But at least with a Web business you'll never have to stand eyeball-to-eyeball with a screamer.

Budget Watcher
On a really tight budget? Offer stock and options to potential new hires and consultants in lieu of high salaries. Silicon Valley is filled with millionaires who have struck it rich with dotcom options.

10. *It's easy to get your message out.* Between your Web site and your smart use of e-mail, you'll have complete control over when and how your message goes out. You cannot beat a Web site for its immediacy, and when a site is done well, it's hard to top its ability to grab and hold the attention of potential customers.

You have other reasons for wanting a Web business? Fair enough. The key is, know your reasons, know the benefits of doing business online, and be persistent through the launch. This isn't always an easy road to take, but it definitely is a road that has transported many to riches, with much less upfront cash, hassle and time required than similar offline businesses. And that's a tough value proposition to top.

CHAPTER 3

Hang It Up: Dashing [Dotcom] Dreams

Read the waves of glum news of Internet hopes gone awry that have washed over us in recent months, and you'd be forgiven for thinking dotcom dreams are just another route to bankruptcy. Probably the scariest finding came from Forrester Research, which flatly predicted (in a report issued in April 2000) that "weak financials, increasing competitive pressures, and investor flight will drive most of today's dotcom retailers out of business by 2001." Yikes, that's rotten news to read over morning coffee. But is it news that should get you thinking about new business directions? Should you tear up your dotcom business plan?

Probably not. Forrester's sourness may be on target, but it's aimed primarily at the heavily funded blockbuster dotcoms that entered the scene spending wildly (buying everything from Super Bowl advertising minutes to multipage spreads in *People* magazine and multiyear exposure deals on AOL) in a madcap race for "mind share," or customer awareness. The big trouble: Many of these dotcoms had little (often no) cash flow and only investment money to spend. As those dollars began to run out, wise heads started looking at the outflow and the income of these dotcom enterprises—and very quickly realized the businesses as presently conceived could never prosper. There is no way around the fact that when you consistently spend much more than you bring in, sooner or later you will find yourself with angry creditors beating down your door.

Case in point: DrKoop.com's auditor issued a statement wherein it questioned how DrKoop could remain "a going concern," which is polite accountantspeak for "the money is going to run out." Whether DrKoop will or won't belly-flop, I cannot say.

I can say I've spoken with the company's CEO, Don Hackett, who's a smart, realistic businessman, so I wouldn't count it out just yet. But DrKoop does have stark imbalances between outgo and income that would be enough to raise any accountant's eyebrows.

All of this surely is grim, but it doesn't have to be the end of your dreams. One area of impact: Venture capitalists and angels lately have gotten skittish—and far more selective about where they will put their money. Raising money has always been tough (despite magazine and newspaper stories that suggest the opposite), but in the near term it will get tougher still as VCs and angels digest losses they've suffered on their dotcom investments.

> ### Budget Watcher
> When you start with little funding, do as small businesses have always done—operate on a shoestring. Dell Computers, for instance, got its start in a dorm room. Apple started in a garage. Your quarters needn't be that humble, but never, ever spend money you don't have to for the sake of "making an impression." If anything, it's the wrong impression you'll make because funders aren't looking to put money in the hands of CEOs who spend like drunken sailors. A little cheapness is always a good thing for a start-up.

You likely aren't a richly funded dotcom and needn't sit around worrying about the day the VCs show up at the door demanding some kind of return. So breathe normally—but don't make the mistakes the dotcoms that are crashing and burning have made. Like what?

○ *Bad balance-sheet math:* At no point did these companies generate financial statements that indicated any reasonable relationship between income and expenses. And yet they spent wildly, renting expensive offices in Silicon Valley and New York's Silicon Alley, hiring deep staffs (and often paying salaries upwards of six figures for minor positions), and buying fantastic exposure in ads of every medium. No genuinely small start-up could long afford these lush business habits. Sure, every start-up has a day or a week or a few months when income lags way behind outgo, but at least the math makes some kind of sense, and in the lean period, spending, too, is lean. You don't need the ritzy office, the high-powered law firm, or the Stanford MBA employees, so you should be able to keep your expenses in some kind of rational alignment with income.

○ *No revenue model:* The core question that's supposed to be asked of dotcom start-ups is, What's your revenue model? This is shorthand for, How do you envision bringing in income? What will be your revenue streams? Potential investors will ask this, as will would-be employees, partners, and anybody thinking about commingling a financial future with your dotcom. Strangely, however, even when the question has gotten asked, the questioners have typically accepted formulaic answers. In the past, dotcoms have vaguely explained their revenue model involved a mix of ad dollars and e-commerce, and in most cases, the answer was accepted. It was a mistake because, as the failing dotcoms are proving, nobody had ever really put flesh on the revenue models.

Never open a business without understanding your source of revenue. This seems so elemental, but in the heady days when vaporous businesses such as Yahoo and eBay quickly snagged multibillion-dollar market caps, so many people abandoned this axiom.

Never open a business **without** understanding your **source** of **revenue**.

Will your predictions be on target? Probably not. They may even be wildly wrong, but that doesn't necessarily mean they didn't serve a good purpose. Simply articulating realistic, workable revenue models is good discipline. In practice, businesses usually evolve in ways the founders didn't anticipate—a fact that is all the more true in the wild and woolly Net—so early drafts of revenue models likely will get discarded, fast. But always know where, approximately, money will originate.

Incidentally, the unspoken revenue model of many dotcoms apparently has been additional rounds of funding—either from VCs or public markets—but, at the end of the day, those spigots will get turned off. Why? Read on.

○ *No clearly defined exit strategy.* Every well-conceived start-up comes equipped with an exit strategy for investors. What this means is, how will investors get their money out of the business and when? Founders with hands-on roles in the business probably don't need to know their exit strategy, but angels, VCs and such do want to know how and when they will get their money back. What are possible exit strategies?

1. *Going public:* a prime choice for many dotcoms

2. *Getting bought by a bigger fish:* not as popular as going public, but attractive when public markets turn turbulent

3. *Bringing in new investors to buy out others:* another option, but rarely used in the years of Net mania, probably because later-round investors have been unwilling to pay the inflated prices sought by early investors

There is no saying which exit strategy is best, but what can be said is that no CEO needs anxious investors calling every few moments to ask when they might cash out. And that happens all too often when there's been a lack of clarity—even realism—about the investment. This means in early talks with investors (even if it's your folks who put up the money), be honest about how you might see them getting their money out and when. Be as pessimistic as possible. Sure, you might spook investors, but better to do it now than have them hassling you as you're trying to build the business.

Smart Tip

You don't need a fancy business plan—it's probably a waste of time and money—but you do need to set down on paper the basics of your business. As the business evolves, and as the fundamental assumptions change, take out the business plan and update it. Are you still on track to hit your targets?

Keep it simple and practical, and a business plan becomes both a road map and a litmus test for the success of your business. Use it to stay on course.

○ *Building market share to the detriment of the business:* Market share is not God, although CEOs of the many failing dotcoms who pursued a strategy of building market share at any cost may have you believe otherwise. Look through the financial filings of many of the best-known dot-coms, and what's stunning is that a common practice is selling merchandise for less than they paid for it. Pay $300 to a wholesaler for handheld computers, and no matter how many you sell for $250, you won't do anything but go broke.

The **only** way to long-term **survival** is to **price** rationally to **begin** with.

Yet a wacky mantra infected Silicon Valley that held that somehow, market share was the end-all. Sure, you will get market share when you sell items below cost because nobody can compete. But when pressures build and you have to tweak prices up to survive, how much of that precious market share will you lose? Lots, you can bet, which is why the only way to long-term survival is to price rationally to begin with. It makes sense to use loss-leader pricing on an item or two if that strategy generates orders that in a short-term horizon will produce profits. But it makes no sense whatsoever to consistently sell goods at below-cost prices. How can anybody wonder why so many dotcoms have nearly slid to extinction with such practices?

○ *Ignoring stakeholders:* Who has a stake in your business? Investors, your community, your employees, management, your vendors and your customers. Long debates can explode around attempts to prioritize these stakeholders—whose stake is meatiest or weakest?—but probably the best strategy for most dotcoms is to assume that all stakeholders carry about equal weight (except for your community, which, in the case of an Internet start-up, likely carries no weight at all).

To succeed, businesses want to satisfy all stakeholders. That doesn't mean all will always get what they want (stakeholders quite commonly are in conflict with each other, and a management task is seeing that everybody gets enough to feel happy), but it does mean you need to keep aware of your stakeholders, their wants, and what you're delivering. You won't last long if investors, employees, management, vendors or customers get and stay cranky. Failed dotcoms often had little or no awareness that any stakeholders existed (at least any that were not on Wall Street), but stakeholders always exist and will always get their due.

○ *Forgetting what industry you're in:* Guess what—your online store is still a store, meaning you are competing in a retail universe. Yet many CEOs of stumbling dotcoms talk as though they are in any industry but retail, throwing terms around like new media, content and consulting. Never fool yourself about your industry.

○ *More ego than profits:* Not only did many CEOs of now deeply troubled dotcoms forget what industry they were in, some seemed actually to forget that they were in business at all, and that the essence of a business is to make money from revenue—not from bedazzled stock market speculators and frenzied angel investors pouring cash into the till. The sad fact about many failed dotcoms is that they could have been successful—maybe not quite on the lavish scale hoped for by the founders, but profitable nonetheless. And they blew it by forgetting that, in the end, business is business. While it might be fun to make it on the cover of a magazine, it's ultimately more fun to be on top of a steady stream of black ink (and it's no fun at all to manage a business that's dripping red ink).

The message for you: Don't be discouraged by the stumblings of the name-brand dotcoms. They had it coming. That sounds cruel, but really, they did. You can avoid their mistakes and thereby create a very different outcome for your business.

Beware!
Of course you will start off in the red—that's the norm. But when can you honestly project seeing black ink? You have got to know that answer and work hard to make it a realistic forecast. So many dotcoms are now being shut down because they never had honest forecasts of when investors could expect to see black ink. Don't let it happen to you.

CHAPTER 4

Dotcom Or Bust: Should You [Shutter] Your Bricks-And-Mortar Store?

Should you shut down your store to focus exclusively on online retailing? That's a question many small-business owners are now chewing on. On the one hand, all the buzz is about the Web and its many opportunities. On the other hand, the question that has to be asked is, Can the Web and offline, traditional retailing co-exist?

E-tailer Sherry Rand has a definite opinion on the subject. "The smartest thing I've done in business is shutting down my store and going exclusively as an online retailer," she says. "Now I have a really neat business. I love it." Rand, 53, has an online store that sells one thing, and one thing only—gear for cheerleaders. You want pompoms in various styles and colors? You want megaphones for leading cheers? Then you want to know about Pom Express (www.pomexpress.com), where Rand has conducted e-business for two years since she shut the doors on her bricks-and-mortar.

"Online I don't have to carry the great overhead of a store, and from a quaint town in northern Massachusetts, I'm selling globally," says Rand. "We get lots of orders from Europe, where cheerleading is really picking up." Rand, herself a cheerleader "from fourth grade until I graduated from college," sold cheerleader supplies as a manufacturers representative until she opened her own store. Now that she's operating solely on the Web, she says, "This is a great niche. And on the Internet, I can conduct business wherever I want to be."

MOVING OUT

Sounds good—good enough to persuade you to dotcom? The temptations are potent. Close a bricks-and-mortar operation, go strictly cyber, and whoosh, you've distanced yourself from monthly rent payments and dealing face-to-face with grumpy customers, not to mention positioned your business to sell globally. At least that's what it seems like in theory. But can you count on it happening for you?

"The decision to dotcom has to be taken on a case-by-case basis," warns Barbara Reilly, an analyst with information technology consulting firm GartnerGroup. "There's no one formula that will work for all businesses, all the time."

What's more, for every dotcom that thrives, there are more that flop, says Mark Layton, author of *.coms or .bombs* (Profits in e-Business, LLC), an analysis of the difficulties in mounting an effective e-commerce site. "Many dotcoms will become dot bombs—they'll fail," says Layton. "Online or offline, you need a sustainable business model. If you don't have that, you don't have a business."

HAVING IT BOTH WAYS

Experiencing second thoughts about burning the lease on your storefront and going strictly virtual? Know that there's another approach to the Internet, one that's not all or nothing. Case in point: Wine Country Inc. (www.winecountryonline.com), the online complement to a Winter Park, Florida, wine store, both owned by 25-year-old Adam Chilvers. Built around the tasty proposition that all wines it sells are $19 or under and all are rated 85 or higher by a prestigious publication (such as *Wine Spectator*), both the storefront (opened in November '98) and the online store (launched a month later) are profitable, according to Chilvers. "Doing business on the Web is a dream," he says. "The costs are very low."

But he has no intention of shutting down his B&M, for a flock of reasons. For starters, an online operation still needs some real-world warehousing for merchandise such as his, and the B&M provides that. But it's the second reason that is the clincher: "On the site we sell to many customers outside our area,

Opportunity Knocks

A big consumer worry about e-tailers: that these cyberstorefronts are fly-by-night scams. When you have a B&M storefront, you also have solidity in the minds of consumers. Don't hide your B&M. Put up a photo of it on your Web site! And definitely show the street address. Bingo, you're an established retailer, and consumer worries will vanish.

but we also get many locals coming into our store with shopping lists they've printed out on the Web," says Chilvers. For those customers, the combination of the Web site and the store offers a great convenience—they hunt for wines they want online, at midnight or 6 a.m., then they can get in and out of the B&M in a matter of minutes. "I'm happy with how the store and the Web site are working together to build this business," says Chilvers. "It's a good combination for me."

DOUBLE VISION

Still, isn't this dual-channel strategy an unnecessary complication that forces an entrepreneur to focus on two distinctly different venues? The experts don't think so, and, in fact, many point to it as *the* way to go forward into the next century. "There are tremendous advantages to be had by leveraging Net sales with a B&M," says Bart Weitz, a marketing professor at the University of Florida, Gainesville. Case in point: "You can use the store to promote the Web site, for instance," and that means printing the URL—Web address—on bags, sales slips and advertising fliers. That can be a big step in overcoming the obstacle facing every dotcom today. "It's gotten very expensive to attract people to a site," says Weitz. "Stand-alone sites incur very high marketing expenses because they have to spend the money to get eyeballs."

"A B&M can be a billboard for your Web site," adds Boston University e-commerce professor Bruce Weinberg, who points to clothier The Gap as a for-instance. It already has massive brand awareness, and whenever a customer walks in—even walks by—a storefront, there's a reinforcement of the URL, www.gap.com. Your business might not be a Gap, but even so, says Weinberg, the fact that you're in a physical location with signage and various advertising campaigns to promote the store means you're also building awareness for a Web site.

Another argument in favor of a dual-channel strategy: "Different consumers want different things," says Bill Gartner, a business professor at the University of Southern California in Los Angeles. "Some customers want the kind of personal interaction that can only happen in a traditional retail setting. For others, it's simpler to log onto the Net. The smart, consumer-oriented business makes it easy to buy, no matter the customer's preferences."

WHO'S MINDING THE STORE?

But the big, worrisome question is, Isn't all retailing heading to the Web anyway? Just last year, that was the buzz, but nowadays—with more dotcoms struggling and few breaking through to profitability—a kind of cautious sobriety has taken hold. Explains Jackie Goforth, an e-commerce specialist with consulting firm PriceWaterhouseCoopers: "There are certain merchandise categories that will be slow to succeed online— women's fashion, for instance. Shoppers will want to try the clothing on, to touch it. With other kinds of merchandise, commodities like consumer electronics, online retailing is the way to go."

Smart Tip
What about returns? They are proving to be a real hassle in online retailing—both to e-tailers and to consumers—and that's where e-tailers with B&M storefronts have a big advantage because consumers who want to return products can simply take them to the storefront. Smart e-tailers stress this perk, so if it's true for you, flaunt it!

Put bluntly, some types of businesses are going to have a tough time prospering if they are not online. Cases in point: bookstores, consumer electronics sellers, and travel agencies. Margins are getting squeezed ever lower as hard-charging dotcoms fight for market share by offering ever-lower pricing, and that means it will only get tougher to succeed in a B&M context. But other

Fortunetelling

Click

Want an easy rule of thumb for assessing how your business might fare online? University of Maryland business professor Jonathan Palmer gives the three factors that shine a green light on this decision:

○ You sell a product line that can be delivered economically and conveniently.

○ You have a desire to market to customers outside your own geographical location and a product with broad appeal.

○ There are significant economic advantages involved in going online.

Chew especially hard on points one and two because if they are on your side, the profits implied in the third point likely will follow.

A fourth decision factor just might be, Can you economically draw customers to your site? Chasing a mass market—and going belly-to-belly against Amazon, Drugstore.com, Priceline, and the like—means you had better bring a seven- or eight-figure advertising-marketing budget to the table to keep up with your competitors. But the good news is that there is still plenty of room for thinly funded players who have targeted shrewd niches and a solid business plan. The experts agree: Those are tomorrow's dotcom companies that will thrive.

---

types of businesses—from furniture sellers to clothiers—just may find the going stays smooth in bricks-and-mortar stores. "Some products are ideal for online; others just work better in a B&M," says Jonathan Palmer, a business professor at the University of Maryland in College Park.

Worried about being a merchandiser in an endangered category? Don't panic, says Goforth: "We heard that catalogs would put traditional retailers out of business, and it didn't happen. In fact, some catalog retailers eventually backed into opening bricks-and-mortar stores. Now we hear that the Web will put B&Ms out of business, and that, too, probably won't happen."

CHAPTER 5

Site Building 101: [Anyone] Can Build A Web Site—Guaranteed!

What's stopping you from putting up a Web site for your business? A big and persistent hurdle is the belief that doing it is hard, technically demanding work. While that might have been true a couple years ago when the World Wide Web first took flight, Web page authoring no longer is the sole province of propeller heads. Plenty of easy-to-use software is on the market, and a Web newcomer usually can get an initial page up within a few hours. Better still, all of this can be accomplished at a very low cost. "Even the smallest businesses can afford to be on the Web," says Mary Cronin, a business professor at Boston College and editor of *The Internet Strategy Handbook*.

Believe it or not, this is probably the least important chapter in this book. Why? Because putting up a Web page has become so simple, it's scarcely worth mentioning. And if you don't have the time to spare, a small outlay of cash will buy you the services of a local community college student fluent in HTML (hyper text markup language). Web page authoring may be fun for purists, but it is no litmus test of your "right" to be on the Web. You have that right just by claiming it, whether you know beans about HTML authoring or not.

But if you want to do it yourself, this chapter gives step-by-step tips for producing your Web site—from picking the right tools and putting them into use to testing your creation. Set aside just a few hours, follow the steps, and you, too, will be in business on the Web.

KNOW YOUR PURPOSE

The starting point for putting up a Web page is to determine what you want it to do—and know what it likely won't do. The bad news is that you won't get rich quick with a Web site. A very few start-ups have achieved overnight success on the Web—the most notable success being Amazon—but for most, profits remain slim or, in many cases, merely a hope. The Web just isn't the fast track to Easy Street that too many commentators have depicted it to be.

The **Web** lets you serve **customers** in **ways** that would be **unimaginable** in a traditional retail **environment**.

Then why do it? Of course, persistence and ingenuity may eventually be rewarded with profits. But there are other sound reasons for putting up a Web site. Such as? Even if the page is little more than an electronic billboard for your company, it's still a powerful tool for building a business. On the Web, for instance, "distance means nothing," says Jerry White, director of the Caruth Institute of Owner Managed Business at Southern Methodist University in Dallas. A small business in the United States can use the Web as a low-cost tool for reaching customers in other states, even other countries.

The clock, too, no longer matters. "On the Web your business can be open 24 hours a day, seven days a week," says Gail Houck, a consultant and Web strategist. Another reason: The Web lets you serve customers in ways that would be unimaginable in a traditional retail environment. Usually it's easy to offer far deeper product selection, for instance, and—with clear thinking on your side—prices, too, typically can be driven down.

All good reasons? You bet, and you may have many more. Whatever your motivations, the single most important step you can take is this: Define your goals and expectations. Do that, and the rest—including the mechanics of a site's design—will fall into place.

Where so many small businesses (and a few very large ones, too) go wrong is that they haven't taken this clarifying step. The resulting sites are fundamentally confusing because nobody ever took the time to specify their purpose. It's perfectly fine to erect a site that amounts to a company information brochure, but that site cannot be expected to function as a retail platform—and the opposite is also true.

Getting Started

In the not-too-distant past, building a Web page meant hours of laborious writing of HTML, but today's leading Web-authoring tools are solidly WYSIWYG, which is computerspeak for "what you see is what you get." Building a page now involves little more than clicking a mouse.

Which tool to use? The top choice—both for usability and affordability—is Microsoft's FrontPage (www.microsoft.com/frontpage, which costs about $125). It's a program that's powerful enough to concoct ambitious sites, but user-friendly enough so that beginners will find the going easy. Another option is WebExpress from MicroVision (about $70), available for download and purchase at www.mvd.com/webexpress. It, too, is powerful but simple to use. Either program will get you live and on the Web in a matter of minutes.

A big plus for both programs: They come bundled with an assortment of templates, or forms, that need only a bit of tweaking and customizing to create your own Web page. Stick with the templates, and a Web page within 30 minutes is a realistic goal. For instance, click "New" in FrontPage and a range of templates pop up, such as "Employment Opportunities," "Meeting Agenda," or a home page. In WebExpress, click "New Web Site," then click "Create

Budget Watcher

Try out WebExpress for free by downloading the software from www.mvd.com/webexpress/download.htm. This is full-featured trialware, about 4.5MB. And even if you decide not to buy, any pages you've created are yours to use on the Web.

Using Web Site Themes," and you're offered a couple of fleshed-out business-oriented templates plus lots of templates created for other uses (but with a little ingenuity, they can be adapted to serve a business).

On A Shoestring

Do you need new software to create a Web page? Not necessarily. Many programs designed for other purposes include basic Web site-authoring tools. Full-featured word processors, for instance, can write Web pages. Case in point: Microsoft's Word 2000 includes handsome templates for erecting business home pages. Click on "New/Web Pages" and a wizard pops up along with a home page template. Other free options include the HTML editor built into Netscape Communicator—actually quite a good tool, though tricky for beginners.

But the truth is, if you are at all serious about getting down to business on the Web, you should spend the $100 to buy FrontPage or WebExpress. Hobbyists and tinkerers can try to coax Web pages out of programs intended for other users— and they may well succeed—but you are too busy for that and you also need more polished tools.

If you're still looking for a bargain, a smarter alternative to diddling with the bare-bones HTML editors stuffed into word processors is to head to Trellix (www.trellix.com) and download a copy of its free Web site-creation software. It's slick, and, better still, through a deal with free Web-hosting service Tripod (www.tripod.com),

Smart Tip

Where the built-in Microsoft Word HTML editor really shines is in converting existing Word documents into Web-ready pages. Click on "File" then "Save As." Under "Save As Type," scroll until you find "HTML." Set that option, press "Save," and, just that fast, the brochure you created in Word is a Web page. You'll probably want to edit it before putting it online— spacing and such is often weird after the translation— but for sheer speed and convenience, you cannot beat this built-in tool.

Image Boosters | Click

When you play with images, you need specialty software that will let you change the image's size, resolution, and more. Good image-editing software will even let you edit photographs. There's a stain on your white shirt in that photo? Whoosh, an image editor will wipe away all such problems.

Used to be such software was tricky to use, expensive, and mainly aimed at professionals working in graphics and photography. Nowadays, there's a boatload of good, cheap, easy-to-use programs. Such as?

A top choice is Adobe PhotoShop Lite (LE), from www.adobe.com. A problem: Adobe sells only the full-bore PhotoShop, which you do not want (it's great for pros, but too expensive and too complex for part-timers). PhotoShop LE is free, but the only way to get it is as a bundle with other Adobe software. If you've bought any Adobe programs, look closely at the CD. PhotoShop LE may be hiding on it, and if it is, you have a free, top-notch application for manipulating, editing and resizing images.

More good choices come from Ulead—www. ulead.com—a Taiwan-based software developer that excels at creating wonderful and very cheap graphics-editing tools. For instance, SmartSaver Pro ($59.95) allows nearly instant changes in an image's format and size. Why is that important? On a Web page you generally want small images that display fast, and with SmartSaver Pro, it's simple to save many versions until you get the right balance of size and graphical quality.

Another must-have Ulead program is PhotoImpact ($79.95). The poor man's PhotoShop, PhotoImpact is the solution when you cannot lay hands on PhotoShop LE. It's easy to use, versatile, powerful, and will allow for creative reshaping of images to suit your Web site.

You can't create quality Web pages without owning image-editing software—but you don't need to

Continued on next page

Continued from previous page

> spend big bucks or enroll in college courses to master sophisticated software. For most of us, less than $200 will buy all we need. A big plus with Ulead is that most of its programs are available for free trial downloads. Next time you wish you could tweak an image, visit Ulead, download the tool you need—and just do it!

users can upload business sites created with Trellix to Tripod. Will this output be as polished as, say, a site concocted in FrontPage? The answer is that it depends. In the hands of a truly skilled user, FrontPage will produce the better site—but for someone who wants a fast solution, Trellix-built sites are good and easy to make. It's worth a look.

PUTTIN' ON THE GLITZ

The Web is a graphical medium—words matter, but images are just as important in attracting and holding viewers. That's why both FrontPage and WebExpress come bundled with collections of free art—textured page backgrounds, buttons, arrows and other visual elements for helping readers navigate a site.

Want to go a visual step beyond? There are plenty of software tools for creating customized graphics. A top choice is Microsoft's Image Composer, a freebie bundled with FrontPage. It's easy to use, and within a minute or two of starting, you'll be cranking out customized buttons, banners and more. You can buy more powerful image tools, but frankly, the learning curve usually is too steep.

Another artistic option: Forget trying to make your own and just roam the Web in a hunt for free art which has been uploaded by graphic artists who are happy just to get their work in the public view and gladly let others download their images. Start enhancing a Web page's graphics with a visit to Webpromotion (www.webpromotion.com), which features several dozen superb animated images that are free for the taking. Use by businesses is explicitly encouraged. Another source: TuDogs (www.tudogs. com), which is a gateway to dozens of graphics houses, most of which provide free clip art images.

Days can be spent downloading images—the Web is swamped with terrific free art. But the chief beef by surfers is about long waits for pages to come into focus, caused invariably by loading up a page with too many graphics. So use images sparingly. A few brighten a page; too many drown it.

Another caveat: Before uploading any images to your Web site, carefully read the fine print on the artist's page. Some prohibit use on commercial sites. If in doubt, ask for permission. That's a sure cure against future complications.

Should you put Java and Active X (both are slick programming languages, much liked by some high-horsepower Web designers) or other fancy Web devices on your pages? Not if you really want visitors, especially repeat visitors. Yes, these tools are eye-catching, and when they work, they are wonderful. But often they don't work reliably or as expected, and they also add considerably to a page's load time. They also often are browser-dependent, meaning they will work well only in specific Web browsers; surfers who arrive without the right browser may be out of luck. Best advice: Leave such devices to designers of high-end, expensive sites and stick to the basics at a small business site. That does not mean your site has to be plain or ugly—think creatively, and you'll make your site both fast-loading and memorable.

Simple is best with a Web page. Better an unglamorous page that loads rapidly than a state-of-the-art page that causes the browsers of half your visitors to crash. When a mania seizes you and you want to "design" pages with fancy looks and the newest bells and whistles, put that stuff on a personal page, not your business site. All those toys are fun to play with—but Web visitors hate them. A reli-

Smart Tip

Don't go crazy with colors—one of the biggest goofs of new Web page designers. Stick with maybe two colors for fonts (words) and use a simple, basic color for the page background (white, off-white and pale yellow are good choices). Always test your page on a laptop with a very cheap screen—don't assume surfers will have $1000, 25-inch monitors. If it doesn't look good on a small, cheap screen, it's bad page design.

able rule of thumb: The more times you say "wow" as you design your Web page, the worse it is. You want to create a page where the wow factor is minimal in terms of design but exceptionally high in terms of functionality.

TESTING, TESTING

Gremlins often play tricks with Web pages, and that's why no professional Webmaster announces a new page to the public before testing it. Surf the Web enough, and, sooner or later, you'll stumble into a test site mounted by a brand-name business that has put it online so that insiders can find the bugs before the public does. Do the same thorough testing before publicizing your page.

A crucial test: Make sure pages work equally well in Microsoft Internet Explorer and Netscape Communicator. Ignore this advice at your own peril. Recently a business acquaintance implored me to look at his site, for which he had paid designers upwards of $10,000. I logged in...and found only blank pages. Incredibly, the site had not been tested on Explorer. When I checked with Netscape, it was indeed a spiffy piece of work, but blocking Explorer, the leading Web browser, is simply nuts. Nor would you want to ignore Netscape, which claims around one-third of the market.

You've found bugs? Few pages get put up without at least some kinks, and a good place to start is to pinpoint things that show up on your screen offline but don't work online. The standard problem is that an image or three isn't displaying, caused by a botched hyperlink. Strip down any Web page to its essentials, and you'll find a little text interspersed with many hyperlinks, which are Web directions to images and other files stored elsewhere. Put in the

Smart Tip

When updating pages, always go through your testing procedure as soon as you put up the changes. It's tempting to neglect this, but don't. Too often I've personally put up updated pages that, somehow, turned out to be bug-ridden. And never do page changes during your peak traffic periods! That's inviting calamity.

wrong hyperlink—and sometimes even Web-authoring programs do just that—and the online page shows up as a jumble.

This is when it's time to do a spot of dirty work with HTML code. Click "View/HTML," and a screen filled with gibberish opens. Hunt for the code pointing to the image or text that's not displaying. A good bet is that the link reads <img src="C:\Windows\temp\bluediamond.gif."> or something near to that. No link that includes directions to local drives—C:\Windows\temp—will work online. The cure? Erase everything that comes before the image's name. The result will read <img src="bluediamond.gif."> And it will work exactly right online.

A **big way** to go **wrong** with a Web site is to **put it up**— and **leave** it there. "If your page is **aging**, static, it says, 'I **don't** get it.'"

Follow the same drill with anything that's not displaying properly. HTML is intimidating at first glance—and at second glance, too. But tinker with it, and soon enough, all images and links will display the way you intended. A big way to go wrong with a Web site is to put it up—and leave it there. To keep viewers coming back, a page needs regular updating. "If your page is aging, static, it says, 'I don't get it,'" says Cronin.

How often does a site need updating? Probably once monthly at a minimum. It does take time, but the investment is warranted, says White: "The Internet is a new frontier with limitless possibilities. Now is the time to experiment...before lack of competency puts you out of business."

MALL MANIA

Pssst. Want to know a shortcut that eliminates much of your need to know how to build a Web site and still puts you in an e-commerce business? Then you want to know about the electronic malls that are sprouting up everywhere. Granted, this option usually is more expensive at the get-go, but the extra cash gives you faster ramp-up time. As quickly as you type in your credit card information, you'll be in business at Yahoo Stores, MerchandiZer or Lycos Shops.

Here's the promise of such services: You don't need to know a speck of HTML code, but within an hour or maybe less, you'll have an online store that looks good—and all you have to do is follow a form-driven set of instructions. Think of it as akin to cooking with a recipe. If you follow the instructions at a mall, the result will be a credible, attractive site. A plus is that malls usually offer easy tie-ins with credit card providers, so you will be truly e-commerce enabled in the bargain.

There is a lot to like about turning to a mall to start your business, especially if you have minimum enthusiasm for Web site design and if your Web ambitions are modest in scope. But you should be aware of the mall site's limitations: Nobody will build a distinctive, one-of-a-kind site using the tools available at a mall. To score a home run of an e-commerce site, you need a unique style and look, something that's both memorable and compelling. All Yahoo Stores look alike and act alike, and that means the crucial element of uniqueness is missing.

Smart Tip

Never underestimate the instant credibility an e-tailer gains from an alliance with a powerhouse like Yahoo—even when it consists of nothing more than putting up a storefront on Yahoo real estate. This name recognition is a real boost.

That shouldn't be a deal killer for all, or even most, aspiring e-tailers, however. Maybe you won't hit a grand slam with a mall store, but you may well hit a double or triple, and that could put real bucks in your pocket. Big pluses with Yahoo and Lycos: Both rank among the Net's most trafficked sites, and both aggressively lure surfers into their malls. Not only are storefronts easy to build at these malls, but—as with any bricks-and-mortar mall—the location is likely to bring a flow of traffic.

Am I recommending malls over stand-alone, do-it-yourself storefronts? It depends on what you want and how much time you're willing to invest. As any surfer knows, the Web is cluttered with millions of poorly constructed, nonfunctional storefronts that get little or no traffic. It is easy to construct a viable store with, say, FrontPage—but "easy" does not mean effortless. Many, many hours go into the job, and your time investment can be slashed dramatically by turning to the templates offered by, say, Yahoo Stores. And at a major mall it is nearly impossible to create a truly bad store, while many aspiring e-tailers manage to do that when they go the do-it-yourself route. So think hard about the mall storefront option. This just could be the solution you need.

Location, Location, Location

What will it cost? Prices are dynamic in this marketplace, but, at a recent glance, here are the price tags for the main malls:

○ *Yahoo Stores (www.store.yahoo.com):* $100 monthly for a store selling 50 items or fewer. No setup fees. You have more to sell? $300 monthly lets you stock up to 1,000 items.

○ *MerchandiZer (www.merchandizer.com):* $79.95 monthly for up to 100 items; $149.95 for up to 1,000. No setup fees.

○ *LycosShop (www.verio-lycos.com):* $129.95 monthly for a robust shop that comes with few limits. $100 setup fee.

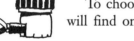

To choose from the many mall providers you will find on the Web, be prepared to spend the better part of a day. Think of that time investment as akin to the hours spent by a B&M merchant hunting for a storefront. In many ways, your process of elimination will be very similar.

Step one is to log onto several malls and find the "store demo" tab. At Yahoo Stores, go to http://store.yahoo.com and click on "How It Works." Then walk through the steps of creating your shop. This is all free so far, so don't fret. What you're looking for is which templates and forms best suit your style and the store you want to build.

Budget Watcher

Want to dabble at e-tailing without a major money commitment? Take a look at Amazon's zShops (www.amazon.com). Think of zShops as auctions without bidding. A merchant lists an item for sale at a fixed price—and pays a listing fee of one dime. That's right: 10 cents. When an item sells, the merchant pays a "completion fee" ($1.25 plus 2.5 percent of any amount over $25). Check it out.

On File Click

You've created umpteen wonderful Web pages, so now how do you get them onto your Web site? You need another piece of software, a program that handles FTP (file transfer protocol). An FTP program lets you shift files from your computer to another via an Internet connection, and that makes it an essential piece of any Net toolkit.

FTP is built into Microsoft FrontPage and many other Web-page editors, but personally, I have long found it faster and easier to use a specialty FTP program. For years I've relied on WS-FTP ($39.95 from Ipswitch Inc., www.ipswitch.com). A free trial version is available for download.

An alternative (and it's free) is Cute FTP, available from www.soar.com/~faq/cuteftp. Hunt for still others at ZDNet's downloads site—www.zdnet.com/downloads. Type in FTP, and you will be presented with dozens of apps that do this work.

Check out several apps, and pick the one that works best for you—and know that, even if you've never FTP'd before, once you get into Web site construction and maintenance, your FTP application will become one that's put to daily use.

A word of caution: FTP software generally seems balky and tricky to use. That's because you need to exactly specify your user name, password, etc., and you must also correctly type everything in the right case (upper or lower). It can be a bit maddening to get an FTP program working right, but once you do, settings will be saved and future transfers will be no harder than making a few mouse clicks. For more tips, head to "Using FTP" (www.interlog.com/~emallay/Interlog/UsingFTP.html), a helpful, free guide that should get you uploading in a matter of minutes.

Oh, a vocabulary point: When you transfer a file to your Web site, that's uploading. When you transfer

Continued on next page

Continued from previous page

a file from a Web site to your computer, that's downloading. Keep those words straight, and all you read about FTP will suddenly make sharper sense.

Once you've found one you like, don't sign up just yet. Take two more steps. First, hunt in the mall for stores similar to yours. If there are hundreds, that might be a negative. But if there are none, that, too, might be a negative. Why? It will be solely your job to get buyers of what you sell used to coming to this mall. Just as The Gap and Eddie Bauer don't mind sharing mall space even though much of their merchandise overlaps, you might find it beneficial to be in a mall with other like-minded retailers.

Step two, before you sign any commitments, is to contact a sampling of current mall merchants. Pick possible competitors, or merchants in entirely different niches, or both—that matters little. What does matter is asking them about their experiences on the mall. How's traffic? How easy is it to update a site? How responsive is the server? How quick is the mall operator to take care of complaints and concerns? In a B&M mall, you would walk from store to store, asking tenants how happy they are, and a shrewd policy is to do the same in an electronic mall. But don't take first answers as definitive. Canvass at least a dozen randomly selected e-tailers.

Budget Watcher
A Yahoo location in particular may be real gold because of how it promotes its stores. Search for "Turkish coffee" on Yahoo, for instance, and it's a fast hop into a couple of small e-tailers selling that brew as well as pots, cups and so forth. Just as a bricks-and-mortar mall brings its merchants traffic, Yahoo attracts shoppers to its stores.

Only when you have satisfactory answers to lots of questions from many different e-tailers should you sign up with a virtual mall. Granted, few impose much in the way of time commitments on your part, but they also know that moving an e-tail store is no easier than moving a bricks-and-mortar store. Once you open up, you are probably staying in place for many months, so proceed deliberately, methodically—make very certain that this is a mall you will be pleased to do business in.

Advanced Tools And Tricks

Your site is up, so now how do you make it special and filled with content that attracts visitors and keeps them coming back? That mission consumes site-builders, both full-time professionals and part-timers, but if there is one fact we now know to be absolutely true, it is this: Simplicity is best.

Case in point: The Web site for a luxury hotel chain based in India features a huge soundtrack of classical music, and it's just annoying. Maybe some sitar tracks—authentic Indian music— might make sense, but classical? It's bandwidth-hogging craziness. Resist the temptation to put something on your site just because you can. Never put up content that slows access to a page but doesn't demonstrably heighten user value.

What does work? Content that gives users reasons to linger, to absorb more of what you're offering. You'll find there are many, many ways to introduce this content, and you are going to have to exercise real discretion here. Pick a few tools, try them out, monitor user responses, then delete the ones that aren't proving valuable. Be ruthless here, and never forget that simple is better.

That understood, here are many tasty tools for you to use in beefing up your site. Just remember, this may be an all-you-can-eat buffet, but the more you put on your plate, the more discomfort your Web site viewers will feel.

○ *Free banners:* A standard of Web design is the banner that proclaims, in effect, a site's name. It can sit at the top of the page, or sometimes at the bottom, but a banner is a necessity. You could make your own from scratch—tools are included with Microsoft's FrontPage, for instance. But my advice is to first try out the free, easy-to-use banner makers on the Web. Usually within five minutes these automated banner makers will produce a spiffy design that you couldn't easily match on your own. A good place to try your hand at this is MediaBuilder's Animated Banner Maker (www.mediabuilder.com/abm.html).

Give it a whirl, and, almost certainly, the result will be so eye-catching you'll want to immediately splash it on your site. MediaBuilder also gives easy-to-follow directions for doing just that.

Smart Tip
Use Web tools sparingly. Best advice: Introduce one, and only one. If it proves popular, leave it up and add a second. If users ignore it, put up another but take down the unloved tool. Always keep it simple, and you'll invariably do better.

○ *E-Mail lists:* You want to experiment with a tool that lets customers talk among themselves about your products and services? An e-mail lists gives you that capability. The smartest, simplest way to create a list is at eGroups (www.egroups.com). EGroups offers many options. Lists can be private, open only to members you approve, or public, open to all who knock on the door. My advice: Experiment with several types of lists, perhaps a private one for existing customers and a public one for all comers.

Either way, carefully monitor traffic. To be useful, a list needs a steady flow of traffic and at least a few messages daily. Initially, you might encourage friends and colleagues to post just to get the list going, but eventually you'll need a site that generates sufficient traffic or your lists will collapse from nonuse. When they work (and they often do), lists are a fast way to spice up a site with the kind of interactivity that keeps surfers coming back.

○ *Polls:* Polls, where surfers register their opinion on an issue, are at the heart of the Net because this is interactivity in its most basic form. Ask any question—"Should pornography be banned from the Web?" "What's your favorite cocktail?" "Who's your favorite Beatle?" It doesn't matter: Surfers will want to register their point of view and see how others voted. AOL, which has to be accounted the slickest Net property of them all, has long used polls as a staple on its pages. Learn from the masters and do likewise.

Writing a poll from scratch is a tricky bit of coding, but free poll templates are readily available for insertion into your site. All you have to do is fill in the blanks in a template, copy and paste a bit of code into your site, and you're in business. Sources of such templates are plentiful, but a good one is from Freetools.com (www.freepolls.com).

○ *CGI scripts:* These are easy-to-use scripts (prewritten code) that you simply pop into your page to create a guest book or the ability to track visitors. CGI (or Common Gateway Interface, a programming tool that lets many small applications run within a Web environment) is one of the Web's oldest resources. Newer, slicker ways to do much of what can be accomplished via CGI are plentiful, but a real plus is their price tag: Scripts put together by enthusiasts are free and available for anyone to use. Always test any CGI script thoroughly before going public with a page, however. In several cases, I simply haven't been able to get some CGI scripts working properly.

> **Smart Tip**
> Keep banner messages very short. How many words might be in one? Aim to limit yourself to three to five words, plus a small image. You want something that grabs attention fast and instantly says what it's all about.

Thousands of these free CGI scripts exist, and one of the best resources for finding the scripts you need is The CGI Resource Index (www.cgi-resources.com). If you cannot find the script you want here, it probably doesn't exist.

○ *Chat rooms:* Wouldn't it be cool if your site had its own private real-time chat room? It's both easy to put up and free from LiveUniverse (http://liveuniverse.com). Just search the page for the link to the chat tool, register, and in a matter of minutes you'll be able to put folks to chatting.

Before you do, however, mull on this: Empty chat rooms look very, very dumb. Will you have enough traffic to put people into a chat room on a regular basis? Do you want to monitor it? How frequently? Know that you won't be on call 24 hours a day, seven days a week—but the chat room will, theoretically, be available that often. My advice: For most small sites, this is a tool to avoid.

Better by far is to set yourself up with an AOL Instant Messenger account (it's free, from www.aol.com) where visitors can fire off questions to you if you're online. This gives surfers an alternative to e-mail for finding information but doesn't expose you to the ridicule that comes with offering an unpopulated chat room. Do this in combination with providing a message board, and surfer needs ought to be very adequately handled.

○ *Counters:* Resources for counters are plentiful, and, with one in place, it's easy to monitor visitor counts. Pick one up at Better Counter (www.better-counter.com). But before installing it, know this: Visible counters usually are signs of amateur page creation, and, worse, if your hit counts are low (as they will be at the beginning), it actually deters viewers from hanging around. It's discouraging to stumble into a page and seeing that you are Visitor No. 112. Any page that's been around any length of time ought to have had thousands of viewers. Another minus to counters: Often they substantially slow down page loading speed. Typically you'll get good counts from your Web host anyway, so leave the counters behind.

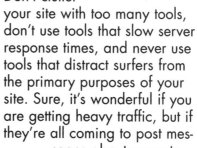

Beware! It's worth repeating: Don't clutter your site with too many tools, don't use tools that slow server response times, and never use tools that distract surfers from the primary purposes of your site. Sure, it's wonderful if you are getting heavy traffic, but if they're all coming to post messages about gangsta rap and your business has nothing to do with music, that's a waste. Keep your site focused, and never stray too far from that focus.

○ *Guest books:* Sure, you could create a guest book using a CGI script, but probably the easier way is just to insert some HTML code into your page—and you will find it at 1-2-3 WebTools (www.freeguest books.com). Why would you want a guest book at all? It's a convenient way to collect more information about your visitors. And incidentally, surfers often like to look through guest books.

○ *News feeds and more:* A secret traffic-builder of the big Web sites is regularly changing content. Usually that means paying writers and other content creators big bucks to produce copy, but you don't need to spend that kind of money. A terrific resource for low-budget Web site builders is iSyndicate (www.isyndicate.com), which makes available thousands of regularly updated pieces of content, including truly readable and useful stuff such as news feeds from leading sources, financial advice, weather reports, even reviews from Wine Spectator.

From sports to news from Kuwait, iSyndicate has material that can be easily put into your Web site and, in most cases, the content is free for you to use. (Some content imposes fees, but that material is clearly labeled.) The upshot is that, with little ado, you'll give viewers a reason to check into your pages often because the content updates automatically.

Smart Tip

When putting up a guest book, create the first six to 10 entries yourself or ask friends and relatives to sign in. This gives the guest book and your site a trafficked appearance. Nobody wants to be the first to sign in.

Is inserting it difficult? Not at all. ISyndicate was created mainly to serve small Web sites, so it provides clear instructions and makes the process quite simple. Check out iSyndicate, and odds are you'll find plenty of material for sprucing up your site. One word of caution: Don't overload your site with this material. It's tempting—so much of it is genuinely good—but use it in moderation so that your surfers still have the time and energy to check out your other offerings, too.

Don't Do This:
The 10 Most [Deadly]
Mistakes In Site Design

This chapter could probably be called the top 100 mistakes—there just are so many goofs site builders make—but let's narrow the focus down to the most disastrous 10. Avoid only these gaffes, and your site will be far better than much of the competition.

1. *Disabling the back button:* Evil site authors long ago figured out how to break a browser's back button so that when a user pushes it, one of several undesired things happen: There's an immediate redirect to an unwanted location, the browser stays put because the back button has been deactivated, or a new window pops up and overtakes the screen. Porno site authors are masters of this—their code is often so malicious that frequently the only way to break the cycle is to restart the computer—but this trick has gained currency with other kinds of site builders. My advice: Never do it. All that's accomplished is that viewers get annoyed.

2. *Opening new windows:* Once upon a time, using multiple new frames to display content as a user clicked through a site was cool—a new, new thing in Web design. Now it only annoys viewers because it ties up system resources, slows computer response and generally complicates a surfer's experience. Sure, it's easy to use this tool. But don't.

3. *Failing to put a phone number and address in a plainly seen location:* If you're selling, you have to offer viewers multiple ways

to contact you. The smartest route is to put a "Contact Us" button that leads to complete info—phone number, fax number, mailing address. Even if nobody ever calls, the very presence of this information will comfort some viewers.

Budget Watcher
Check your site for broken links, automatically and free, with a stop at NetMechanic (www.netmechanic.com). Type in your URL, and, whoosh, you'll get a report on broken links and page load time, and even a freebie spell check.

4. *Broken links:* Bad links—hyperlinks that do nothing when clicked—are the bane of any surfer. Test your site—and do it weekly, to ensure that all links work as promised.

5. *Slow server times:* For personal and hobby sites, slow server times are the norm, and since much of this Web space is free, there's really no complaining. But slow times are inexcusable with professional sites. It's an invitation to the visitor to click away. What's slow? There's no easy rule, but I'd say that any click should lead to something immediately happening. Maybe a new page or image will take some seconds to come into view, but at least the process should start immediately.

6. *Outdated information:* Again, there's no excuse, but it's stunning how many site builders lazily leave up pages that long ago ceased to be accurate. When information changes, update the appropriate pages immediately—and this means every bit of information, every fact, even tiny ones. As a small business, you cannot afford the loss of credibility that can come from having even a single factual goof.

7. *Scrolling text and marquees:* It's an odd fact: Netscape and Microsoft Internet Explorer do not display pages identically, which is one way these site-design tools get easily screwed up by browsers. They can also be maddening to the viewer who wants to know, now, what you're offering. . .but the information keeps scrolling off the page. Use these tools in personal pages—they are fun and add liveliness to otherwise static pages—but put these tricks aside when building business pages.

8. *Too many font styles and colors:* Pages ought to present a unified, consistent look, but novice site builders—entranced by having hundreds of fonts at their fingertips plus dozens of col-

ors—frequently turn their pages into a garish mishmash. Use two, maybe three fonts and colors per page, maximum. The idea is to reassure viewers of your solidity and stability, not to convince them you are wildly artistic.

9. *Orphan pages:* Memorize this: Every page in your site needs a readily seen link back to the start page. Why? Sometimes users will forward a URL to friends, who may visit and may want more information. But if the page they get is a dead-end, forget it. Always put a link to "Home" on every page, and that quickly solves this problem.

10. *Using leading-edge technology:* Isn't that what the Web's all about? Nope, not when you are guaranteed to lose most of your viewers whenever your site requires a download of new software to be properly viewed. 3-D VRML pages are way cool, no question about it, but if nobody actually looks at them, they are just so much waste. Never use bells and whistles that force viewers to go to a third-party site to download a viewing program. Your pages need to be readable with a standard, plain-Jane browser, preferably last year's or earlier. State-of-the-art is cool for techno wizards but death for entrepreneurs.

Smart Tip

OK, there are exceptions to the "no orphans" rule. If you want a special page set aside only for invited viewers, send out the URL, but offer no links to the page from any of your other pages. When might you use it? For instance, if you're offering big discounts to a special group of customers, that price list might be put on an orphan page.

CHAPTER 7

e-Chat

OneTravel.com
Michael Thomas, CEO and founder
Location: East Greenville, Pennsylvania
Year Started: 1995

T ime out. So far, you've absorbed the theory of building a Web site, but to really understand what is going on, you need to hear from the experts—the entrepreneurs who are really doing it. Throughout this book, you will find two types of interviews—some with top executives at the Net's most distinguished sites and others with folks at wanna-be sites that show promise but still have a long road in front of them. Why both types? The top execs tell how to get there, but it's the wanna-be top execs who give us insight into the raw nitty-gritty of the process. Mix them together, and what you have is the reality of success.

You want to stick with learning how to build a site into a monster business success? Skip over the next two chapters and carry on. But I strongly recommend you read the words from the real builders because they truly know where you are at and how you can get to the next level. Even if you jump over this material now, come back to it later—because what you learn will pay big dividends.

To start, meet Michael Thomas, founder and CEO of OneTravel.com. Usually ranked among the Internet's best travel sites, OneTravel.com is at the forefront of the race to dominate what is likely to be among the Web's richest sectors. Nine million households booked travel online in '99, but by 2003 that number will nearly triple to 26 million, says Forrester Research, an Internet research firm. Maybe 3 percent of travel now is booked online, says Jupiter Communications, another research firm, but Jupiter projects sharp growth, from $4.2 billion in '99 to $16.6 billion in 2003. Plenty of money is at stake here, and Michael Thomas intends to get a thick slice. He explains how.

Robert McGarvey: *How much money did you start OneTravel. com with back in 1995?*

Michael Thomas: Unlike many dotcom business strategies which center on securing OPM (other people's money) as fast as possible, I decided to build the business out of cash flow. I know that it is a little old-fashioned in this day and age, but I just felt more comfortable that way. My outlay was about $150,000. In 1995 I had purchased five strategic keywords from Yahoo, and these initially represented my largest monthly outlay.

McGarvey: *You started OneTravel on a sheep farm in Zionsville, Pennsylvania—miles from anywhere. Was this location a disadvantage?*

Smart Tip

Ever wonder why when you search for, say, "health insurance" on Yahoo, the results page features a banner ad from a health insurer? Those positions are for sale, for prices starting around $500 monthly, depending upon the word (high-traffic words naturally cost more). Most Web search engines sell these spots, and, often, they are good buys. Get more information by clicking "Advertising" on your favorite engines.

Thomas: We had a lot of fun on the farm. In the spring it was hard to get the employees focused on work as they all wanted to go out and play with the foals, lambs and kids. Watching and helping babies being born was a lot more fun and exciting.

Our office was located in the loft of a wagon shed on a sheep farm. We did a good job using this as a differentiator in the marketplace and secured significant media and PR as a result. Our loft was only one and a half hours from New York and one hour from Philadelphia, so we could reach civilization easily but did not have the daily hassles and expenses associated with major urban areas. The biggest difficulty was finding employees that were comfortable using an

Fighting The Good Fight `Click`

Who are the big players in the travel market? Expedia, recently spun off from Microsoft, and Travelocity, recently spun off from Sabre, which, in turn, is largely owned by American Airlines, are both very big, very smart companies—and they have lots of money. But as Michael Thomas proves, an entrepreneur with guts and determination can find a place to thrive even on fields that have been well staked out by 900-pound gorillas.

Don't ever assume that because some giant is in the way, your idea will never prosper. What if Jeff Bezos had felt that way about Barnes & Noble's dominance of national bookselling? There'd be no Amazon. Instead, Bezos is well on his way to beating Barnes & Noble. If your idea is good, fight it out—and let the marketplace pick the winners.

outhouse. We finally outgrew our space and moved to a much larger facility with "real" plumbing in February 1999.

You can see the location of our humble beginnings at www. 1travel.com/ponylady/welcome.htm (building next to yellow truck).

McGarvey: *What's been the biggest challenge you've had in building out OneTravel.com?*

Thomas: I knew that it was not going to be easy. Nothing worthwhile ever is. The biggest challenge has been the securing of preferentially priced product/inventory and the development of the tools to easily bring it to market.

McGarvey: *How do you broaden your product mix outside airline tickets—i.e., it's hard to make a profit with a $10 commission cap [the prevailing rate on airline tickets]?*

Thomas: Since we have built OneTravel.com out of cash flow, we pride ourselves on having a lean operation. We never had the luxury of fattening up on OPM. We have been smart to ensure that our labor-intensive operations are in low-cost locations. Our ticket fulfillment is being done out of Odessa, Texas, which provides us with a great labor market. I believe that we are one of the few operators that can make money at $10 per ticket.

Having said that, we are and have been very proactive in diversifying our revenue streams with the addition of other product lines. Our next-generation hotel product, which allows hotels to manage their own inventory and pricing on our platform, is going to significantly enhance our revenue stream. In addition, we are starting to make money with our new auction platform. Our business is firing on all cylinders.

> "This **game** is **really** about who **can** paddle **faster**."

McGarvey: *The big guys in your space are getting bigger. How will you find your niche against Travelocity and Expedia?*

Thomas: Proportionally, we are actually growing faster than they are. In 1999, the online travel industry grew at 173 percent. I think Expedia exceeded the pace somewhat with growth of approximately 200 percent. We grew by 248 percent!

This game is really about who can paddle faster. As opposed to focusing on narrow niches, which by definition have limited appeal due to a limited potential market, we have sought out niche opportunities within the primary travel markets. In the air market with our "White Label," we have conceptualized a brand-new type of fare, which we have integrated into our existing continuum of negotiated, consolidated, sale and regular tariff fares. [White Label fares are offered to the public without identifying the airline and some details of the route.]

We think that our approach to the marketplace and implementation is unique, and we have filed for a patent. You can expect to hear a lot more about our White Label fares in the near future. It is the ultimate air product for the flexible and cost-conscious traveler. The White Label represents a very extendable platform for us that we are introducing into our hotel, car and auction platform. Even beyond travel, it presents some very interesting opportunities.

McGarvey: *Why haven't you gone public?*

Thomas: It was not that long ago that we were still in the barn with an outhouse. When all the underwriters started to call regarding an IPO, we were simply not ready. Now that we have fleshed out the management team, got audited financials, and are carving out a differentiated position with our White Label strategy, an IPO is very real possibility. We are currently evaluating our options.

McGarvey: *How do you up the look-to-book ratio?*

Thomas: We are working on a number of initiatives on this front. The math is simple: 2 percent to 3 percent of the people that look buy. Of the other 97 percent to 98 percent, 70 percent will eventually buy, and the rest are just lookers. The game is about increasing conversion on those 70 percent. Without divulging secrets, we are implementing techniques that are used successfully to generate sales and create urgency to make the buying decision in the offline world. Let's face it, the art of selling product is the same as it has been for thousands of years. The only difference is the medium and interface.

McGarvey: *How do you market the site? What works; what hasn't?*

Thomas: Given our limited resources to date, we have utilized guerrilla marketing techniques and public relations extensively. Now that we have greater resources, we will market much more aggressively using conventional media. OneTravel.com has been the best-kept secret in the online travel marketplace. Obviously we will not keep this secret from the marketplace much longer.

CHAPTER 8

Cheap Tricks

> BlueSuitMom.com
> Maria Bailey, president and founder
> *Location:* Pompano Beach, Florida
> *Year Started:* 2000

I t is amazing, the opportunities that still exist on the Web. Ask Maria Bailey. A onetime marketing executive with AutoNation, she launched BlueSuitMom.com on Mother's Day 2000 with the aim of meeting the needs of executive working moms. Her take on the Net was that there were sites geared for working moms in general—but none aimed specifically at executives who also happen to be moms.

So she decided to build one, BlueSuitMom.com, which offers opportunities for networking, news geared for executive moms, and tips (how to manage time, for instance). Brilliant as the idea for BlueSuitMom may well prove to be, the ramp-up of her site wasn't always smooth. Read on for Bailey's candid—and helpful—comments on building a site.

Robert McGarvey: *How much funding did you start out with? Where was it raised?*

Maria Bailey: We started out with a commitment for $1 million from a former boss—but, unfortunately, the money did not became a reality. So we truly began with $100,000 raised from personal savings and a few friends.

McGarvey: *What were the first big obstacles you encountered in building a Web business?*

Bailey: Our biggest obstacle has been getting interested investors to actually write the check. That stems from a historical obstacle: Career women have done such a good job at proving to the wealthy/powerful men they work with that they have obtained work and family balance that it is difficult to help my potential investors understand the needs of our market. And on top of it, these men are most likely not married to a woman who is a vice president or CEO. So you say mother, and they envision their spouse, who is normally a stay-at-home mom.

There has been a bit of challenge in learning to manage the young technology pros who you need to grow your site. There is little loyalty, and they convey an attitude that they have you by a leash and without them you wouldn't be able to execute your business plan. They realize that their talents are in demand and are used to changing jobs often. Also, their confidence in technology has led many of them to believe that they also know how to run a business based on that technology. There is a short learning curve to adapt your management style to the new breed of employee you find in the Web world.

Opportunity Knocks

Building a Web business is a road filled with ups and downs for any entrepreneur, but a wonderful thing about it is that it provides a space of genuinely equal opportunity. Color, race, gender, creed—none of it matters because all cybercitizens are created equal. Better still, whatever you are, if there are others like you, that's the basis for creating a Net community that just may become a profitable business.

McGarvey: *How do you promote the business?*

Bailey: We promote our business mainly by creating very strategic partnerships. For instance, we have a partnership with Stork Avenue, the largest retailer of birth announcements. They were willing to put our logo on 15 million catalogs in exchange for driving traffic to their site. We are relying too on the strong word-of-mouth network moms and businesswomen create and networking within women's professional organizations, human resources departments and parenting organizations. Also, we are sponsoring events such as parenting conferences and distributing our content to other Web sites to build brand recognition, and we have been very lucky in creating great press.

McGarvey: *What's the business's goal? What's the end game?*

Bailey: Our exit strategy is not to go public. Our goal is to create a prequalified niche market that may be attractive to content aggregators, such as iVillage or Women.com, or a search engine. Because there is no one out there exclusively targeting our market, we feel we have a good shot at it. We monitor the women's market regularly and watch the Internet strategies of others so that we can identify possible acquirers.

McGarvey: *What unique advantages do you have vis-a-vis other Web sites?*

Bailey: We felt the best advantage we could have was to be the first to market— and we were. Because we are the first site aimed at executive working mothers, it has allowed us to create all the great press we've received. The other advantage we have is that any time we are working with a woman to make deals or create partnerships, we almost always get what we need because the woman on the other side of the phone relates immediately to the elements of our site.

> "I **never** thought raising **money** would take so much **time** out of each **day**."

McGarvey: *What's been your biggest surprise in building this business and your biggest disappointment?*

Bailey: The biggest surprise has been how quickly the site and idea have grown. The response we have gotten from other Internet companies and offline retailers, marketers and associations has been overwhelming. We can't keep up with the people who want to do business with us. Also, the international response we have received has been incredible. We receive e-mails from women all over thanking us for our vision to create something that is valuable to them.

The biggest disappointment, or the biggest surprise I didn't anticipate, was I never thought raising money would take so much time out of each day. I don't think I would have started any differently, but I would have anticipated differently the time it would take. It's a constant "chicken or the egg" game when you are juggling raising money, hiring good talent and getting the product to market.

CHAPTER 9

The Host With The Most: [Nuts And Bolts] Of Web Hosts And Domains

With your Web site authored, you need a place to stow it so that visitors can access it—and you have hundreds of choices. Many of these hosts are free, and few cost more than $20 per month. Truth is, setting up your own host—a dedicated computer that's permanently wired into the Net—wastes money and time and, for most small businesses, is a bad idea. Better to outsource hosting to folks who specialize in it.

You could use the free space that comes with your ISP account—all providers, from AOL to EarthLink, offer users at least some space as part of the basic package of services. Frankly, though, this space rarely is suited to running a business. Servers often are slow during peak traffic hours, and domain names can be cumbersome (http://members.aol.com/rjmcgarvey is a for-instance). This space may be great for putting up test pages and fiddling with a site before you are ready to go live, but when you want to get down to business, you will need a dedicated host.

Where to find one? A quirk of the business is that while big-name national online services have emerged to dominate much of the Internet (AOL, for instance), hosting remains the province of thousands of usually tiny, home-brewed, mom-and-pop shops. Paradoxically, however, there's little advantage to using a host that's based in your neighborhood. I honestly don't know where my host (ProHosting.com) is located and cannot imagine stopping in for a visit.

The only potential benefit of using a nearby company is that many hosts do not offer toll-free customer service. You'll pay your long-distance provider whenever you run into a snafu and need to call the company. Probably, though, hitches will be few. In the past year, I believe I've called my host one time, incurring maybe $1 in phone charges. Might you have more phone contact? Not likely: Low-budget hosts are just not geared up to provide the in-depth handholding that would involve many phone calls. So, in most instances, you can put host location out of your mind.

When picking a host, you first and foremost want to know if a host can handle e-commerce activities. Some of the most barebones companies simply aren't equipped. Other criteria that are important to most users: setup and monthly fees (a typical range is $9.95 to $49.95 monthly, with a setup fee equal to one month's fee); amount of available storage space (you want at least 10MB to start as well as the option to add more space as your needs expand); and connection speed (some very low-budget hosts rely upon slow 56K modems, while most business-level hosts have high-speed T1 connections).

Smart Tip

Want a fast take on comparative features of Web hosts? Log onto Compare Web Hosts (www.comparewebhosts.com), where a few mouse clicks let you specify what's important to you and check out which hosts likely will serve your needs.

For a second opinion, head to TopHosts (www.tophosts.com), a site with a bit less functionality but more layers of detail— meaning it's not the easiest resource to use, but it has lots of information.

Comparing hosts is difficult, so a good policy is to quietly set up an account and test the host—kick the tires, so to speak—for several weeks before announcing your presence to the world. Isn't that expensive? You bet, when setup fees are factored in. But more expensive—and embarrassing—is to make a big push for traffic, only to have your host drop the ball and leave you with cranky visitors who cannot quite make it in. Better to know your host is operating smoothly before inviting guests to the party.

MASTER OF YOUR DOMAIN

Before setting up your site, you also need to stake out your domain name, which is the word in between "www" and "com" or "net" in Web addresses. So, what name suits you? Come up with some possibilities, then surf into Network Solutions (www.networksolutions.com). Other businesses now offer domain registration, but this place was the first, and it has the technology down pat.

The drill is simple: You try a name, and Network Solutions tells you if it's available. When you strike out—that is, the names you want are taken—Network Solutions shifts you to "My Name Finder," a spiffy tool that asks for keywords, then offers up possibilities that are available for registration. Mind you, Network Solutions traffics only in the main U.S. top-level domains— "com," "net" and "org." Find a name that suits you, and the charge is $70 for two years. After that, you own the name.

Don't believe doomsayers who talk of a shortage of good names. Yes, most easily remembered "com" names have been snagged, but entrepreneurial genius spawns new possibilities faster than old ones are foreclosed—and that catchy name may be within your reach after all. How? Every country gets its own country code, and that's created the possibility of registering a name abroad that may be already spoken for at home. A Tonga name, for example, would use the domain "to"; Niue would be "nu"; or "st" for São Tomé. You don't have to be in those places to register a domain there—you don't even have to know where they are. All that's required

Opportunity Knocks

What's a good domain name worth? Stories abound of names selling for seven figures or more, but proof of such transactions is hard to find. Nonetheless, if you think you have a zingy, sellable name that you want to market, try Yahoo Auctions (Yahoo, Auctions, Computers, Domain Names—http://auctions.yahoo.com/27751-category-leaf.html). If you are really curious about the market, GreatDomains.com sometimes has as many as 1 million domains up for sale.

is authorizing a credit-card charge—$189.95, in the case of Tonga, for a one-year registration of a Web site with a Tonga address.

Here's where matters get strange or funny, depending upon your perspective. Your site may be registered in Tonga, but your Web host needn't be there (and probably you'd have a tough time finding one there that met your needs anyway). All you need is a host that handles uncommon locations (which you can find out by asking them).

Not every country is quite so cavalier in its sales of domains. Greece ("gr"), for instance, requires a physical presence in the nation (with the only satisfactory proof being a certificate from a government agency). Hong Kong ("hk"), too, requires a physical presence. In fact, most bustling nations want to hand out domains only to their own businesses.

Where to find out about registering your name in a foreign country? Head to Alldomains (www.alldomains.com), a company that sells non-U.S. domains, such as Tonga's "to." Prices usually will be higher than a standard U.S. registration, but for a zingy name, what's a few extra bucks?

What's In A Name?

There's wide agreement that nothing matters as much as a good name. Yet who would have thought Amazon was one? What most matters in a name is that it's easy to

Beware!
Can you "park" a domain name for free? When you park a domain, you reserve it, but haven't yet mounted a site.
Many outfits tout that they offer free parking, but that's not exactly true: You still have to pay the $70 registration fee. Free parking only means they'll put up an "under construction" sign that anyone who hunts for your domain will find. Big deal, you say? Yeah, that's how I see it, too. You could put up the same sign in 30 seconds on free space you already have access to (at an ISP, for instance).

spell and easy to remember. For my money, that's an argument against using a catchy name with an unorthodox country code suffix. Most U.S.-based computer users just automatically type "com" or "net" or "edu" or "gov." Throw a weird ending at them, and you may lose them. So I would recommend a clunky name with a "com" or "net" ending.

Another argument against really offbeat endings: How stable are some of these countries? In revolutions, it's common to nationalize—that is, grab—holdings of foreign companies. What's to stop a new government from nationalizing its Web and taking back all the names sold by a prior government? Here we're venturing into speculation. It hasn't happened, but it could. Don't forget that when picking your domain. You want something that will last, that's worth investing time and money into in building its traffic. And "com" and "net" names just may be the best bang for those dollars.

No Business Like Business-To-Business: The [Scoop] On B2B e-Commerce

U sed to be, the dream was starting the next McDonald's, or maybe inventing a new widget that everybody would need—putting you on the fast track to wealth so immense it could scarcely be counted. Today, of course, the dream is to come up with the new Amazon or Yahoo—but just possibly that's the wrong dream.

Isn't this book all about launching the Next Big Thing? Nope. It's about building businesses on the Internet. Nowadays, a very good argument can be made that there's a smarter way to go than scouting around for the idea that will spawn a new Amazon.

TAKING CARE OF BUSINESS

Consider Walt Geer. It was in late '98 that Geer, a partner in an Atlanta promotional products company, faced up to reality. His little business—which sold logo merchandise such as pens and coffee mugs to companies to hand out to employees and customers—was chugging along OK, but it was just one of 19,000 promotional products companies in the country. Plainly put, Geer's company was lost in the mob. So he decided to take the plunge. He cut the cord on his traditional company, dumping his existing customers and then placed his business online as eCompanyStore (www.ecompanystore.com).

Opportunity Knocks

Do you buy anything for your business that could be more efficiently purchased over the Web? That thought alone can be the trigger to launch a B2B Web site. Get thinking about what you buy and where—and whether the Net would make the process cheaper and faster.

How is he doing now? Well, there were a couple months of hard swallowing: "We had no revenue coming in," recalls Geer, "but we had to focus our energy on the Internet because we didn't have the resources to do it and run our traditional business." But, he says, "in just a few months, the Internet let us move from being a small company to a national player. Before, we serviced lots of little accounts. Now we have AutoNation, the country's biggest car dealership. The Internet is what lets us go after big accounts."

ECompanyStore is just one of hundreds of a new breed of business-to-business (B2B) enterprises, where companies sell not to consumers but to other businesses. These Internet companies may not be winning wide press attention, but they are creating real buzz in big-money circles. Listen up, because Forrester Research—a technology consulting firm—predicts that the B2B sector is going vertical, with an explosion from an estimated $43 billion in revenue during '98 to a jaw-dropping $1.3 trillion in 2003.

Meantime, Forrester predicts that online retail—that's the business-to-consumer (B2C) market—will also grow, but the numbers are piddly in comparison. In '99, says Forrester, B2C e-commerce reached $20.2 billion, and by 2004 it will hit just $184 billion. Do the math: B2B will generate seven times the cash—and that's a multiple that demands attention.

Just why the rush by businesses to purchase on the Internet? Simple, says Ben Smith, a consultant with global management consulting firm A. T. Kearney: "This represents a fundamental change in how companies purchase, and they are using the Internet to drive out costs."

How much cost? "Shift purchasing to the Web, and a business can eliminate 90 percent of the cost of a transaction," says Dean Whitlock, vice president of information technology consulting firm ICL's eBusiness Solutions group.

Another estimate comes from Chris Cogan, CEO of GoCo-Op. com (www.gocoop.com), a Maitland, Florida-based Internet purchasing solution for hotels and restaurants. "We estimate the average cost of executing a paper purchase order is $115," he says. "We get that cost down to $10. When companies buy through our system, they will see immediate savings."

But more than just cost savings are propelling this mushrooming of business trade on the Net, says eCompanyStore's Geer. "The real drivers are speed and efficiency," he says. "And besides, our Web store is always open. These advantages are as attractive to our customers as are the savings. The Internet is a better and faster way for businesses to shop."

THE MANY FACES OF B2B

Just who is making it in B2B e-commerce? Sure winners have yet to emerge, but lately the Web is filled with enticing players that illustrate the breadth of this marketplace. That's because B2B e-commerce offers diverse opportunities, with some players seeking to establish themselves as exchanges—where buyers and sellers meet to do deals—while others are positioning themselves to provide services and products to business customers in a wholly new, Web-based way. The bottom line: B2B e-commerce entrepreneurs are limited only by their own imaginations. There are plentiful possibilities in this exploding space.

Want concrete for-instances of how businesses on the Web are serving other businesses? Read on for a sampling of the strategies B2B Web sites are pursuing.

○ *BizBuyer.com:* When Bernard Louvat was hired to help set up Disney's

Opportunity Knocks

In early 2000, the major automobile manufacturers rocked their multibillion-dollar world by announcing a plan to shift, as soon as possible, much of their buying to the Web. Why? To save money and gain time and flexibility. The point here is just this: When tradition-bound behemoths like the automakers say that B2B e-commerce is the way to go, no longer can there be any doubt that it's so.

Opportunity Knocks

If it can be sold by phone or by mail, it can be sold, probably better, on the Web. E-commerce may never completely replace face-to-face selling (who wants to rent an office space over the Web?), but it sure will take a huge bite out of telemarketing and direct-mail sales.

operations in his native France, it seemed like it would be a simple job—but it took innumerable hours to identify sellers of the products and services he needed, from computers to telecommunications, and then get bids, compare them and make deals. There had to be a better way, thought Louvat, and that's why a few years later he founded Santa Monica, California-based Biz-Buyer.com, a Web-based marketplace established with a mission to streamline buying—and selling—on the part of small businesses in particular. "The Web will allow everyone, buyers and sellers alike, to achieve more efficient pricing," says Louvat. "We help vendors reach new buyers and buyers hear from new suppliers, and we estimate that our system will save buyers 25 percent."

The model is simple. A buyer logs onto the site and indicates an intention to make a purchase—say a wireless telephone plan and a new company car. BizBuyer.com then submits that request to suppliers, and those who want to bid pay "a nominal amount," says Louvat. If the buyer likes a bid and makes a deal, "BizBuyer.com collects a commission from the seller on the transaction," says Louvat, who adds that even after paying the commission, a vendor's costs are lower because the Web creates slick efficiencies.

More than 17,000 vendors already are enrolled in BizBuyer.com, and Louvat anticipates strong growth. "Web-based procurement benefits everybody," he says. "Everybody wins with this system."

○ *ProduceOnline.com:* What do you do with a few tons of butter lettuce and no buyer in sight? That's just the dilemma Chuck James, CEO of Pasadena, California-based ProduceOnline. com, wants to solve by creating a narrowly focused online exchange that brings buyers and sellers of produce together. "In this business, you sell it or you smell it," says James, who last year shut down his family's 166-year-old bricks-and-mortar produce distribution business to build his Web site. "This is an opportunity to reinvent the produce industry."

The way business is done in the produce industry, adds James, has scarcely changed from when his ancestors set up shop back in the 1830s. It's a business that revolves around lots of scraps of paper and "many small players," says James, who points out that while production of grains and livestock is increasingly in the hands of large corporations, "produce remains a business of small farmers."

At ProduceOnline.com, sellers list their available fruits and vegetables, and buyers use search tools to hack through the mountains of broccoli and rutabaga in search of the cherries they need. Neither pays any subscription fee, with ProduceOnline.com's revenues coming from a 1 percent fee on completed deals. In the process, says James, buyers may get lower prices and sellers reap higher margins because "our system cuts transaction processing costs by 70 percent."

Will farmers take to this model? You bet, says James: "Farmers already are very entrepreneurial, and they are eager to find ways to increase their returns."

○ *Ubrandit.com:* Who would be nuts enough to go head-to-head against e-tailing giants like Amazon and CDNow, which are fast on their way to devouring the online market for books and music? Meet Jeff Phillips, CEO of Del Mar, California-based Ubrandit.com. Phillips, who intends to make his profits selling the same books and CDs as the big boys, just may not be nuts at all. That's because he has tilted Ubrandit.com not toward

Opportunity Knocks

No medium has ever been as fast at moving time-sensitive merchandise as the Web. If it will rot or become terribly dated if it doesn't sell fast, the Web is the best sales agent there could be. What besides produce can you think of that's extremely time-sensitive? Come up with possibilities, then search Yahoo to see if that niche already has players. Maybe you'll hit upon a real gusher of a new B2B play.

readers and music fans, but at media properties, such as radio stations and local newspapers.

Phillips explains: "They want to participate in e-commerce, but most don't have the resources to mount a fully functioning e-tailing site. We offer them a turnkey site that doesn't cost them a dime. In fact, they'll get revenues from it."

The Ubrandit.com pitch? Pretty much any media property can take the Ubrandit.com storefront, slap on its own logo, and in a matter of minutes be in the business of selling books and music. On every sale, the radio station or newspaper gets 5 percent of the gross, with Ubrandit.com pocketing the rest for handling every aspect of the transaction.

Even so, don't e-tailers like Amazon offer affiliates—who bring in sales by posting, say, Amazon logos on their sites—commissions upwards of 5 percent (see Chapter 17 for more on affiliate programs)? Yes, acknowledges Phillips, but "our key difference—what we sell our customers—is that the site features their brand, not ours. When a radio station sends a customer to Amazon, it gets a commission, but Amazon owns the customer. With our service, the station's name is up front and they are earning money."

So far, 50 radio stations and a handful of newspapers have signed up with Ubrandit.com, but Phillips is projecting rapid expansion. "With our model, we are not competing against Amazon," he says. "Our partners are, and in their markets they have well-recognized brands. When you hear a radio interview with a book author, why wouldn't you buy the book from the station's site? That's why we believe this model will work, for our partners and for our company."

○ *SeminarSource.com:* Every day, across the world, hundreds of seminars,

Opportunity Knocks

What's the best news about B2B e-commerce? Launching a site is significantly less expensive than trying to create a winning consumer site. Usually it's cheaper to target an audience and pursue it in B2B. If you've narrowed down a business niche and know how to cost-effectively target it, a B2B site can gain traction fast and on a minimal budget.

conventions and workshops aimed at businesses are held. For potential attendees, the problem is finding the right ones. For seminar producers, the problem is much the same: getting out the word to the target audience in a cost-effective manner. That's where Kim Folsom's SeminarSource.com enters. "We list over 25,000 seminars and meetings," says Folsom, CEO of the San Diego-based company, "and we're getting over 250,000 page views per month from potential seminar attendees."

SeminarSource.com charges neither seminar producers nor attendees. Its revenue sources are services offered to seminar producers—from online registration to Webcasting of programs—and selling advertising on the site. "We're not profitable yet," admits Folsom, who says SeminarSource has raised more than $1 million from angel investors. "The size of this market is $35 billion annually, and the Web is the

> "**Venture** capitalists are **investing** $100 million each week in **new** **B2B** properties."

perfect solution, both for meeting organizers and attendees. It's low-cost and efficient. This market will take off. Our only obstacle is getting enough people, attendees in particular, aware of what we're offering. As more people learn the advantages of online booking, more will look to us for solutions."

Want yet more for-instances of B2B sites? Just surf the Web—nowadays, new B2B players are popping up everywhere. "We hear venture capitalists are investing $100 million each week in new B2B properties," says A. T. Kearney's Smith. "There is a lot of excitement about the potentials here."

A Slam Dunk?

If you think B2B sounds too good to ignore, the news gets better: "There will be thousands and thousands of successful B2B e-commerce sites," says Smith. "There will be many fewer B2C sites that succeed."

A crucial reason: "Customer loyalty will be higher in B2B e-commerce," says Smith. Why? Consumers shopping on the

In The Know Click

What industry do you know, and know well? Substantial expertise is needed to create a viable B2B. What industries have you worked in? Which ones interest you enough so that you'll enjoy the long hours of research you'll need to put in?

The irony, though, is that you could probably pick any industry and do well—if it truly interests you and your ideas are good. That's because just about every industry will go through massive structural changes in the next decade as the underlying business processes are impacted by the Internet. Savvy entrepreneurs need to be watching for the turf where their ideas can make a difference.

Marketing glitz doesn't go as far in a B2B context as getting down to the nuts and bolts of what you have to offer businesses that will positively affect their bottom line. Business executives tend to be more cold-blooded about these things, so show them where they will save time and money, and they will follow you.

Internet so far are proving to be price-driven. They want the best, rock-bottom deal and will switch vendors in the click of a mouse to save a few bucks. Businesses won't be so fickle. "Once you lock in a B2B customer, he'll be less likely to switch sites because as the B2B site integrates into the customer's way of doing business, it simply becomes difficult to switch," says Smith. The hassle factor of switching—coupled with the risks involved in any new vendor relationship—outweigh the benefits of small cost savings.

That's why "first-mover advantage will be very important in B2B," adds Ubrandit.com's Phillips. "The players that establish early market dominance will retain it."

Hold on, however, because the sailing for early entrants won't be entirely smooth. In key respects, the bar may be higher in B2B e-commerce than it is in B2C, and the requirements for succeeding likely will be stiffer. "B2B is different from B2C," says John Sviokla, a vice president with e-commerce consulting firm Diamond Technology Partners. "To succeed in this space, you'll need deep domain knowledge." You don't need to know much about farming to successfully peddle peaches to consumers, but to build an exchange for farmers, you have to grasp the fundamental issues in that industry. Lack that, and there will be no trust on the part of your target audience.

Another hitch: B2B involves long selling cycles, and, likely as not, before big deals are nailed down, you'll need to do face-to-face selling. It is one thing to buy a $10 book with a mouse click. It's an entirely different matter to buy $100,000 worth of coffee mugs. "A Web site won't close deals for you," stresses eCompanyStore.com's Geer. "To make B2B deals, often you've still got to put feet on the street."

A third hitch is that while B2B sales are expected to take off, that fast growth is in the future. For now, few B2B e-commerce sites report profitability. But Mark Hoffman, a vice president in the e-business group of consulting firm Booz-Allen & Hamilton, says that's about to change, fast. "B2B is still nascent," he says. "We're now just seeing the tip of this iceberg. Mainstream big businesses had been skeptical about the Web, but no more. They're now jumping on the Internet. We'll be seeing many, many successful B2B sites. There is every reason to be optimistic about this market."

e-Chat

$$
\begin{bmatrix}
\text{Autobytel.com} \\
\text{Mark Lorimer, CEO} \\
\textit{Location: } \text{Irvine, California} \\
\textit{Year Started: } 1995
\end{bmatrix}
$$

Do you wish you could get in the head of a successful dot-com CEO and find out what he's thinking? Read on. Mark Lorimer, CEO of Autobytel.com, here offers an in-depth look at the dotcom world. A onetime corporate lawyer who jumped into the Web first as Autobytel's in-house counsel and later won promotion to the top job, Lorimer is bright and articulate. His perspective is not that of a techie, but of a business executive, and he is candid about the business challenges he faces.

Just what does Autobytel do? In essence, it's a middleman in car buying, but in a way that benefits consumers and dealers. When birthed, the company saw the telephone ("Auto-By-Tel") as a big part of its selling process, but, almost immediately, the computer took over. Log onto Autobytel, tell it what you want—say, a 2001 Camry with a 6-cylinder engine, dark green, ABS, no sunroof—and it routes your request to a dealer in your area. The dealer gets back to you with a firm quote that usually is far below the sticker price. The dealer makes money here because its advertising-marketing costs—a big spend for dealerships—plummet since Autobytel brings in customers. And Autobytel gets paid flat fees by participating dealers that are far lower than dealers would otherwise spend to market. So it's win-win-win for Autobytel, the dealer and the consumer.

Recently, in the face of new competition, Autobytel has begun directly selling cars to consumers (with prices agreed to online, dramatically reducing the roles of dealers). Watch this space: More changes will emerge because automobile retailing remains a dynamic, toughly contested marketplace. That puts Lorimer in a very hot seat, but it also places him in an ideal spot to share insights on running a dotcom today.

Building **brand** **loyalty** and **trust** among consumers on the **Internet** is hugely **expensive** and extremely **difficult** in a space that is **chock** full of **dotcoms** du jour.

Robert McGarvey: *What advantage do you (as a dotcom) have over the big automakers?*

Mark Lorimer: First of all, it is interesting to note that after only five years, Autobytel.com is the sixth-largest generator of automotive sales in the United States, behind GM, Ford, DaimlerChrysler, Toyota and Honda.

[Among the other advantages, we have:]

O *First-mover/brand equity:* Autobytel.com was the first out of the box with the idea of selling cars via the Internet, leveraging not only the efficiencies inherent in e-commerce, but also the empowerment that the Internet gives to consumers, putting them in control of the purchasing process. While manufacturers were trying to come to terms with the Internet, Autobytel.com was already establishing its brand as a trusted third party in the automotive-buying process.

Autobytel.com has established the biggest brand name for car purchasing on the Internet. Building brand loyalty and trust among consumers on the Internet is both hugely expensive and extremely difficult in a space that is chock full of automotive dotcoms du jour. It would appear that the manufacturers have not as yet been able to establish any significant brand following—or purchasing trust—in the e-commerce space.

O *Consumer trust:* Studies show that most consumers view automakers' Web sites as advertising, not as places to actually enter the purchasing process. While manufacturer sites offer consumers extensive and beautifully produced information on specific vehicles, when it comes to the dotcom purchasing process, most consumers choose to go to a third party such as Autobytel.com, where they are offered unbiased information. Furthermore, consumers are looking for what we call "selection protection" in their car-buying process. Autobytel.com's brand stands for protection from bad providers in all phases of the automotive life cycle, much as *Good Housekeeping* has its seal of approval or Underwriters Laboratory has its seal.

○ *Choice:* Choice is oxygen on the Internet. Autobytel.com provided consumers choice from the outset, something manufacturers' Web sites are simply unable to do. Consumers can comparison shop across brands at the Autobytel.com site. A consumer who is shopping for an SUV can view all the SUVs that fit their specs and review invoice, as well as MSRP, pricing; option packages; and rebates and incentives, as well as configure lease and loan payments. Additionally, Autobytel.com consumers can comparison shop for insurance and financing, something they cannot do at manufacturers' sites.

○ *Speed:* As a dotcom, we are used to a territory that is constantly evolving. We have built an infrastructure—without entrenchment in bricks and mortar and nearly a century of business practices—that allows us to move fast, adapt, and change at the "speed of Internet."

McGarvey: *What's been the biggest surprise you've had in building out Autobytel.com? The biggest challenge?*

Lorimer: Rapid worldwide acceptance of the Autobytel.com approach. We're now on four continents and have been in business just under five years. We knew that this multitrillion-dollar, entrenched, global business needed re-engineering, but we've been very surprised at how rapidly it is unraveling and reinventing itself—exploding conventional wisdom on almost every front.

The auto industry in the year 2000 is in the throes of a profound self-scrutiny at both the factory and dealer level. We take credit for helping to propel these much-needed changes. While many are

> ### Opportunity Knocks
> Read Mark Lorimer's words again: "Choice is oxygen." How does your site give customers choices? How can you give more choices? Come up with shrewd answers, and you're on the fast track to riches on the Net.

bemoaning the fact that the Internet bubble has burst—that perhaps e-commerce is not all it's cracked up to be—the mostly salutary effects of the Internet and e-commerce on one of the world's largest industries are unmistakable and will reverberate for quite some time to come.

The biggest challenge is a clear offshoot of the biggest surprise. As the impact of the Internet on this powerful industry became apparent, and as Autobytel.com became a force to be reckoned with in the industry, myriad copycat sites and auto dotcom wanna-bes came scurrying out of the bushes to take a stake in this multitrillion-dollar industry.

Make no mistake: There is plenty of room for a variety of players and plenty of room for billions and billions of dollars to be lost in the automotive dotcom sweepstakes. We believe that competition is a veritable life force in a territory that is evolving every day, and we welcome it—there is no room for complacency in this space. We have been competing successfully for years (centuries in Internet time) with quality companies like Microsoft [owner of CarPoint.com, another leading auto-related Web site] and Cox Communications [an owner of AutoTrader.com], none of whom have come close to our share of market.

However, of late, there has been tremendous confusion in the space as more and more players have climbed on the auto dotcom bandwagon: software prodigies with no automotive knowledge attempting to take over a business with Byzantine legal trappings; companies subsidizing car prices and confusing consumers about what they can and cannot do online; fancy Web sites luring consumers back into the same old process; newspaper classifieds gussied up and posted online; and manufacturers joining forces for back-end software deals that masquerade as new e-commerce initiatives. The net result of this is a dilution of quality for consumers that is deleterious to all players in the automotive e-commerce space, while at the same

Beware! Success breeds nearly instant imitation on the Net. That's the irony: The more you prosper, the tougher you have to fight. How will you stay a step—better still, two steps—ahead of those who will follow?

time brewing a backlash among very strong dealer lobbies against automotive OBSs (online buying services).

Our biggest challenge is to keep our brand promise clear and alive above this fray for all our customers. We will meet this challenge by continuing to support and strengthen a dealer and technology infrastructure that is second to none in the space, and by leapfrogging ahead of all the noise to continue to set the standard for consumer fulfillment in automotive e-commerce.

Opportunity Knocks

Can you deliver the best combination of user experience and price? That's what Mark Lorimer says is the winning experience, and he's unquestionably spot-on. Great prices on a site that's difficult to use won't make a winning business. But pricing cannot be too high, either. Net shoppers are price-sensitive, a fact that can never be ignored.

McGarvey: *What's your strategy in coming out ahead of competitors?*

Lorimer:

○ To continue to leverage our powerful brand both domestically and globally

○ To continue to deliver on our brand promise

○ To fully exploit our superior domain expertise and automotive mastery to expand market share

○ To rapidly scale our business and move from share of garage to share of wallet

○ To deliver, deliver, deliver

McGarvey: *Is price the deciding factor in buying online? If not, what is?*

Lorimer: The three deciding factors are process, price…and price. Our parents' generation spent time to save money; today's generation spends money to save time. Generation Next will be willing to spend neither. Our business is contingent on offering savings in both. We have engineered our business to provide consumers process and price (as well as information) advantage.

Our business is about leveraging the Internet to create distribution efficiencies, providing advantages for both consumer and dealer that result in a better purchasing process and more competitive pricing. Nearly 31 percent of the cost of a car is in getting it from the factory gate to the consumer's door. It is that 31 percent that we are attacking. Autobytel.com has focused on driving costs out of the process at the dealership level so that the dealer can pass on savings to the consumer. We are carrying this philosophy of providing price and process advantage into all of our products, attacking traditional inefficiencies in services such as finance and insurance.

> ## Smart Tip
> One reason Autobytel is a market leader is that the company hasn't fallen in love with how it does things. As market conditions change, Autobytel quickly adapts. That way of thinking and acting is essential for any dotcom, so once you have launched a site, prepare to change its basic approaches a week after launch...and the next week...and the next. That's the only way to survive on the Web.

Our success in providing price and process advantage to the consumer is evident in the nearly $13 billion in car sales we generated in 1999, and in the fact that we have the largest brand in the online automotive space and nearly 50 percent of the online new vehicle market (more than three times that of our nearest competitor). If consumers were not getting price and process advantage at Autobytel.com, we would not be the market leader.

McGarvey: *What stops a customer from buying a car online? And how will you persuade them?*

Lorimer: A car is the second-largest purchase most consumers will make. It is an important financial commitment that most consumers do not take lightly. In addition, there still is a whiff of suspicion about the Internet among consumers, creating a reluctance to transact.

However, perhaps more powerful than consumer reluctance to purchase a car online is consumer revulsion about the traditional car-purchasing process, a process that is universally considered to be on a par with getting a root canal. It is the dissatisfaction with that process that Autobytel.com has tapped into, and it is the ease and information advantage that the Internet provides that will persuade more and more consumers to shop online for cars.

It is anticipated that more than 60 percent of consumers will use the Internet to shop for a car this year. While it is true that studies project that a relatively small number, around 6 percent, will actually purchase a car online in 2000, it is double the percentage that purchased online in 1999. Our numbers, anecdotal evidence and experience certainly show that acceptance of the Internet as a safe and efficient channel not only for car purchasing, but for the full range of automotive products and services, is rapidly growing.

Ultimately, the biggest persuader will, of course, be trust. Autobytel.com will continue to draw consumers by delivering on our brand promise and by continuing to engineer our business from the customer backwards. Consumer trust is our lifeblood, and we work aggressively not only to gain, but to maintain it. We have what we consider to be the best customer service department in all of e-commerce because we believe that all e-commerce consumers need a strong safety net, one that acts like a trampoline, rebounding them back into the process. We have set the industry standard for dealer training and fulfillment and work aggressively to ensure that our dealer body is delivering on our brand promise. And it is working—our closing ratio is the highest the industry has ever seen.

> "Consumer **trust** is our **lifeblood**, and we work **aggressively** not only to **gain**, but to **maintain** it."

We have developed the infrastructure and distribution network to deliver the car-purchasing and ownership processes that consumers demand. For example, because of our strong dealer relationships and solid infrastructure, we were able to rapidly launch AutobytelDirect, a click-and-buy purchasing process that, our research showed, many consumers wanted to migrate to. This process provides consumers with more information than ever before—a virtual car lot with searchable dealer inventory and upfront pricing posted right on the Web site.

McGarvey: *When do you stop evolving your business model?*

Lorimer: Never is probably the safest answer I can give at the moment. No one knows where this industry will be next year (and ten years is real crystal-ball stuff). As technology develops and the territory shifts, we will continue to evolve. However, our core values will never change—and have not since day one. We will always strive to drive cost out of the distribution process and work to create efficiencies on both the B2C and B2B ends of the business; but, above all, we will always be committed to providing the best possible car-buying and ownership experience for consumers.

CHAPTER 12

Cheap Tricks

AllWords.com
Fred Weiss, founder and owner
Location: Ann Arbor, Michigan
Year Started: 1998

Fred Weiss is a one-person Web site machine. In a few years, he's erected three successful sites—AllMath.com (with flash cards, games and more for math junkies); AllWords.com (an online dictionary); and AllLotto.com (results for state lotteries nationwide). Along the way, he's mounted a site that didn't prosper (AllFree.com) and bought a number of domain names he hasn't had time to flesh out. But when you want insight into doing Net business on the cheap, Weiss is a man you have to talk with.

Robert McGarvey: *What were your start-up costs?*

Fred Weiss: My start-up costs were minimal. Originally (during 1998), I paid about $200 per month for hosting and spent about $5,000 to license content. Between March 1998 and the end of 1999, I raised about $75,000 [from investors] and spent about $70,000 of it by the end of 1999. In early 1999, I began to host my own sites and spent money on office space, Internet connectivity, hardware and software. Below are estimates of my monthly costs:

○ *Office, phones, etc.:* $500 per month

○ *Internet connectivity:* $600 per month

○ *Hardware:* $450 per month

○ *Software (Microsoft NT server, SQL server and other tools):* about $700 per month

○ *Licensed data:* about $1,000 per month

○ *Contracted services:* about $800 per month

McGarvey: *How do you accumulate content?*

Weiss: I purchase content through various publishers—news services, Houghton Mifflin—and we also create content, such as our Word of the Week column on AllWords and our tools (flash cards, metric converter and magic square game) for AllMath.

McGarvey: *How successful are your sites?*

Weiss: My sites generated more than 150,000 unique visitors [statistically identifiable individuals who visit a site; a site may have five page views by one visitor or by five unique visitors, for instance], 1.3 million page views, and more than $7,500 in revenue in January 2000.

McGarvey: *Your revenue comes from advertising. How do you sell it?*

Weiss: I am a member of a number of ad networks, including

Ad It Up Click

Can you generate cash by putting third-party advertisements on your Web site? You bet. Smarter than chasing down individual advertisers (and trying to collect!) is to join a Net ad network, an intermediary that brings Web sites and advertisers together. Cases in point:

○ *Engage Media:* www.engage.com

○ *i-clicks Network:* www.i-clicks.net

○ *eAds:* www.eads.com

○ *DoubleClick:* www.doubleclick.com

Find many more at Yahoo by following this link: http://dir.yahoo.com/Business_and_Economy/Business_to_Business/Marketing_and_Advertising/Internet/Advertising.

Literally dozens of companies want your business. Before signing any deals, check references, asking the following questions: Is payment prompt? Are advertisers as promised? Can you ban certain kinds of ads from your site?

Opportunity Knocks

Wow, $7,500 in revenue in one month from several simple Web sites! What can you do that's in the same vein? Yes, there are many millions of Web sites already up, but there also remain many millions of opportunities for smart entrepreneurs. Making a profit on ad sales alone is tough—mighty Time Warner essentially folded its ambitious Pathfinder site because it realized that it couldn't live on ads alone—but when expenses are kept low, the model just might work, as Weiss' sites prove.

Flycast [www.engage.com—which pays sites to display third-party advertiser banners]. I also receive advertising from several agencies that cater to online casinos (for our AllLotto.com site only) or sell directly to interested parties.

McGarvey: *Where did you get the idea for the sites?*

Weiss: In January 1998, I was working as a programmer when a colleague mentioned how useful it would be if the *CRC Handbook* [an engineering reference work] was available via the Web. This gave me the idea of developing automated, reference-focused sites. The first idea was for AllMath.com, which I felt could be developed over time while still providing useful tools as development continued. AllMath was launched in September 1998. I also launched AllFree.com as a political magazine, but I stopped updating that site in January 1999 because there was a lack of traffic.

McGarvey: *Why did you build other sites?*

Weiss: I built AllWords.com and AllLotto.com based on a serendipitous event and my belief that they could be developed at a low cost ($5,000 to $10,000 or less) and operated at a profit. When looking for math biographies for AllMath.com, I found that the same publisher had a dictionary available for licensing. This looked like a simple task to implement, so I registered AllWords.com and launched the site in January 1999.

I had also registered as many "All" domains as I could think of, and one happened to be AllLotto.com. I met a salesman from Flycast who had a friend who ran a lottery site. He put us in contact with each other. I eventually contracted with this gentleman to host my site, using his software. Some months later, in spring 1999, I wrote my own software and relaunched the site using my own hosting facility. I also arranged to resell the result data to other Web site publishers as another leg to my business.

CHAPTER 13

Nothing Ventured, Nothing Gained: [Secrets] Of Venture Capital Funding

As 1997 neared its end, Jed Smith—a Boston-area computer entrepreneur who had founded CyberSmith, a chain of computer retail stores—began looking at e-commerce. "What categories haven't been taken?" Smith asked himself.

"I first looked at the grocery space," Smith recalls. "But the model didn't work. The gross margin to cost-of-shipping ratio was unattractive: You're shipping bulky, heavy products with low margins. Then I looked at the health and beauty aisle. Good margins; small, easy-to-ship products. A lot of this is regular, repeat purchases that don't need to be touched. To me, this category worked well, much better than books because this is a $158 billion market. That's six times bigger than the book market. I realized, this is a big opportunity. And I knew I needed to move fast."

First on Smith's list of must-gets: money. "I knew I needed money because this space was going to get crowded, fast," he says. "And I needed smart money that would help my company get more competitive."

That meant one thing. Smith needed some of the venture capital that's ponied up by the hundreds of firms—mainly around San Francisco, but increasingly in Austin, Texas; Boston; Seattle; and New York, too—that specialize in putting cash into untested businesses. How much venture money is there? Lots. The usual estimate is that more than $36 billion was invested in start-ups by venture capital firms during 1999. Around 3,000 start-ups divvied up that money, according to research firm VentureOne Corp.

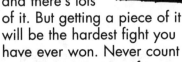

Beware! Venture capital is real, and there's lots of it. But getting a piece of it will be the hardest fight you have ever won. Never count on a penny of venture funding until the check is in your hands.

The good news for e-tailers: In 1999, 80 percent of venture funding went to Internet-related businesses, according to VentureOne. The bad news: For every firm that wins venture funding, probably 100 go away empty-handed...and probably another 100, maybe more, didn't even get their foot in the door.

MAKING CONNECTIONS

Just getting in front of a major VC firm is an accomplishment, but that's where Smith had an edge. Around ten years earlier, he had worked at Oracle—one of the globe's biggest software companies—and, as luck would have it, a co-worker had a roommate that Smith clicked with. In the intervening years, Smith had kept in touch with that roomie, Dave Wharton. When Smith had his nascent idea for a cyberdrugstore, he bounced it off Wharton—by then an associate at Kleiner, Perkins, the Silicon Valley VC firm that usually is ranked at the top in Internet investments because it put early money into Netscape, Healtheon, Amazon, and many more major successes.

"I didn't even know who Kleiner, Perkins was when I first talked to Dave," Smith says. "Call me somewhere between naive and lucky, but maybe that's why I was successful. I didn't grovel. I just thought I had a neat idea. What I said to Kleiner was: I have an idea. It's yours to invest in if you want. I'm not shopping it around. Let's work on it together and create something big. I didn't say, 'You want to invest? I got other guys who want to.' I asked Kleiner to collaborate with me."

Kleiner, Perkins liked what it was hearing, including Kleiner partner John Doerr. If any Kleiner, Perkins partner likes an Internet idea, the entrepreneur has got a golden future to look forward to. But Doerr is the partner who jumped into Netscape, Healtheon, Amazon—most of the firm's big Web plays—so if he climbs on board, it's tantamount to the kiss of a god.

But Smith hadn't gotten kissed yet, not by a long shot. He presented to Kleiner in January 1998, but they weren't ready to put money into the idea quite yet. "They asked me to come out to the [San Francisco] Bay area, spend some time working on my plan and meeting people like [Amazon founder] Jeff Bezos," Smith recalls. So he did, and a few weeks later, Kleiner said, "Stay a bit longer and flesh out your idea more." Weeks went by, Smith kept tinkering with his plan...then bingo: "In April, Kleiner put up seed money, and by June they funded it."

That is how Smith's idea became Drugstore.com (www.drug store.com)—but there is still more to this story. Kleiner, with its connections throughout the tech industry, soon persuaded Microsoft vice president Peter Neupert to leave that company and become CEO of the new Drugstore.com. ("I told John Doerr no and I told him no again, but eventually I said yes," Neupert recalls. For an interview with Peter Neupert, turn to page 159.)

How did that sit with Smith? "My perspective is, what's best for the business is what we should do," he says. "Controlling every piece of this company is not the most important thing to me." That is a shrewd position to take because once VC money comes aboard, much of the control usually begins to slip away from the founder. Neupert had run much of Microsoft's online operations and, as a vice president, also had experience managing a large staff. That made him perfect for running an online drugstore that aimed to be the biggest in its huge sector.

Opportunity Knocks

Don't assume that you have to have all your ducks in a neat row to win venture funding. Quite the contrary. In many cases, VCs like helping to shape a business idea, to put their marks on a plan. And as they get more involved, their willingness to fund increases. You still need to be savvy—and to have good answers for questions—but keep your ears open to VC suggestions and be ready to incorporate the good ones.

And Neupert inspired confidence in outsiders, too. A major

investment from Amazon.com followed, as did more money from Microsoft co-founder Paul Allen's Vulcan Ventures. Drugstore.com went from idea to heavily funded company in the space of a year.

One footnote: In mid-1999, Smith left Drugstore.com to pursue unspecified interests. A bad ending? Not at all. Along the way, Smith picked up 950,000 shares in the company, which went public in mid-1999. With share prices ranging from around $8 to $70, Smith emerged a millionaire many times over. Even at $8 a share, that stake is worth more than $7 million—a pretty good payday for a guy who happened to think that, just maybe, there was a Net opportunity in drugs.

Beware! Bring in VC money, and you will probably lose control of your business. That's just a reality. For every Jeff Bezos who stays on top, there are several entrepreneurs with ideas that are good enough to get funded who don't personally inspire confidence—and they get pushed aside. Ironically, it happened to probably the most fertile tech idea man of the past 15 years, Jim Clark, the founder of Netscape and Healtheon. Before those two companies, he had the idea that gave birth to Silicon Graphics, a maker of high-performance computers, but he got nudged aside. It happens.

LOOKING GOOD

Landing VC funding is not just about money. It doesn't take a rocket scientist to realize that fantastic wealth has been made in a very short period by Net entrepreneurs, and, in that universe, billions of dollars (not millions) are the target. Wealthy individuals know this, and many are on the prowl for Net start-ups to fund. Their money may be welcome (see Chapter 14 for more on angel financing), but it is not as good as money from Kleiner, Perkins; Benchmark; Flatiron Partners; and a handful more firms. What makes VC money better? When a major VC signs up, it adds intangibles such as class and prestige.

Talk to a start-up, and an early question is "What's your funding?" And the person who asks the question wants to hear names he recognizes. Ask Will Clemens, CEO of Respond.com (www.respond.com), an e-mail buying service, who his investors are, and Clemens fires back with The Barksdale Group, Benchmark Capital and Hummer Winblad Venture Partners—all top-tier venture capital firms, proof that Respond.com is in it for the long haul.

VCs also like to leverage their contacts—witness Amazon, a Kleiner, Perkins-funded company, joining as an investor in Drugstore.com. That's no fluke. Kleiner, Perkins, for instance, talks about its "keiretsu"—a linking of companies it's funded—and members include bookstore Amazon.com, freelance marketplace eLance.com, search engines Excite and Google, health information provider Healtheon, human resources provider Icarian.com, home improvement site HomeStore.com, women's site iVillage.com, financial manager myCFO.com, retailer OnSale.com, and dozens more. Cross-pollination (where members make deals with each other and exchange ideas) is common. That's a big boost for a Net start-up. Not just anybody can pick up the phone and call Amazon's Bezos with a business question—but members of the Kleiner, Perkins keiretsu know that's doable.

Other VC firms do much the same, and the upshot is that smart Internet entrepreneurs look for prestige VC money even when they don't really need it. $10 million from Kleiner, Perkins is worth a whole lot more than the same amount from your rich uncle, and that is a Silicon Valley reality.

Opportunity Knocks

Who do you know? If you want a hearing at a VC firm, find a way in via friends and friends of friends. The "six degrees of separation" theory claims we all know everybody else—or at least we know somebody who knows somebody who knows somebody. Check it out. When a friend told me about this idea, I scoffed and said, "No way I'm within six degrees of the Pope." She told me: "You know me, and the father of a good friend of mine has met the Pope many times." The lesson: If you really want VC money, find out who you know who knows somebody. That's the way in the door.

GOING FOR THE GOLD

On paper, scoring VC funding looks simple. You write up a business plan, wherein you pay very close heed to the possible payday ahead (typically this is made vivid with charts that forecast revenue and profits). VCs do not want to hit singles. They swing for the bleachers, and to win funding, an idea has to have the clear potential to be a major winner.

Smart Tip

Sometimes companies bring in VC money even when none is needed. EBay, for instance, brought in Benchmark Capital because the founders believed the sanction of a leading Silicon Valley firm would be a big boost in recruiting a name-brand CEO who, in turn, would be a major asset to a future IPO. EBay was right: Benchmark helped recruit Meg Whitman to run the company—and eBay's stock offering in turn scored a home run for all involved.

Why do VCs want big winners? Simple. They are realists who know that out of every 10 ventures they fund, maybe eight will vanish without a trace, one will be a modest success, but that one home run will generate so much cash, it makes all the losses forgettable as it propels the firm deep into black ink. So don't be conservative. Think big.

Also think of the exit strategy. That's key. VCs don't invest to hold; they want a way to translate a business success into an economic success. Usually, that means the company gets bought by a big fish (as, for instance, auctioneer uBid.com was bought by CMGI, a holding company for many Internet businesses, for around $400 million in stock) or it goes public. Either way, early investors want to know how they will get out of this deal before they go into it.

Once you've got your plan in hand—with an exit strategy and a payday spelled out—you look for every way possible to get it (and yourself) in front of VCs. It isn't easy. So often Internet entrepreneurs complain to me, "I have a great business plan, and nobody will fund it." Maybe the plan is great, maybe it isn't, but step one in proving you have what it takes to prosper in the rugged Internet economy is finding a way to get in front of VCs.

You've tried and cannot land VC money? Take what cash you can from anybody, of course. Get the business afloat, and then maybe VCs will come calling with cash in their hands. Even better, once a business is prospering, you can usually get much more favorable terms from VCs. The earlier they come in, the bigger piece of the company they want, which means second-stage VC financing may actually be more desirable.

MATCHMAKER, MATCHMAKER

Curtis Giesen knew he had a cool idea for a Web site. His childhood buddy was Dr. Drew Pinsky. You don't know who Dr. Drew is? Everybody who tunes into MTV does, because Dr. Drew has a regular show where he dispenses advice on health, sex, love and emotions. Giesen figured the youthful demographics of MTV-watchers paired up perfectly with the demographics of heavy Net users, so he put the idea of a Web site to Dr. Drew. Pinsky signed on in a flash. That left just one problem—money.

Launching a major, national site costs megabucks, but Giesen figured it was a slam-dunk with Dr. Drew on board. Except in his first round of contacting VCs, nobody would put up a dime. "They didn't know who Dr. Drew was," Giesen remembers. "They knew Dr. Koop, but not Dr. Drew, who is the Dr. Koop of the MTV generation."

Giesen was striking out until he heard about Garage.com, a Silicon Valley firm that aims to match up good ideas with funding. Garage.com does not itself invest in firms, but it serves as a financial matchmaker, and in 1999 it helped 40 start-ups get around $100 million in capital.

Giesen also had a bit of luck. A junior staffer at

Smart Tip
Monogamy isn't practiced by VCs. Rarely will a major VC firm act as sole funder. It seems strange, but it is a fact that frequently a VC firm will agree to fund if you can get another firm also to fund. Keep in mind: VCs like to minimize risk, and one way to do it is to share investments.

Garage.com knew about Dr. Drew, saw the potential magic in building a Web site around an MTV personality, and told his bosses what he thought. One thing quickly led to another, with Garage.com finding Giesen the money he needed to get started—about $1 million raised from five investors.

Giesen is effusive in his praise for Garage.com: "What sets Garage.com apart is its philosophy of making its entrepreneurs successful," says Giesen. "Garage.com not only helped us raise capital, it helped us build a framework for success. Garage.com provided us with multiple resources to move our company from business plan development through the funding phase and beyond to building our team, finding strategic partners, and creating a buzz around our business."

Good news for you is that Garage.com isn't alone in provid-

Read All About It　　　Click

VCs are not kindly money sources—they are in business to make piles of cash. It's an unwary (read: dumb) entrepreneur who doesn't approach VCs cautiously. Read about VC greed in Charles Ferguson's *High Stakes, No Prisoners* (Times Books), a book that tells how Ferguson took an idea and transformed it into FrontPage, the ubiquitous hypertext editor now owned by Microsoft. Also worth a read is Michael Wolff's *Burn Rate* (Touchstone Books), a brutally funny book, and Michael Lewis' *The New New Thing* (W.W. Norton), a vivid recounting of how Jim Clark (co-founder of Silicon Graphics, Netscape, and Healtheon) utterly rewrote the rules of venture funding to put more power in the hands of entrepreneurs.

Maybe the best book of all about VCs is Randall Stross's *eBoys* (Crown), because Stross won access to partner meetings at VC powerhouse Benchmark Capital, the funder of WebVan, eBay, Ashford.com, and many others. In the book, Stross gives readers a behind-the-scenes look at the decision-making process as Benchmark decides to put cash into start-ups or to decline investing. It's a well-told story, full of useful insights.

ing this financial matchmaking. Other Web sites are coming on stream to serve as intermediaries between entrepreneurs and investors. Check out The Elevator (www.theelevator.com), iMinds Ventures (www.iminds.com), and Artemis Ventures (www.artemisventures.com), for instance. And angels—friends, family, friends of friends—remain a viable source for seed money.

The moral: When the idea is good, the money will follow.

Smart Tip
Where to find venture capital firms? Check out FinanceHub (www.financehub.com) and vFinance (www.vfinance.com) for leads to many VC firms.

INSIDE INFORMATION

Don't get discouraged about finding VC money. Garage.com, for example, encourages submissions of business plans at its Web site (www.garage.com). Here, its co-founder and CEO Guy Kawasaki (a onetime Apple Computer marketer) eagerly tells how to win funding from Garage.com. Kawasaki's trademark is irreverence—his wit is quick and pointed—but read between the lines in this Q&A, and you'll discover he is telling you what your chances are and how to make them better.

Robert McGarvey: *What does an entrepreneur need to get venture funding?*

Guy Kawasaki: Most investors look for unfair advantages in three areas: team, technology and market. It's not that the start-up has to have everything, but there needs to be some compelling reason to believe the company will succeed.

McGarvey: *What's your ballpark estimate of the percentage of business plans that get funded?*

Kawasaki: Half a percent [Note: That's 0.5 percent—meaning 1 in 200].

McGarvey: *How many plans do you look at in an average week?*

Kawasaki: Personally, I see about 50. Our company gets about 200 per week.

McGarvey: *A typical complaint is "I know nobody—where do I start looking?" What's your answer?*

Kawasaki: Garage.com.

McGarvey: *What's the minimum (realistic) funding for launching a B2B site? A B2C site?*

Kawasaki: This is tough to answer because you can't glom all B2B- or B2C-type businesses together. You could start a company with $250,000 or $250 million. It all depends. Having said this, too much money is worse than too little.

McGarvey: *What's the one thing an entrepreneur can do that's sure to turn you off?*

Kawasaki: Ask me to sign an NDA [nondisclosure agreement].

McGarvey: *What's the one thing an entrepreneur can do that's sure to catch your interest?*

Kawasaki: Have a presentation that's less than 10 slides.

What has Kawasaki told you? Develop a plan that emphasizes your unique strengths—the compelling reasons to fund it—keep it short, don't ask for too much money, and never ask potential funders to sign an NDA. Why the last point? NDAs—which bind the signer not to reveal what you show or tell him about your plan—are unenforceable in many cases, and, just as bad, a busy investor probably has heard much the same idea from multiple sources already.

"Too **much** money is **worse** than too **little**."

On the other hand, complaints that investors sometimes steal good ideas are epidemic. Are the beefs founded? Hard to say—but a Silicon Valley legend is that when Sabeer Bhatia shopped his idea for what became Hotmail, he lied to would-be funders in initial meetings, telling them about a totally different business idea. Only when they passed some kind of test for Bhatia did he lay out his real idea. Paranoid? Bhatia became a very rich man when Microsoft bought Hotmail—and proof that, in his case, caution panned out.

Do you need to be as cautious as Bhatia? Quite probably, most entrepreneurs who take that closed-mouth route will simply strike out with funders. A better route is to tell what you need to tell to spark interest, then keep offering more details as investor interest looks ever more genuine. Besides, if you treat people sincerely and honestly, more often than not, you'll get much the same in return. Sure, there are crooks in Silicon Valley—but most folks are decent, well-meaning and well-intentioned. So play things straight, and usually you will indeed get the results you deserve.

CHAPTER 14

Angels Of Mercy:
Financial [Angels] Explain
Why They Fund Start-Ups

D o you believe in angels? After you read this chapter, you just might: With a little luck and lots of persistence on your part, angels—of the flesh and blood variety—may fund your Internet venture. Want to know more? Keep reading.

In the last couple years, the traditional ways companies have won funding have blurred substantially. Not long ago, step one was for the entrepreneur to bootstrap the business, using his own resources (savings and credit card debt usually). Step two was to seek angel funding from seasoned professionals who typically put in not only money but expertise, mentoring and guidance. Step three saw the business pursuing venture capital. And in step four—taken after several years of profitability—the company went public.

That scenario is laughable in today's fast-paced e-commerce world, as companies with scarcely any track record and no profits (nor much in the way of revenue) go public, and venture capitalists increasingly take on a mentoring role.

But a place—a big one—remains for angels. Where do you find angels? Usually through personal connections, because angels, generally, are friends of friends or parents of friends. Why do they invest? Many angels thrill in getting involved in a start-up. Maybe they don't want personally to run one, but they nonetheless are excited about being on the periphery and offering advice in addition to capital. Of course, there is also the real possibility of hitting a major home run.

Opportunity Knocks

Sky Dayton, the story goes, got in touch with angels Kevin O'Donnell and Reed Slatkin through mutual friends who all belonged to the same church. Are you a churchgoer? A member of the American Legion? In the PTA? Share a background, and angels are much more likely to give your idea a hearing. In Silicon Valley, there's an active group of angels from India who seek out young Indian techies with bright ideas. Connections and roots do matter.

Just ask Kevin O'Donnell and Reed Slatkin. Entrepreneur Sky Dayton approached O'Donnell and Slatkin in the early 1990s with his hopes for an easy-to-use Internet service provider that would deliver high levels of customer service. They liked what they heard and invested very early on in Dayton's idea. That was in '94, and in the six years since, those angels have watched their investment multiply in value many, many times as Dayton's EarthLink rose to become the premier independent ISP, second only to gargantuan AOL. O'Donnell and Slatkin are still on the board of directors and are major shareholders, with stock worth upwards of $30 million apiece.

How do you hook up with an angel? What can you reasonably ask of an angel—and what are you likely to get? The following two angels—Lori King, CEO of angel Web portal NVST, and Steve Fu, founder and CEO of Angeltips—readily agreed to provide insight into what they do. Their methods and approaches differ, but that's the norm: No two angels have exactly the same motivations. But if you understand who angels are and how to persuade them, you just might get one to put cash into your company.

> *Lori King is CEO of NVST (www.nvst.com), a Web site for angels and entrepreneurs. She also is CEO of the Business Exchange Center, a firm that helps companies through the merger and acquisition process, and is herself an angel through a network called Seraph, a Seattle-area group of female tech executives who hunt for promising start-ups to fund.*

Robert McGarvey: *Why are you an angel investor?*

Lori King: I have the experience that gives me the confidence that I can choose good candidates for success, so the opportunity to participate financially and to join in the excitement that surrounds emerging technology companies is irresistible. Similar to others who have been entrepreneurs, I view angel investing as a way to expand on that experience.

McGarvey: *What do you see as the difference between an angel and a VC?*

King: The main difference is their agenda. A venture capitalist manages a fund of other people's money under a predetermined investment focus, so the VC's agenda is to get this money invested and make the largest return as quickly as possible. The angel investor does not have a predetermined investment focus that must be adhered to and probably has money invested and producing a good return already. So the angel must weigh liquidating a current investment and possibly paying taxes on the gain to invest in a higher-risk investment. Thus, a desire to get involved and promote an entrepreneur's vision can often be the deciding factor when the financial reasons are compelling.

> "The **angel investor** does not have a **predetermined** investment **focus** that must be **adhered** to."

McGarvey: *How many plans does Seraph look at in a typical month?*

King: Seraph Capital receives 10 (and often many more) executive summaries in a month. The entrepreneurs submit their plans online at seraphcapital.com so that members can review them directly from the secured-access Web site. A review committee considers member comments to choose three presenters for the monthly meeting.

McGarvey: *What's a typical investment?*

King: A typical investment is $25,000 to $50,000 per angel, and, in most cases, more than one Seraph member will invest in a presenting company. Depending upon the amount of capital being raised, it may be 100 percent met by the Seraph Capital members.

McGarvey: *How can an entrepreneur find angels?*

King: In the past, this has been the hardest part for entrepreneurs. Now there are Internet-based networks such as NVST.com. At NVST.com we have amassed the largest database of experienced angel investors in the world. An entrepreneur can search by region and specific investment criteria or utilize the NVST team to locate and meet with appropriate angel investors out of the 9,000 pre-IPO investor database. Key to receiving an investment from appropriate angel investors is this opportunity for an entrepreneur to present to them in person.

McGarvey: *What can an entrepreneur do to win a "yes" from angels? What's sure to win a "no thanks"?*

King: To win a "yes," an entrepreneur needs a succinct presentation that communicates the vision and gives potential investors confidence that the management team can execute the plan.

A sure "no thanks" will result from a presentation where the entrepreneur does not acknowledge competitors and does not provide the reason his or her plan is going to be the clear winner in the space.

> **Steve Fu** *was a top interactive ad agency executive when he decided to take the entrepreneurial plunge to found Angeltips (www.angeltips.com), a Web site designed to provide a place for entrepreneurs to link up with angels. So he's been through both finding angel financing himself and helping others find theirs. He readily talks about the business of angel financing.*

Robert McGarvey: *What is the difference between an angel and a VC?*

Steve Fu: An angel is an individual investor, while a VC is an institutional investor with a charter/mandate to invest in a predefined manner. When a VC raises a venture fund, the fund prospectus states the type of investment by sector and by stage (dollar amount), etc. An angel investor is

Smart Tip
Practice, practice, practice. Before you go into any meetings with VCs or angels, really hone your presentation on your business—this can prove a lot more crucial than your business plan in the funding decision. Why? Investors invest in people who inspire them. Go in with a pitch that wows listeners, and you may walk out with a big check.

not constrained by these boundaries. VCs have to invest their money; angels do not. That's important in trying to understand their motivations.

VCs provide management support as do angels. Today we see an increasing blurring of the line between angels and early-stage VCs, especially in the technology sector where angels have sufficient capital to compete against VCs.

> "Angels **invest more** than $50 billion **annually** vs. VCs, who **invest** only $25 **billion**."

The original definition of "angel" was someone to whom a playwright would go to get funding for a Broadway musical. An angel did not necessarily have expertise in the area in which they invested. Subsequently, we saw the rise of business angels (retired or working businessmen who had capital, expertise, free time and a personal interest in helping start-ups).

Today, we see an increasing interest in angel investing. Angels invest more than $50 billion annually vs. VCs, who invest only $25 billion. There are currently 250,000 active angel investors, but the potential pool is actually 6 million. That is why Angeltips.com was invented, to bring the other 5.75 million potential investors into the market through the Internet, the most efficient medium to bring people together.

McGarvey: *What's the biggest mistake entrepreneurs make in approaching angels?*

Fu: Entrepreneurs make the same mistakes with angels and VCs:

O they do not have a refined business model or plan;

O they've not done sufficient due diligence (market size, competitors, etc); and

O they do not select the right angels. For instance, if you're starting a portal for teens, why would you go to a real estate mogul who has no experience with either the teen market or the Internet? You're better off going after the publisher of a teen magazine as an angel.

McGarvey: *What's the one thing entrepreneurs can do to make their case stronger?*

Fu: They can do a number of things, including building a solid management team and targeting the right angels. Find the angel with the experience and Rolodex: The experience will help them better understand the competitive landscape, and the Rolodex will help them initiate business partnerships with companies, recruit management and advisors, and get introductions to VCs.

Smart Tip
Don't delay. Check out both www.nvst.com and www.angeltips.com and see if there's anything there for you. Do not submit material too early—wait until it's polished. But once your business plan is solid, get a move on!

McGarvey: *How many business plans come through your door weekly? How many do you think get funded by anybody?*

Fu: We launched on January 31, 2000, and here are the site metrics: Six hundred accredited investors signed up in about 45 days and 350 business plans were submitted in the same period. We anticipate growth to be about 25 percent monthly in terms of sign-ups.

We are looking to find about 10 to 15 deals per month in the next 12 months. As for outside our network, 1.2 million businesses get started each year, and less than 10 percent get angel funding.

McGarvey: *What are investors looking for in start-ups?*

Fu: A differentiated product, first-mover status and a solid management team with experience in the field they are looking to start a company in. Investors are also looking for entrepreneurs who can recognize their strengths and weaknesses and who know to bring in support in their areas of weakness. Investors are looking for hungry entrepreneurs with flexibility and adaptability—people who can change their business models to respond to the marketplace.

CHAPTER 15

e-Chat

> WorldRes.com
> Greg Jones, founder and CEO
> *Location:* San Mateo, California
> *Year Started:* 1995

When you travel, you need a place to lay your head at night when you get there, right? While the big online travel agencies (Expedia, Travelocity) have aggressively sold airline tickets, they have been less successful in selling hotel rooms—even though the global hotel market is a $220 billion business. Why? Many reasons, but mainly it's that only a tiny percentage of hotels have real-time, online booking capabilities, says Greg Jones, CEO and president of San Mateo, California-based WorldRes.com, an online reservations service that includes hotels in its offerings.

"The vast majority of hotels aren't online anywhere—around 40,000 out of 220,000 properties worldwide," estimates Jones. But that's good news for Jones, whose aim—fresh off a $30 million financing round that includes funding from online reservations system architect Sabre and industry giant Starwood Hotels—is to sell those hotels a back-end system that will get them online fast. There are no upfront costs. Fees are collected on a pay-as-you-go basis, with a transaction fee collected whenever a room is booked through the WorldRes system. Sound good? You bet, and that's why Jones' WorldRes ranks as an up-and-coming B2B e-commerce star.

Robert McGarvey: *What's been your biggest surprise at WorldRes?*

Greg Jones: After two months of negotiations, we went to collect a check for an investment, and the investor backed out, leaving us with two weeks of cash. I borrowed $200,000 secured by my house and asked our 20 employees to work without pay. Eight weeks later, we closed on our first round of $4 million in venture capital.

McGarvey: *How hard has it been to raise funding? What did you do right in approaching investors?*

Jones: It was very difficult early on, 1995 to '98. I have probably presented the business plan to more than 70 venture capitalists over the past four years in raising $60 million. We were early for a B2B e-commerce company. It has only been in the last six to nine months that the financial markets have discovered the attractiveness of B2B.

McGarvey: *How is building a B2B site different from building a B2C site?*

Jones: A B2B e-commerce business requires building a network of supplier (e.g., hotel) relationships, core transaction processing technology (e.g., an Internet central reservation system), and a network of distribution partnerships (e.g., travel Web sites). There is a difficult chicken-and-egg dilemma in starting these businesses. For example, hotels want to join the system with the best distribution and vice versa. One needs to get enough suppliers and distributors onto the system to reach the "critical mass" that will result in transactions (reservations and revenue).

> "One **needs** to get **enough** suppliers and distributors **onto** the **system** to reach the **'critical mass'** that will **result** in transactions."

A B2C business is primarily focused on using the Internet as a low-cost marketing channel to build a brand for existing products and services. For example, the major online travel agencies (e.g., Travelocity/Preview and Expedia) are Web front ends of the existing travel agent GDS (Global Distribution System;

distributes airfares, cars and chain hotel rooms). They are spending millions to build a brand that will cause consumers to visit their sites and access exactly what a travel agent could do for you. The Internet has removed the branding and logistical constraints of the bricks-and-mortar travel agency business. Basically, you pour a ton of money at building a brand in B2C.

McGarvey: *Is there a potentially bigger payout in B2B? Why?*

Jones: The total B2B markets are estimated to be eight to 10 times the size of the B2C markets. There are natural monopolies/oligopolies for B2B companies in highly fragmented markets. The company that captures the first-mover advantage in building the most supply and distribution relationships has a very strong competitive advantage.

McGarvey: *What advantage do you have against the many competitors in your space?*

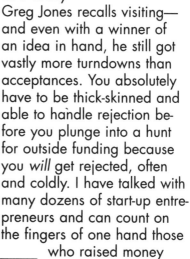

Beware!
Seventy VCs! That is how many Greg Jones recalls visiting—and even with a winner of an idea in hand, he still got vastly more turndowns than acceptances. You absolutely have to be thick-skinned and able to handle rejection before you plunge into a hunt for outside funding because you *will* get rejected, often and coldly. I have talked with many dozens of start-up entrepreneurs and can count on the fingers of one hand those who raised money easily. Pain is just part of the game.

Jones: There are not many real direct competitors in our space. Since we're focused on building "the plumbing" to the hotels, most travel Web sites that are perceived as competitors are actually partners. We had a significant head start in building the technology and network, which has allowed us to establish 12,000 hotels and 1,200 distribution partners today with strong positive momentum.

CHAPTER 16

Cheap Tricks

oneNest.com
Durreen Shahnaz, co-founder and CEO
Location: New York City
Year Started: 1999

he idea is brilliant: Create a marketplace that unites artisans and craftsmakers around the world with buyers who will be able to purchase the latest in scarves, jewelry, pottery and whatnot from places like Russia, Indonesia and India. Think of oneNest.com (www.onenest.com) as a wired version of Pier One, a chain that's thrived by selling Third World goods to U.S. buyers. But with oneNest, the seller usually gets more for his or her goods and the buyer pays less because most of the costs associated with a middleman have been eliminated. Here, Durreen Shahnaz, a Bangladesh native and oneNest's co-founder and CEO, tells the site's story.

Robert McGarvey: *What were your start-up costs? How did you raise funding? How long did it take to get funded?*

Durreen Shahnaz: The first six months of the business, we ran on $100,000. The money was spent primarily on developing technology and on salaries. The three founders put in that seed money.

In late 1999, we raised an additional $1 million from outside investors. We started raising the first round of outside financing in October and closed the round in November. This round was focused on personal contacts. We got very positive feedback from investors. The feedback was encouraging not only because we

Opportunity Knocks

Be realistic: Building a Web site and nurturing it until it succeeds is usually tough work. A few years ago, sites launched with little funding and within days were Net hits. No more. But the struggle—and it will be a struggle—to win success for your site will be much easier if you are doing work you believe in. Of course the founders of oneNest hope to make money for themselves, lots of it, but at its core this is a Web site inspired by a passion. Such sites are those most likely to survive the dark, tough periods along the way to success.

were able to raise the $1 million in a short time but also to think that people believed in my dream and my passion.

Having said that, raising the first round of financing is always the toughest. So it took some convincing and persistence to raise all the money for that round. With investments ranging in size from $15,000 to $100,000, it takes a lot of investors to total $1 million. Even with a very positive response, for each person we contacted who invested, there were probably two more who didn't.

McGarvey: *Where did you get the idea for the site? When did the site go live?*

Shahnaz: The idea of oneNest has been with me since my days of working in the villages of Bangladesh. Working with the Bangladesh Rural Advancement Committee, I saw what difference a small amount of credit made to the otherwise destitute lives of these women. I wanted to take that a step further. I wanted to help these women who were trying to make a living by providing them with a market in which to sell their products. I wanted to give all the artists and artisans of the world the ability to sell to a store or an individual on the other side of the world. Such trade can really make this world one community. OneNest's goal is to do its part in that mission.

The oneNest.com Web site was launched on December 21, 1999. The site features a self-service model for selling independently produced products, with an initial listing more than 500 products from every continent. Items for sale include fine art, decorative items, home furnishings, sculpture, music, photography, clothing, jewelry and fashion accessories, both new and vintage. OneNest does not carry inventory but instead relies for fulfillment on the individuals and businesses that offer products for sale on the site.

McGarvey: *What's the financial upside?*

Shahnaz: The market objective of oneNest is to achieve total revenue of approximately $80 million over the next five years. The business mix is projected to be approximately 40 percent retail-related revenue and 60 percent wholesale revenue. We'll also get some revenue from advertisers.

McGarvey: *What challenge do you face in making this site grow?*

Shahnaz: The challenge lies in getting the right message across to the global audience. The international market potential is so large that it will be crucial to not get the branding message diluted.

CHAPTER 17

That's What Friends Are For: [Cashing In] On Affiliate Programs

Want to generate cash, now, from your Web site? Even sites that aren't e-commerce enabled—meaning they retail nothing—can put money in your pocket through the many affiliate programs now found on the Web. From Amazon to OfficeMax, leading online retailers are eager to pay you for driving sales their way. How? You put up their banner on your site, and for every click-through that results in a sale, you earn a commission, anywhere from 1 percent to 15 percent.

A variation that's popped up in recent months puts money in your pocket even if visitors don't make a purchase. Case in point: Put up an AltaVista (www.altavista.com) banner on your site, and every time a visitor clicks into that portal, you earn 3 cents. Or join the GoTo (www.goto.com) affiliate program and earn $5 for every 1,000 searches your visitors perform.

IT ALL CLICKS

Supposedly, the idea for affiliate programs—where big merchants enlist small sites as a de facto sales force—got its start when a woman talking with Amazon.com founder Jeff Bezos at a cocktail party in 1996 asked how she might sell books about divorce on her Web site. Bezos noodled the idea, and a light bulb went on. He realized the opportunities for both to benefit were great, and the upshot was the launch of Amazon's affiliate program, one of the industry's most successful.

The appeal to small-business Web sites is plain: "Small Web sites want to monetize their page views, and affiliate programs let you make money just like a big Web site," says Kris Hagerman, CEO of Affinia.com, a Mountain View, California-based company that specializes in bringing name-brand affiliates to small Web sites.

How much money is involved? Forrester Research, a company that tracks Web trends, interviewed 50 leading online retailers and discovered that, on average, they have more than 10,000 affiliates apiece who collectively generate 13 percent of these retailers' online revenue. What's more, big growth is anticipated, with the

Working The System — Click

Is joining an affiliate program an instant way to get yourself discounts on the stuff you intend to buy anyway? It might seem that way. Put up an Amazon logo, and, bingo, whenever you buy a book, you get a 5 percent commission (or discount, since it's you shopping).

Except affiliate program owners aren't that stupid. Read the fine print, and, in most programs, there's a clause that says you won't get a commission on your own purchases. End of story? Maybe not: Whispers in the industry are that few affiliate program operators enforce that exclusion. Sources insist that although the program operators know it's you when you're buying—cookies make your identity known—they pay the commission anyway because they don't want to alienate affiliates and, furthermore, are fearful of driving business to competitors.

Is that true? Try it for yourself when next a major purchase looms. Don't frivolously buy, say, a computer just to get that 3 percent discount—buy only because you want to—but if a check does come, pop a celebratory bottle of wine for us. Not only is the vino in effect free, but you've paid for this book, too. What a deal!

leading merchants expecting affiliate programs to produce more than 20 percent of revenue by 2003, according to Forrester.

For you, getting a share is simple. You put up a few links on your site (to any of the thousands of e-tailers that offer commissions to affiliates), and, as surfers click from your site into your affiliated site, you earn money. All of this sounds so new, but think about it. Basically, you're getting paid for leads, a practice as old as selling that makes sense for everyone involved.

ADDING IT UP

Sound good? Understand that affiliate programs rarely generate big bucks for small Web site owners. In many cases, they generate no money at all, even when sales occur. Why? Amazon's affiliate program, for instance, pays up to 15 percent commissions, with most sales generating at least a 5 percent commission. But Amazon won't issue a check until commissions hit $100. Do the math: At 5 percent, you have to sell $2,000 in books to see a check. That's a lot of dead trees.

At Priceline, affiliates get $1 for a lead they generate *if* the lead posts "a reasonable offer" at Priceline, with checks issued once your balance reaches $50. PC Connection pays its affiliates 3 percent on every computer and peripheral sale they generate, which means you sell a $1,500 computer and get only $45—and checks aren't cut until a $100 balance is hit. At GoTo, the minimum check issued is $25—which means your site has to generate 5,000 GoTo searches for money to land in your mailbox.

> You **need** brisk **traffic** for any affiliate program— no **matter** how **generous—** to actually **send** you **checks**.

The inescapable conclusion: You need brisk traffic for any affiliate program—no matter how generous—to actually send you checks. And don't believe the affiliate proponents who promise that somehow, just by signing up with an affiliate program, you'll see a jump in traffic. It won't happen—the Web is awash with places to buy just about everything imaginable.

None of this means that affiliate programs are bad news. For some small Web sites, they genuinely produce cash. But before signing up, take out a calculator and do some realistic forecasting. How long will it take your site to generate, say, 5,000 searches? Say you get 100 visitors daily—not bad traffic for a tiny site. That's 9,000 in three months, which means more than half your traffic would have to initiate a search for you to get $25 from GoTo. Unrealistic? Yep. So do some hard-eyed forecasting before pasting an affiliate link into your site.

SOLID LINKS

How hard is it to create an affiliate link? The job is simple, and you'll have it done within a minute or three. It works like this: You select the logo or link you want to show at your site (most e-tailers offer many choices, sometimes dozens, so you can get exactly the look you want). Click the logo you like, and the e-tailer automatically generates HTML code that does two things: It links to the e-tailer and includes your affiliate ID so you can

---

A Touch Of Class | Click

A couple years ago, the secret reason many small Web sites slapped on a banner from, say, Amazon was to gain a kind of legitimacy. It was hoped that the hard-won (and expensively bought) credibility of Amazon would anoint a start-up with a species of classiness. Maybe it even worked—once. But if that's what you think affiliate programs will do for you now, forget it. With so many banners out there, nobody any longer will think anything more than that you took the time to copy and paste someone's HTML code into your Web page.

This strategy may even backfire. Sites festooned with affiliate banners simply look cheesy, the very opposite of legitimate. The bottom line: The only valid reason to join affiliate programs is if they put cash in your pocket.

---

earn commissions. Then you copy that code and, using any HTML editor (such as Microsoft's FrontPage), paste it into your site.

Doing all this is grunt work, not rocket science, and inside a few minutes the link should look spiffy. Want to see this procedure in action? Head to Amazon's excellent resources for affiliates. One page covers the nitty-gritty in vivid detail: www.amazon.com/exec/obidos/subst/associates/join/basic-links.html.

Smart Tip

Once you have pasted in affiliate code, always preview the revised page before going live. Oftentimes, the placement will not be where you thought it would be (centering a logo can be downright tricky—just use trial and error), and, sometimes, the link is dead (usually because a tiny bit got cut off in the copying and pasting).

Even sites with heavy traffic won't necessarily see big profits resulting from affiliate programs. To make money, you have to follow the rules. Rule No. 1? "You cannot make affiliate links your content. That will generate no sales," says Affinia's Hagerman. The advice seems obvious, but the Web nonetheless is cluttered with pages that consist of nothing but banners from affiliates—and nobody is apt to buy anything from these sites. That's why a basic element in setting up a thriving affiliation deal is to strictly limit the number of programs you join. You don't want a blizzard of banners on your site.

Rule No. 2: "Do contextual placement, with products you personally recommend," advises Hagerman. Be sparing—rarely should there be more than a single affiliate link on any page—and if you explain why you are endorsing this merchant and merchandise, you just may get visitors to check it out. A saloon owner, for instance, might recommend a cocktail recipe book, or a Web site design firm might endorse a Web hosting service.

The third rule is to seek feedback from your site visitors. Do they find the links to affiliates useful? Distracting? An annoyance? Pay attention to what they tell you—and if they are *not* clicking through to your affiliated merchants, that, too, tells you something. Put up different banners, or take them down altogether.

THE DARK SIDE OF BANNERS

You've digested the warning that, at a site with modest traffic, you're unlikely to see an affiliate check in this century (which runs for another 99 years!), but there's more bad news to consider.

For starters, whenever a visitor clicks the affiliate link, he or she clicks away from your site. You may make the commission, but you'll lose the visitor. Is it worth it? That's your call, but this is an issue every site—no matter how heavy or light the traffic—has to ponder. Winning traffic just isn't easy in today's cluttered Internet marketplace, and justifications have to be strong for you to willingly show a visitor the way off your site.

Then why does Amazon, one of the undisputed kingpins of e-commerce, routinely do it? The Amazon front page features links to Drugstore.com, but Amazon is a major investor in Drugstore, which in turn has paid Amazon for this prime chunk of real estate, so the payoff is plain to see. For you, the choice is more difficult. An affiliate link might put money in your treasury, but would you make more money keeping the visitor at your site? Think hard on that.

Beware! Never forget that a bad shopping experience at an affiliated site will tarnish you, too. Choose affiliates cautiously, monitor them (check into their sites), and carefully heed any feedback you get from your visitors. Better still, shop yourself at your affiliated merchants and swiftly eliminate any that don't measure up. You simply cannot afford links to bad affiliates.

A second problem: Every banner you insert takes time to load, meaning there will be more delay in how long your page takes to come into a visitor's view. *Always check affiliate banners to make certain they load swiftly.* Amazon banners usually pop rapidly into view, while those from lesser players sometimes can take many seconds. Ruthlessly delete slow-loading banners. You cannot afford to waste your visitors' time.

And what if a site visitor clicks into an affiliated merchant and has a bad experience? Whom do you blame when your pal Joe recommends his barber and the haircut you get makes you look old, tubby, and poor? The barber, of course—but also Joe.

When affiliate programs work, they work, but when they don't, no Web site owner should hesitate to take down the links and call it a noble but failed experiment. Check out affiliate programs, absolutely, but don't be shy about pulling the plug if you are not seeing meaningful returns.

Smart Tip
Find more information on affiliate programs at CNet's Affiliate Center, www.builder. com/Business/AffiliateCenter. Get still more of the scoop at Lycos' Webmonkey, http:// hotwired.lycos.com/ Webmonkey/guides.

Want to discover more about affiliate programs? Good sites that offer speedy sign-up for multiple quality programs include LinkShare (www.linkshare.com), which offers deals with The Disney Store, J.C. Penney, OfficeMax and plenty more; and Be Free (www.befree.com), including deals with Staples, eToys and more. Other top sites are CashPile (www.cashpile.com) and Top 10 Affiliates (www.top10affiliates.com).

Crave more obscure programs for your site? You'll find them at ClicksLink (www.clickslink.com), which provides a searchable directory plus tools for signing up with everything from astrology vendors to watchmakers.

New Alliances

The old-fashioned approach to affiliate relationships—and still the Web's most prevalent way—is to pop some HTML code onto one of your pages and hope that produces a ringing cash register for your affiliated merchant. But the drawbacks involved in doing e-commerce this way have prompted creation of a new style of program.

Case in point: Five or 10 minutes after registering for free at Affinia (www.affinia.com), you'll have built on your site a separate storefront stocked with merchandise from Affinia's e-tailer partners, including many name brands such as eToys, Barnes & Noble, Garden.com and OfficeMax. Affinia provides the storefront building tools and the server space for hosting the page, and you get paid for every lead you send to participating merchants. How much? That varies from merchant to merchant, with the current range running from 3 to 15 cents per click. A check is cut when your balance hits $25.

The benefit to this storefront is that it's a separate page in your site. Rather than cluttering your pages with merchant banners, you put up a little button that suggests to visitors that they drop by your storefront. It's neat, nondistracting to visitors, and just may put dollars in your account.

Teaming Up: Partnering With Big Bricks-And-Mortar Companies

It was June 1999, and Andrea Reisman had a problem, a huge "Is this the end of the business?" crisis. Just a few weeks earlier, the 30-year-old CEO of San Francisco-based Petopia.com—an online pet supplies store—had been on top of the world. She had scarcely closed a venture financing round that pumped $9 million into her start-up when her world tilted upside down. Archcompetitor Pets.com announced it had snared $50 million in venture funding that included a strategic alliance with Amazon, meaning that visitors to Amazon would be peppered with reminders to buy kitty litter and 100-pound bags of dog chow at Pets.com.

That news easily could have meant lights out for Reisman and Petopia. In today's bullet-paced e-commerce battlefield, there is no nostalgia for yesterday's leaders. But shazam—Reisman pulled a fabulous rabbit out of cyberspace, and within a month, she closed a $66 million funding round that included buckets of cash from pet store powerhouse Petco, not to mention an exclusivity agreement with the retailer in the bargain.

"It's been a wild year," Reisman says. "The Petco deal enabled us to leapfrog over many competitors. It's really given us a head start."

GOING CORPORATE

Applaud Reisman's success, but also learn from it. She is not alone—in fact, forming alliances with major corporations has become a common strategy for dotcom companies seeking to carve out a niche for themselves in an ever more brutally competitive marketplace. Why? Nowadays branding is crucial—it takes a name and a sizable share of consumer mind share to win eyeballs, and getting there is an expensive proposition.

The days when a little start-up could go it alone—the way Yahoo and Amazon did—are waning, and a new philosophy is taking hold. "If you are a small dotcom, you have to build alliances with bigger companies," says Phil Anderson, an associate professor of business at Dartmouth College in Hanover, New Hampshire. "You have no choice. You need to build share, fast, and that means you have to leverage more resources than you can get your mitts on by yourself."

> "If you **are** a **small** dotcom, you have to **build alliances** with **bigger** companies."

"Speed to market is critical today," agrees Jim Datovech, president of e-commerce consulting firm ComVersant, "and that's why alliances make so much sense. An alliance brings more strengths together."

Align with a big partner and, immediately, you get multiple pluses: cash, deep management expertise and—when it benefits you—a name you can use to help open doors. Those are very real, very substantial benefits, and that's why partnering is epidemic among dotcoms.

What's in it for the big company? Plenty. Many have been battered by stock markets that want to see the next act—that is, how the traditional business will cope with a world that's ever more centered around the Internet. Building a viable in-house dotcom operation has proven tough for old-style companies, and an alliance with a brash, youthful dotcom is a fast answer to the question, How will you succeed tomorrow?

Back at Petopia, Andrea Reisman heartily concurs with the benefits of teaming up with a big company. Besides providing money, the partnership with Petco transformed Petopia overnight into an online bruiser. "This partnership gives us so many advantages," says Reisman, who ticks off a few:

○ "We get better pricing on products because we're pooling our procurement with theirs."

○ "Every Petco store will feature marketing materials for the Web site, and we'll have access to their database of 5 million customers."

○ "We are using their distribution centers, so we can get products to customers more efficiently."

○ "We're doing our media buying in conjunction with Petco, so we'll get better deals on advertising."

But best of all, says Reisman: "We remain an independent company. Petco is a partner, not the owner. We retain complete freedom to run this business. Petco is good at bricks and mortar, we're good at the dotcom space, and their management knows it."

RISKY BUSINESS

Good as some of the news is about the partnerships that are proliferating throughout the dotcom world, there's a dark side, too. "Partnerships can be an incredible opportunity, but for the relationship to work, you have to work at it," says ComVersant's Datovech, who cautions that oftentimes big companies put up their money but are unprepared to offer anything more: "They are looking to learn from you but aren't prepared to put much into it."

Another trouble spot is pointed out by Dartmouth's Anderson: "Almost definitionally, you are taking the larger brand where it hasn't been before. That's a recipe for conflict." Chew on that because it's at the paradoxical core of small-big alliances. The big company wants the little partner for its creativity, its innovation, and its ability to plunge into terrain previously unexplored by the

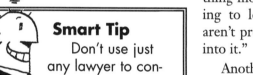

Smart Tip
Don't use just any lawyer to consult with when a tech marriage looms. Find one in a tech center—Silicon Valley, San Francisco, New York City, Austin—with prior experience in doing deals, and be prepared to pay fees upward of $500 per hour. Look at that money as an investment in your future, because that's exactly what it is.

big fellow. But once the deal is done, the risk aversion that is at the core of virtually all megacorporations kicks in—and, suddenly, the partner is counseling caution and slow forward motion.

Then, too, "it's easy for small-business management to take their eyes off the ball," adds Larry Lenhart, a consultant with Deloitte & Touche's high technology practice. Bluntly put: Once an infusion of cash from a large partner eases the pressure to perform, some small businesses get lazy, or—just as bad—they suddenly adopt the methodical "big company" thinking of their partner and lose the hard-charging drive to succeed that once gave them their edge.

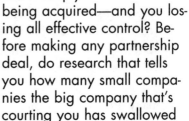

Beware!
Are you concerned about simply being acquired—and you losing all effective control? Before making any partnership deal, do research that tells you how many small companies the big company that's courting you has swallowed in the past year. If the number is high, that doesn't mean back away from the deal. But it does mean you need to be sharply aware of the possible outcomes.

A chilling potential byproduct: "Often the little company's best employees will quit," says Ed Roche, a vice president with technology consulting firm The Concours Group. Why? They were attracted to the fast pace of a small business, but as more bureaucracy takes root in the aftermath of a partnership, they just might bolt.

A last worry to gnaw on is that "the big company may acquire effective control of the little company," says Roche, meaning that although a straightforward acquisition hasn't been done, by taking command of key functions—accounting, say, or by assuming multiple board seats—the big company simply grabs control.

Budget Watcher
Get lots of good information about alliances, free, from Larraine Segil's Web site, www.larrainesegil.com. She offers a thick sampling of freebie articles crammed with sage counsel.

"Small companies usually don't have the expertise to negotiate a fair deal. You absolutely need a third party to assist you."

That recommendation is seconded by Ken Burke, founder and CEO of Petaluma, California-based Multimedia Live, an e-commerce tool developer that in 1998 brought in publisher R.R. Donnelly as a sizable partner. It took eight months to negotiate the deal—which, according to Burke, left him still "controlling the majority of the company's ownership; Donnelly has no real decision-making power"— but, he says, a key for him was "hiring good lawyers. They found many things in the deal we had to get revised or deleted. You don't want to negotiate this sort of thing alone."

Don't pop the cork to celebrate a business alliance too soon—55 percent of alliances fall apart within three years, says business consultant Larraine Segil, author of *Intelligent Business Alliances*. Just why do these marriages unravel? Incompatible corporate cultures were cited by 75 percent of the executives surveyed by Segil, 63 percent pointed to incompatible management personalities, and 58 percent said differences in priorities contributed to the falling-out.

Beware!
Toysmart, www.toysmart.com, thought it had a primo deal when Disney acquired it in 1999 for an undisclosed amount. Except those hopes turned to dust in mid-2000 when Disney simply unplugged Toysmart, shutting down the site to stop its losses. Big companies may have deep pockets, but they may have shallow patience—and that's a real pitfall. The cruel fact is, just as they have the resources to quickly make substantial investments in a little dotcom, they can also—without a shudder or even any hesitation—afford to write all that money off and walk away.

That's why Segil tells small companies to ask themselves: If this marriage ends in divorce, do I have the resources to recover? If you don't, get moving on developing a separation strategy. Maybe it will never be deployed, but with more than half of corporate marriages ending in quickie divorces, prudence dictates having on hand a scenario for survival without the larger partner. Cautions Datovech: "Partnerships can prove life-threatening to small businesses that aren't prepared for the day when the wheels come off the alliance."

FORGING AHEAD

Know that it won't be easy to create a partnership with a big company—no matter how good your dotcom is. How tough will it be? Here's a true story that ends with success, but the going was rugged along the way.

Picture this: You have a great idea for a dotcom. You will sell gift certificates that can be redeemed at many major retailers, and you will make a little bit on every transaction. Sounds terrific, except there's a problem: How do you talk retailers into letting you sell their gift certificates?

Jonas Lee, CEO of GiftCertificates.com (www.giftcertificates. com), knows—and he also knows how hard it was to do the persuading. He now has relationships with more than 100 major retailers, but "we knocked on many doors before we signed the first deals," he says. Why? Start-ups are potentially pathways to wealth, but they may also be fly-by-night concerns. Major, established businesses don't want to risk tarnishing their brand by partnering with a start-up that goes bust.

Eventually Lee got his initial commitments from a couple of

Getting Hitched	Click

Want to pursue alliances? Make up a list of potential partners, and make very sure that you see the deal from their perspective as well as yours. Then put yourself in those partners' faces. Talk to them at trade shows, for instance, and take every step that comes to mind that will increase their awareness of you. But let them make the first move.

In every instance of successful partnerships I've heard about, the big company made the initial suggestion. Maybe there's no jinx involved in taking a direct approach, but maybe there is. So wait to be wooed. Hold on, you may be protesting, didn't Petopia effect its own rescue by bringing in Petco? As it happens, it was Petco that made the first advance, according to Andrea Reisman. The rule still holds true.

name-brand shops—Barnes & Noble and The Sharper Image—"but it took me two or three months of persistent calling and explaining," he says. "You may have a good idea, but you have to also convince people you're a good businessperson, and that takes time." The broader point: Partnerships can be wonderful, but persuading partners to ally with you is about as hard as building a winning Web site in the first place.

e-Chat

$$\left[\begin{array}{l}\text{Guru.com}\\\text{James Slavet, co-CEO and co-founder}\\\textit{Location:}\text{ San Francisco}\\\textit{Year Started:}\text{ 1999}\end{array}\right.$$

Guru.com
James Slavet, co-CEO and co-founder
Location: San Francisco
Year Started: 1999

One of the Web's leading exchanges for matching free-lance talent with businesses that need them, Guru.com has quickly become a hot, richly funded Net property. The revenue model is in flux but apparently will revolve around fees from companies listing jobs as well as from advertising agreements. Early acceptance of Guru.com has been brisk—list-ings and job seekers both number well into the thousands. Guru.com looks as though it's hit a sweet spot in the market, and co-CEO and co-founder Jim Slavet tells how it all happened in a matter of months in 1999.

Robert McGarvey: *Why did you get the idea to launch Guru.com?*

James Slavet: The impetus for Guru.com came primarily through our own personal experiences—I think that's the source of most good entrepreneurial ideas. Jon [co-founder, co-CEO, and Jim's brother] and I have both worked in the Internet indus-try since 1994. We both had a lot of experience trying to find and hire independent contractors to staff up project teams quickly. There was no trusted place to go to find freelancers and consult-ants, and finding them through word-of-mouth was inefficient and time-consuming.

As we developed our business plan, our concept became increasingly "guru-centric." We both have lots of friends and colleagues who've left traditional corporate jobs to work as independent professionals. They are some of the most dynamic, resourceful, intelligent and interesting folks we know, and we thought they'd be a great group of customers to serve.

"Today, companies **are** **forced** to **grow up** so **quickly."**

While freelancers and consultants work in a broad range of industries and professions, we came to realize that there's a tapestry of concerns that connects their everyday lives. People who work on their own want the ability to market themselves better; better deals and information on products and services (like insurance); support with easing their day-to-day back-office hassles (like billing); and a sense of community and connection with other folks who work on their own.

At a broader level, we believed that making a market in services—a market in human capital—is a great, leveraged use of the Web. Building scale in our community, and then connecting fragmented buyers and sellers of contracted services, was exciting to us.

McGarvey: *How long did it take to go from idea to funding to launch?*

Slavet: We developed our original concept in January 1999, incorporated in April 1999, closed our first round of financing (a $3 million angel round)—and launched our preview site—in July 1999, closed our second round of financing in November 1999 ($16 million venture capital round), and relaunched our service in January 2000.

McGarvey: *What's been the biggest surprise you've had in building out Guru?*

Slavet: How compressed company development cycles are in the age of the Internet. Historically, companies would take years to progress and mature. Today, companies are forced to grow up so quickly. Team building, financing, product development and brand development—all these things have to come together so quickly for an Internet company to compete and win these days. You go from infancy to adolescence to adulthood in a matter of months.

McGarvey: *What's been your biggest challenge?*

Slavet: Rapidly building our management team while simultaneously setting the bar extremely high on the quality of people we hire. We refuse to dilute the gene pool, and sometimes that forces us to hold off on filling key positions until we find the right person.

McGarvey: *How many VCs did you meet with before you got a funding commitment?*

Slavet: My strong advice is to take an initial seed round of financing from individual angel investors to get the business going. Venture capitalists prefer not to invest in two guys with a business plan; they usually like to get involved a little bit later, after the company has already demonstrated some traction. We raised our first round of investment through individual angel investors, who were willing to bet more on the team and take more of a risk based upon a promising concept.

When we raised our first round, the major questions were, "How will you get the gurus and can you acquire customers cost efficiently?" When we raised our second round (our first from venture capitalists), we'd launched our beta site and already preregistered more than 20,000 gurus. That went a long way toward answering investors' questions. We met with six venture capital firms and received term sheet commitments [written offers showing how much money a VC will invest in return for what percentage ownership] from four of them within one month of our initial meetings.

Opportunity Knocks

Who can you bring together in an online marketplace? Find two groups that need to talk but aren't, build a Web site where that can easily happen, and you have a formula for success à la Guru. Incidentally, when you get nearer to launching your own site, Guru.com is a rich hunting ground for talented Web site designers.

McGarvey: *What is your strategy in coming out ahead of competitors?*

Slavet: It starts with people: Our management team, investors and board of directors are talented, and they're passionate about building a great company. Beyond that, here are our strategies:

○ *We are guru-centric.* We exist to empower independent professionals and to make their working lives more productive, more lucrative and more fun.

○ *Our intent is to rapidly build our brand and scale our community.* We'll do this through establishing a brand that resonates with our customers, aggressively investing in customer acquisition, brand-building both online and offline, and establishing key strategic distribution partnerships with other leading brands.

CHAPTER 20

Cheap Tricks

> No Brainer Blinds
> Jay Steinfeld, founder and CEO
> *Location:* Houston
> *Year Started:* 1996

Who actually likes buying window coverings? Probably nobody, a fact that Jay Steinfeld—founder and CEO of No Brainer Blinds (www.nobrainerblinds.com)—has turned into a thriving Web-based business that was started with just $3,000 and has been profitable from day one. Steinfeld tells his story here:

Robert McGarvey: *Where did you get the idea for the site? When did the site go live?*

Jay Steinfeld: My wife and I own a full-service bricks-and-mortar window coverings store [in Houston]. We've owned the store for about 14 years, so we know the window coverings business inside and out. But we wanted to expand into a different niche—the price-sensitive do-it-yourself market.

No Brainer Blinds.com has been live for four years, which is two years before the Web was a proven entity. We figured if we hustled and used the same service-first, high-touch philosophy; kept our personality present on the site; and made it fun, then customers would react favorably.

We wanted to make it easy, too—a no-brainer. So we called it No Brainer Blinds.com. That name occurred to me in about two minutes. As soon as I said it, I knew it would work. It made sense, it's descriptive of our mission, and people get it.

McGarvey: *Why haven't you sought outside funding?*

Steinfeld: We might later this year. Lately, we've been barraged by requests from other sites that want us to sell blinds for them. Once those deals are inked, our valuation will go up significantly. There are some blinds factories that have hinted they want to buy us...so who knows? This is my baby, so it would be hard to sell. On the other hand, I suppose, everything is for sale.

McGarvey: *How do you attract visitors to your site?*

Steinfeld: We use all the guerrilla tactics—newsgroups, link building, search engine optimization—and we encourage our existing customers to tell their friends. Most (65 percent) of our volume these days is either repeat customers or referrals.

McGarvey: *What's your look-to-buy ratio?*

Steinfeld: About 5 percent to 10 percent usually.

McGarvey: *How big is the average purchase?*

Steinfeld: $460, which is about three times the industry average.

McGarvey: *To the consumer, what's the advantage in buying online?*

Steinfeld: They save a bunch of money, and they can read up on the options/products at their own pace. No pressure. And we've just created our own private-label product line, too. All of those products are custom-made in just one day and have lifetime warranties.

Budget Watcher

Do you have $3,000 and a decent idea? Check out what No Brainer Blinds did with just that. It's not a Web site that's likely to win prizes for spiffy or artsy design, but it's functional, fast, and helps buyers get in and out quickly. And it's profitable. What can you sell on the Web? Look for products that aren't being sold very well (maybe not at all), get your budget together, and start working. No Brainer Blinds is real proof that if you dream it, you can make it real, with very little money or technical know-how.

McGarvey: *What challenge do you face in making this site grow?*

Steinfeld: Keeping it fresh and out ahead despite other far better funded companies.

Rush Hour: Web Site [Traffic] Builders

Here's the bad news: Search engine Inktomi recently surveyed the Web and reported back that it had counted a mind-numbing 1 billion Web pages. Wow. Just a decade ago, the Web didn't exist. And even five years ago, it remained a playpen for super-nerds. No more. Now every business needs a Web site—but just because you build it doesn't mean a soul will ever visit. "Putting up a Web site can be like opening a store in a back alley," says Jim Datovech, president of IT consulting firm ComVersant. "You've got to work to win visitors."

What's more, traditional marketing campaigns don't necessarily produce results for Web sites, warns Mark DiMassimo, CEO of DiMassimo Brand Advertising, an agency that handles many dotcom clients. A case in point: "Generally, television advertising for dotcoms, although expensive, has been very ineffective," says DiMassimo, whose agency surveyed consumers and discovered that only 6 percent of heavy Web users said they had ever visited a site due to a TV ad. "Offline advertising hasn't always worked as well as the dotcoms had hoped."

That's because these companies are ignoring the cardinal rule of Web site marketing: "Put your dollars where your customers will be," urges DiMassimo. Seems basic? Not to the dotcom companies that plunked down tens of millions of dollars to buy Super Bowl ads. "Having money is no excuse for spending like a drunken sailor," says DiMassimo, who adds that the critical test always has to be, Will my potential customers see the material?

BAITING YOUR HOOK

What will work in luring visitors to a site? Although heavily funded Internet companies can make seven- and eight-figure deals to buy prime advertising real estate on the major Internet portals and online services like Yahoo and AOL, you're likely priced out of that race. So winning visitors becomes a matter of creative, persistent marketing. And the good news is that it's still the little things that will bring plenty of traffic your way.

There are fundamental steps that too many businesses neglect. For instance? "Always put your URL on letterhead, business cards, in e-mail signatures—wherever potential visitors are likely to see it," says Datovech.

The e-mail signature is an especially powerful—and absolutely free—tool. Recieve e-mail from me, and at the bottom you will see a link to www.mcgarvey.net. Click it, and whoosh, you are at my page. It took me a few seconds to create this signature, and it brings in visitors every day.

Think you need to be extremely clever to market your site? Not so. Often it's the simplest things that matter most. "Don't ignore the obvious opportunities to promote yourself," says DiMassimo, whose clients include Kozmo.com, a delivery service. "Kozmo delivery guys are moving advertisements," adds DiMassimo, who explains their clothing is covered with ads for the dotcom. "You cannot ignore these opportunities to promote the brand."

Another low-cost traffic builder: "Get active in online discussion groups and chats, and, where appropriate, always give out your URL," says Shannon Kinnard, author of *Marketing With E-mail: A Spam-Free Guide*. Sell bird toys? Scout out the many groups that focus on birds—a

Beware!
A strong bias against overt advertising remains on the Net's newsgroups. Sigs are OK with postings, but be careful to use a sig that's informational. "Best parrot seeds on the Net" is out; "Seeds for parrots" is fine. The lines seem blurry? They are. But if you cross them, hostile postings from anti-ad folks will tell you the difference.

Snazzy Signatures

Click

Pretty much every e-mail program offers the ability to include a signature that goes out with every e-mail. Think of a signature—"sig" in tech-speak—as a teaser, a fast ad for your Web site. How do you create a signature? In Microsoft Outlook, go to "Tools/Options/Mail Format/Signatures." In AOL, click "Mail Center" then "Set up e-mail signatures." On Yahoo Mail, click "Options/Signature."

Some advice: Short is better than long with signatures. Rarely should you use more than six short lines, and three or four are better.

What to include? If your Web site sells foreign language tapes, for instance, you might use this sig:

> *John Smith*
> *President, TapesRUs.com*
> *"Learn Languages by Tape"*
> *www.tapesrus.com*

Once you've set it up, that signature will appear on every e-mail you send out (unless you override the default), and if you send out 20 e-mails in a day, that's 20 repetitions of a fast ad message. It's one of the Net's best marketing bargains.

good place to find them is at www.deja.com/usenet, which archives discussion lists—and get active. That spreads the word about you and your site, and "you'll get traffic coming to you," says Kinnard.

THE MOST BANG FOR YOUR BUCK

Another big-time traffic builder for any Web site that retails: posting items for sale on the major auctions such as eBay, Yahoo and Amazon. Those sites let you identify yourself to viewers, and a few dollars spent on putting out merchandise to bid just may bring in lots of traffic from surfers seeking more information.

Many small e-tailers tell me their entire advertising budget consists of less than $100 monthly spent at eBay, but they nonetheless are seeing traffic counts above 500 daily, with most of those viewers coming via eBay. My advice: Put up a few items for bid on each of the leading auction sites, then track traffic. Even if you sell the auctioned goods at no profit, the traffic jams you may experience could well justify your efforts.

Classified ads offer more possibilities for traffic generation on the cheap. Check out both Excite and Yahoo. Ads run free there, and viewership is high. I have run ads for Taos County, New Mexico, land that I'm selling, and a stream of leads keeps coming in, at no cost to me. Listing is simple—just follow the steps at the sites—and, again, you can insert your URL so that readers who want more information can get it with a click.

For my money, classified ads—at least the freebies—represent one of the very top ways to generate no-cost traffic, yet many businesses ignore them. Why? The complaint is that such sites have too many listings—hundreds of thousands—but don't let that stop you. Put up some ads, and watch your hit count climb.

Should you buy ads on other Web sites? Absolutely, if you find sites that you can afford—and, increasingly, that's getting easy. Many sites are selling off ad slots for a few dollars. For $150, for instance, Microsoft's bCentral (www.bcentral.com) offers a package of 19,000 banner ad exposures on LinkExchange. Is that money well-spent? If you have a quality banner ad, even though there's no guarantee of a payback, my advice is that it's worth a plunge. With a large number of exposures on premium sites, you just may see a traffic jump.

With any ad campaign you purchase, closely monitor results. Renew only the deals that are generating traffic to your site, and know that Net advertisers have a big plus over advertisers in offline media, such as

Budget Watcher

Get your current visitors to recommend your site to their friends and colleagues—and don't pay a cent for this clever marketing ploy when you sign up with Recommend-It (www.recommend-it.com). It's a clever concept that just might increase your visitor counts.

magazines, because on the Net it is very easy to track—via your log files (see Chapter 32)—which ads are producing which results. That takes the guesswork out of decisions to renew media buys.

What is a fair payback? If small businesses goof, it's in wildly overestimating the results they can anticipate from a media purchase. If you spend $100 on ads that bring in sales that produce $110 in profits, consider it money well-spent. Expecting more than that is just fantasy.

When it comes to offline advertising, expert opinion is mixed. Some pros advocate big spends on traditional media, while others will tell you to fish where the fish are, and that means advertising online to promote an online store. I split the difference here, and my advice is to incorporate your URL prominently into all offline advertising you are doing—never overlook a chance to plug your Web site—but don't launch an offline campaign for an online-only property. Sure, many of the big guys, such as MotherNature.com and PlanetRx.com, extensively advertise in offline media, but these are businesses with heavy venture capital backing and the dollars to experiment with. When money is tighter, go where you know you'll find surfers—and that means hunting online.

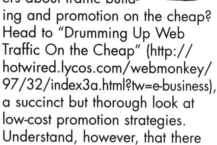

Budget Watcher

Want more pointers about traffic building and promotion on the cheap? Head to "Drumming Up Web Traffic On the Cheap" (http://hotwired.lycos.com/webmonkey/97/32/index3a.html?tw=e-business), a succinct but thorough look at low-cost promotion strategies. Understand, however, that there are no magic formulas. No-money promotion can work if you work at it, and that means consistent, solid effort. Do that, and you'll see the results in a rising daily visitor count.

A Direct Approach

For many businesses, direct mail—good old e-mail—may be the surest and certainly the cheapest tool for building traffic. "E-mail still gets results," says Hans Peter Brondmo, chairman of Post Communications, an e-mail marketing firm that numbers Victoria's Secret, Palm Computing, and Wells Fargo among its clients. Who reads spam? Nobody, says Brondmo, but well-constructed e-mail is "informative and personal, and people will look forward to getting it and reading it."

Spam, Brondmo adds, is "unwanted and unsolicited, by definition. But customized e-mail can generate response rates upwards of 6 percent— sometimes as high as 30 percent. No reputable company would send out spam, but we're seeing more companies using individualized e-mail in their marketing campaigns."

Smart Tip
Ever wish you could use your handwritten signature in your e-mail? Check out Signature e-mail (www.signature-mail.com), where $14.95 buys you five different handwritten signatures to insert into your e-mail.

News Flash

A key to making e-mail effective: Use "opt-in" sign-ups, where Web site visitors are asked to indicate if they want to receive e-mail from you. How to get sign-ups? "Offer a free monthly newsletter," says e-mail expert Shannon Kinnard. "The key is to give really good information."

About what? Content is wide open, but effective newsletters usually mix news about trends in your field with tips and also updates on sales or special pricing. Whatever you do, "keep it short," says Kinnard, who advises that "600 words is probably the maximum length. The rule is, the shorter, the better." Another key: Include hyperlinks so that interested readers can, with a single mouse click, go directly to your site and find out more about a topic of interest.

How often should you mail? Often enough to build a relationship with your readers, but not so frequently that you become a pest. "Monthly works for most mailing lists," says Kinnard, but she notes that "every other week is okay for some businesses."

Daily updates are a big mistake, and probably a weekly frequency is, too. The reason: Recipients will ask to be deleted from the list or, worse, they'll simply delete each of your e-mails unread as soon as they come in. I am personally on a couple lists whose daily incoming e-mail goes straight into the trash unopened. Don't make that mistake.

Some mailing list drawbacks: Maintaining a list can be time-consuming. Worse, most Internet service providers put limits on the size of outgoing mailings (a maximum of 50 recipients is common) to keep spammers away, so mailing to a large list can be an aggravation involving use of many small lists. When I recently mailed to a charity's list of 1,000 as a do-good deed, I had to break the master list into about 25 minilists. When I tried to use more than, say, 50 names at a crack, the server just rejected the whole mailing.

SPECIAL DELIVERY

A solution to common mailing hassles is to "use a mailing service," says Kinnard, who suggests eGroups (www.egroups.com) and Topica (www.topica.com), services that provide free list hosting, meaning they maintain the mailing list and, on your schedule, send out the mailings you provide. Mailings go out with a little third-party advertisement, but with eGroups, a payment of $4.95 monthly kills that ad. It's a smart expenditure to make sure the mailing conveys your message—not that of other companies.

A lot of the drudge work involved in mailings gets handled by these services, which leaves you to focus on the fun part: your message. Keep it simple, keep it sharp, and always use e-mail to drive traffic to your site. Don't make the big mistake of trying to cram your Web site's entire message into every e-mail. Nobody has the patience for that. E-mail should stick to "headline news," with the full story residing on your Web site.

Is your list succeeding? There is no reason to guess the answer.

Smart Tip
Always give e-mail recipients an easy way to "opt out" of future mailings, too—and whenever anybody asks to be removed from your list, honor that request immediately.

Just track site traffic for a few days before a mailing and a few days afterwards. Effective e-mail ought to produce a sharp upward spike in visitors. How big a spike? That answer hinges on your usual traffic, the size of your list, and your personal goals. A good target, though, is the 6 percent response rate mentioned earlier by Brondmo.

Smart Tip
Don't want to take on the task of producing a regular e-mail newsletter? Contact a local college or university. There you'll find plenty of students in communications or journalism departments who would be glad to write up your newsletter for a small monthly payment. But make sure you give the student plenty of direction—it still has to be your newsletter.

If you do not see an increase in traffic, take a real hard look at what you are mailing. Is it succinct? Focused? Does it encourage the readers to click through for more information? If not, odds are you need to do more buffing of your message to encourage recipients to click through.

Another possible reason for less-than-desirable results: Your mailing list is bad. Send a vegan mailing to a list of self-proclaimed steak lovers, and probably you are knocking on the wrong door.

The best way to build up a targeted mailing list is to make it simple for visitors to your site to sign up to receive it. By doing that, they show they are interested in your message—enough to indicate they want to hear more from you. Those are the folks who should be stimulated by your e-mail newsletter to click through for more info, at least sometimes. Keep working on both your newsletter and your list, and it will happen for you, too!

STICK IT TO ME

"Sticky" is the dream that keeps Web site builders going. When your site is sticky, visitors hang around, and that means they're reading and buying—and you can bet every minute a surfer sticks to your site translates into greater brand awareness for you. Whether you are in a mall or your site is stand-alone, sticky is the Holy Grail—but making your site sticky doesn't have to be that elusive. "When the information, the content, is there, people will stick to your site," says Bill Razzouck, former CEO of online healthcare and pharmacy company PlanetRx (www.planetrx.com).

Is he right? For a measuring stick, poke around NetRatings (www.netratings.com), and you'll tumble into a chart headed "Top 10 Web Properties"—and there is no better measure of which sites truly are sticky. In a recent week, eBay (www.ebay.com) held each visitor for more than 48 minutes! When the exit is just a mouse click away, that is amazing, and no other heavily trafficked site rivals eBay's stickiness. In second place, Yahoo (www.yahoo.com) holds its visitors on average a bit more than 27 minutes. Numbers go down from there, with sites like Lycos (www.lycos.com) and AltaVista (www.altavista.com) keeping their visitors less than 10 minutes.

Sticky is the Holy Grail— but making your site sticky doesn't have to be elusive.

Still, even 10 minutes merits a big "Wow!" because most sites I know are happy when visitors stay longer than three. So what do the winning sites have in common? "It's all about content," reiterates ComVersant's Jim Datovech. "Good content and a site that's easy to navigate will keep them coming back."

Of course, content is lots easier to say than it is to deliver. Following are concrete building blocks for making any site stickier:

○ *Fast loading time:* Surfers are impatient. Force them to watch a stagnant screen as dense images (gif's or jpg's) or fancy Java applets load, and they will be out of there before your cool bells and whistles ever come into sight. It's tempting to use these gizmos—you might think they'd increase your visitor stays because just watching them load eats up minutes—but forget it. When you force surfers to wait until meaningful stuff happens, they won't. They will simply leave, often in a huff—and that means they won't be bookmarking your site for future visits.

○ *Good copy:* "The Web is still about text, words," says Motley Fool co-founder David Gardner, and he's spot on. You're not a writer? That doesn't necessarily matter—not when you stick to your field of expertise. Are you a criminal lawyer? Put up a list of the "10 Dumbest Mistakes Defendants Make." An accountant could do likewise. An electrician could put up a list of terribly dangerous goofs made by do-it-yourselfers. Think snappy and useful, and try to create info readers cannot easily find at thousands of other Web sites.

○ *Free stuff:* Surfers still love freebies, and they'll keep coming back if you offer a smorgasbord of goodies. What can you give away? Try your favorite freeware programs. (Always check with the developer before making an app available for downloading from your site. Most developers will thank you, but asking first is both good etiquette and a wise legal precaution.) Find links to plenty of free stuff (both software and nontech stuff) at the About.com Freebies page: http://freebies.about.com

Budget Watcher

Worried that your copy won't be up to snuff? You may be right. A sure way to make a site look amateurish is to post stuff that's riddled with misspellings, bad grammar and worse. The good news: The leading word processing applications (Microsoft Word and Corel WordPerfect) both will meticulously check your copy. Use these tools! Doing so takes a few minutes, but the improvements in writing come instantly.

○ *Lists of favorite links:* Surfers come to you for information in your field of expertise, so are there other related sites you can point them to for more information? Sure, showing a surfer the way out of your site might seem a wacky tool for upping stickiness, but ask sites to give you a reciprocal link, and you'll get traffic from them. Besides, what's Yahoo—the Web's second stickiest site—but a collection of links? There are many much bigger search databases on the Web than Yahoo offers, but its visitors prize the editing that's gone into its listings.

Your visitors, too, will appreciate a concise, intelligent listing of "Sites for More Information," and they may bookmark your site just because they know you offer intelligent links. Note: Keep your links current, relevant to your business, and fresh because how good they are will shape how good visitors think you are.

Oh, and never forget the second half of Datovech's prescription: easy navigation. Every pro webmaster has a few "favorite" awful sites that in fact offer great content but nobody will ever see it because it's too hard to find. Simplicity has to be a byword for any site builder, because the price of boring or confusing a visitor is that surfer's quick exit.

In Search Of: [Secrets] Of Search Engines

I t's simple: If your site isn't listed in the major search engines, Web surfers won't find it. Proof of the importance of search engines is in a recent survey by researchers at Georgia Tech's Graphic, Visualization & Usability Center, which asked surfers how they found new sites. Eighty-five percent pointed to search engines, second only to links found on other pages (88 percent). That says it all: You have to get yourself listed.

But the problem is, with more than 1 billion pages on the Web, how do you win a high ranking in search engine results? "It's almost a black art," says Rob Crigler, the CEO of FatTraffic.com, a Ft. Lauderdale, Florida, consulting firm that specializes in helping clients win top rankings. The inside scoop is that many engines use algorithms—mathematical formulas— to rank sites. Not only do they all use different algorithms, but they don't reveal them, and, worse still, "they change them often, sometimes weekly, but usually monthly," says Crigler. Figure out the formulas—which is what clients pay Crigler to do—and next month you still have to start all over because the rankings have morphed.

Should you just shrug your shoulders and give up? You can't. Every expert agrees that search engines have to figure large in any Web site's marketing plan because they are where users hunt for the information they want. So hunker down, and follow these steps.

Express Delivery `Click`

You want a listing in Yahoo now? Pay the service $199, and you qualify for its "express business submission" plan. The hitch is, payment does not guarantee entry into the index. What the money buys is priority handling: Yahoo guarantees that you will hear a verdict within seven business days of filing. You can get more information at http://help.yahoo.com/help/bizex.

LookSmart offers a similar deal, at the same $199 price. For more information, you can go to http://submit.looksmart.com and click on "Express Submit."

Are these good deals? If you get into the directories, yes, because you'll be weeks ahead of the game (in many cases, perfectly good sites simply get overlooked in the crush of applicants). But it's a risk—you may not get in and will have wasted the money. My advice: Pay the money to Yahoo. It remains far and away the most trafficked search engine. You can prosper without LookSmart, but it simply is very hard to win heavy visitor counts if you are not in Yahoo.

GETTING LISTED

Just about every search engine provides tools for easy registration of new sites. Just look for an "Add URL" or "Add Site" button, then follow the directions (ordinarily no more complex than typing in the address and hitting "Send").

There are hundreds of search engines to choose from. For-hire site registration services typically say they submit to more than 100 engines. But there is little value in being on an index no one uses, which is why Crigler advises clients to focus on a handful of high-traffic engines. Crigler ticks off those where his firm puts its energies: AltaVista (www.altavista.com), Lycos (www.lycos.com), Go (www.go.com), WebCrawler (www.webcrawler.com), Excite (www.excite.com), and Google (www.google.com). Get in them, and you'll reach most surfers, he says.

Want to know which engines have the heaviest traffic? Stop at Media Metrix, a traffic-monitoring firm (www.mediametrix. com). In a recent look, the top engines were Go, Lycos, Excite and AltaVista. But any in Media Metrix's top 10 list are worth pursuing.

For those interested in going slightly off the beaten track, Yahoo offers up a full page of offbeat listings, such as Yep (www. yep.com), but traffic at these sites is scarce. If you personally use a few—or know your customers do—get listed. But don't sweat the many dozens of engines you won't be in. Probably this omission won't amount to much, so long as you are in the biggies.

Do you use Ask Jeeves (www.askjeeves.com), DogPile (www. dogpile.com), or Mamma, the Mother of All Search Engines (www.mamma.com)? Don't try to list with them. These are "parallel engines" (sometimes called meta engines) that query various search engines with your question. They don't index sites; they aggregate information from other sites. DogPile, for instance, queries LookSmart (www.looksmart.com), GoTo (www.goto.com), InfoSeek (www.go.com), Google, DirectHit (www.directhit.com), Lycos, AltaVista, and a couple of others. These parallel engines are handy to use when searching, but put them out of mind when seeking to get listed.

ENGINE TROUBLE

One hitch in the listing process: Expect delays. AltaVista is quick to add new sites to its listings—historically they have shown up in the database within a few days—but

Smart Tip

Usually the "Add Site" button is at the bottom of the page, sometimes in tiny print. A few engines hide theirs. At Google, for instance, it's under "About Google." The only major engine that does not seem to offer this option to users is Fast Search (www.fastsearch.com), which seemingly relies upon its own spider (a search tool that automatically moves from site to site, following all available links) to add listings. Find out more about spiders later in this chapter.

Spider Webs | Click

User submissions are not the only—or even the main—way search engines compile their indexes. The chief tool used by the engines in scoping out the lay of the Web are spiders—also called crawlers—which meander from site to site, following links, and reporting findings back to the search engine. Has your Web site been spidered? Check your log file (see Chapter 32 for more on logs), and you'll easily see a spider's trail.

A recent look at the log for www.mcgarvey.net revealed that AltaVista had paid a visit. I knew that because this showed up on the log: scooter.pa.alta-vista. net. "Scooter" is the nickname used by AltaVista's spider (cute names are the norm for spiders. Inktomi calls its spider "Slurp," while Northern Light calls its "Gulliver"), and in this sweep it took in about one-third of the pages at mcgarvey.net. That can be a sign that it needs to be reminded about the other pages. Whenever you see a spider has missed key pages, resubmit them to that engine. Maybe the engine already knows them, maybe it doesn't; either way, resubmitting is good policy.

A sure tip-off that a spider has come is when the log file reveals a request for the "robots.txt" file—a file that tells a visiting spider what parts of a Web site are off limits. If you don't have one, that request is put in the "errors" bins. Do you need one? Probably not. If you have nothing that's meant to be strictly private stored on your Web site—and you shouldn't because if a file is on the Web, it's in the public domain—there's no need to tell a spider hands off.

weeks, sometimes months, will pass before a site appears in Lycos or Excite. What can you do to expedite this? Sadly, nothing. Engines list new sites in their own time frames, and as they've been hit with a tsunami of new Web pages, backlogs of sites in the "to be added" queues have grown long. But just maybe some engines will take a clue from Yahoo and offer those willing to spend cash the option to buy expedited entry. So look around the sites for news about "express entry," and you may find that prayer answered. (For more on the express option offered by Yahoo and LookSmart, see "Express Delivery" on page 146.)

In the listing of Web sites, nothing is automatic. The most comprehensive search engine of all is Fast Search (www.fast search.com), which indexes only about 30 percent of the Web. Second place in a recent survey was AltaVista with about 24 percent. Excite and Northern Light (www.northernlight.com) each had around 20 percent. And Lycos (www.lycos.com) had only 5 percent.

Why aren't more sites listed? Most engines seem to ignore Web pages put up at free Web hosts (such as AOL's member pages). But the big reason just may be that the site owner didn't take the time to submit the URLs.

Make it a habit. Submit all your URLs to all the main engines every couple months. Nobody knows why, but sometimes sites fall out of a listing. Even if you're already listed, you'll rarely be penalized for resubmitting a site. Don't spam the indexes—by submitting junk pages or deceptive content—and you'll be fine.

RANK AND FILE

Getting listed is the easy part. Scoring high in the ranking is another story, but that's where the money gets made. It does little good to be the 212th business-plan writer in the rankings at Go. Who will wade through 21 screens to find you? Nobody, maybe not even you, would likely read that many pages of information. You'll only look at perhaps 30 results from any given search; maybe 50 or 100 if the quarry is proving elusive. Patience runs only so deep, and a surfer's attention span is not infinite.

That's why big dol-

Smart Tip

Get the scoop on using meta tags to maximum advantage by doing some reading. Search Engine Watch offers a full discussion at www.searchenginewatch.com. Or visit Cyber Eye at www.meta-tags.com.

lars are earned by consultants who specialize in tweaking sites to maximize ratings. But legitimate consultants make no empty claims. "We cannot promise you a specific ranking or a high ranking," says Crigler, whose FatTraffic charges clients $49 per keyword they want to show up high in the ratings. That is just being honest. With search engine architects so frequently tinkering with their algorithms, nobody can truthfully promise you the placement you want. Professionals who are expert in artificial intelligence and search engine logic can go far toward boosting your ranking, but any promises are just hot air.

Beware! Don't put in the names of big competitors in your meta tags. Some small companies have tried that, to boost traffic, but when big companies get annoyed with this, they are starting to sue. Even if they don't ultimately win in court, who has the time and resources to fight back against a Fortune 500 behemoth? Be scrupulously honest about content in your meta tags, and you will do fine.

Can you do some of this yourself? You bet. The secret of pro webmasters is clever use of meta tags, which is computerspeak for text the search engine reads but surfers don't see. Use this tool wisely, and a site can find itself climbing high in the ratings.

Sounds tricky? It's not. When constructing any Web page, just insert simple meta tags high on the page. For example, a computer discounter might insert the following tags:

<META name="description" content="discount prices on name-brand computers"> and <META name="keywords" content= "discount computers, computers for sale">

Many search engines use keywords and relevancy—how directly a site relates to particular keywords—to determine how high you show up in the ratings, and meta tags are the surest way to let search engines know what you are about.

Not all engines recognize meta tags, but many do. That makes this a powerful tool, so keep tinkering with your meta tags until you come up with a short summary that fully captures your site's mission—that's a big step toward scoring high.

Here's the big warning about meta tags: "Don't go wild with

meta tags; you'll get penalized," says Crigler. That's because some site developers are deceptive, and they insert meta tags that have nothing to do with their own content. Case in point: the heavy use of celebrity names in meta tags of porno sites. (Search for, say, "Julia Roberts," and don't be surprised if many of the "hits" are X-rated sites with no obvious relationship to Ms. Roberts—other than a meta tag that includes her name because a slick webmaster is aiming to lure in traffic.) Search engines are always on the hunt for such abuses, and page designers who purposely deceive can find all their pages deleted from the rankings.

DIRECTORY ASSISTANCE

There's another way to get your site in front of users' eyes: directories at Yahoo, LookSmart, and Snap (www.snap.com); and the Open Directory Project (www.dmoz.org), used by Netscape, Lycos, and HotBot (www.hotbot.com). They aren't search engines as such but rather directories compiled by human editors.

By all means, submit your site to these indexes, but know that the tweaks the pros use to maximize search engine placement won't work with these human-edited directories. Especially important: "Good, relevant content and design are the secrets with the human-edited directories," says Crigler.

Getting into any directory, however, is tough. The biggest, Yahoo, indexes around 1.2 million pages, a tiny fraction of the Web's content. Heavily trafficked Snap indexes just 600,000 pages. But don't dwell too much on the complicated nuances involved in getting ever higher rankings. Put that energy into building a spiffier, more user-friendly site, and, odds are, you'll get a payoff.

Smart Tip

Want to know more about search engines and rankings? Head to Search Engine Watch (www.searchenginewatch.com), where all the ins and outs are explored. Other sites worth a look include Understanding Search Engines (http://Web.hamline.edu/administration/libraries/search/comparisons.html) and Search Engine Showdown (http://searchengineshowdown.com).

How do you get listed in a human-edited directory? Just go to the sites and—as with search engines—look for an "Add URL" tab. At Snap, for instance, click "List Your Site," and that takes you to a fast form. Fill it out, cross your fingers, and you just may show up in that directory.

CHAPTER 23

Trade Ya: [Boosting] Traffic With Banner Exchanges

Use the Web to build the Web: That's a guiding philosophy for jump-starting Web traffic to your site. There are two main ways site owners help each other gain more traffic: banner exchanges and link exchanges. A root belief behind these arrangements is that the best audience for any Web site is the person who's already online. Think about it. You could tell Great Aunt Molly back in County Cavan, Ireland, how wonderful a site is, but if Molly has neither an Internet connection nor a computer, what possible good does that do?

Talk to the architects of great Web successes, and they all are big advocates of seeking to gain more traffic through online marketing campaigns The good news is that exchanges are priced right for any small business: They are absolutely free. But they are not without some drawbacks. To discover more about the pluses and minuses, read on.

HOLD YOUR BANNER HIGH

How can you turn down free advertising for your Web site? That's what banner exchanges offer. Usually, the deal is that you put a third-party banner on your site, and with every two exposures, your banner shows up on another site. The cost to you: zip, other than the minute it takes to paste the banner exchange's code into your site. What's in it for the exchange? It sells a banner slot for each one you get for free.

"These programs can really benefit a small business," says Peter Krasilovsky, a vice president with tech consulting firm The Kelsey Group. But they aren't merely the province of small businesses. Look closely at your computer screen, and you will see big names—Drugstore.com, E-Trade, even lofty Microsoft—using banner ads to drum up traffic.

"**Good** banners are **billboards** **on** the information **superhighway**."

The catch: Increasingly, surfers just ignore banners. "Three years ago, it was easy to get people to click on banners. Now it's tough," says Ben Neumann, CEO of iBoost.com, a Los Angeles-based Web site-hosting firm. "If you are really good, you might get a 2 percent click-through rate," meaning that it will take 50 exposures of your banner to get one visitor to your site.

That's if your banner is top-notch. Mundane banners fare still worse: "We're seeing click-throughs averaging 0.6 percent," says Deborah Bayles, an e-commerce consultant. At that rate, a site needs almost 200 exposures of its banner to snare a lone visitor.

In a banner exchange where I participate, my current average click-through is an anemic 0.3 percent. Maybe it's just a bad banner, or maybe the subject matter is uninteresting, but whatever the reason, it takes 1,000 exposures to bring three visitors to the site. Is that worth it? So far, my judgment is yes, because those are new visitors. What's more, even surfers who don't click through perhaps absorb the ad. And that's all to the good when promoting a site.

A CLEAR MESSAGE

You may be able to do dramatically better than that. "Banners are ineffective for many sites, but they don't have to be," says Ed Ziv, a consultant with Flash Creative Management, a tech consulting firm. "Good banners are billboards on the information superhighway. They are short, with just a few words, and offer a clear message. And you'll increase your results if two of those words are 'Click Here.' We've seen big jumps in click-throughs just by including those words."

Another pointer: Modest use of animation still catches eyeballs. Note the word "modest." Animation can be overdone, but a bit of motion does catch the eye, and that's the first step in creating a successful banner.

And think short and sweet. Best guesses are that if a banner is noticed at all, it only has a couple of seconds to grab a viewer's attention. Simple messages work: "Tax Consulting, Low Cost, High Results" is much better than the more complicated "Our tax lawyers are the county's best. We keep you out of jail and save you money." The latter might work in a 15-second radio spot, but forget it in a banner ad. If you cannot read your banner in a couple of seconds, it needs pruning.

Easy Does It — Click

A big question: Should you put banner exchange banners on each of your pages, or only a few? Most exchanges leave that call in your hands, and my advice is to be judicious in slapping third-party banners on your pages. Keep them off pages that already take a long time to load. Every banner adds seconds to the loading, and on the Net every second counts with impatient surfers. Keep them off critically important pages, such as the page where visitors complete sales—who wants distractions at that time? Use your own judgment, but always keep in mind that your message is paramount, and anything that gets in the way has to go.

In that same vein, many banner exchanges offer you a deal: Put their ads at the top of your pages, and your ads will display on the tops of others' pages. I say take the deal sparingly or not at all. The evidence is plain that banners near the top of pages do draw better, but that's because this is where a visitor's eyes go first. And that's where you want your company to be instantly visible. Building your brand identity is more important than chasing click-throughs from third-party sites.

Don't have a banner, or don't like the one you have? There are software tools that will help you through this task—see Chapter 5 for some tools and tricks. But you may be able to do this job, easily and for free, using the Web to snag free banners. Plenty of sites that offer do-it-yourself online tools are on the Web to serve you, including GraphXisle (www.graphxisle.com), Banner Generator (www.coder.com/creations/banner), and MediaBuilder's "Amazing, Instant Online Animated Banner Maker" (www.mediabuilder.com/abm.html).

Wherever you go, you will have a usable banner in hand within a few minutes. These tools are simple and designed to be used by nontechies. And while you're at it, make several banners. Why? A key to any advertising program is testing, and much as you may love a banner, your target market may ignore it. Test several, and use the one that consistently brings in the best results.

Keep tinkering—with banner design, text and placement—until you win a click-through rate that at least tops 1 percent. A big plus of banner exchanges is that all the major ones tell you your exposures and click-throughs, so knowing how you score is just a matter of checking in.

One more tip: In any banner exchange, closely watch the banners that show up on your site. You don't want to display banners that drive off customers. Like what? Well-run exchanges let you ban "adult content"—that means porn—and no matter where you stand on free speech, make sure to check the "No Porn" box. Religion, too, is a sensitive topic, and many businesses will want to keep it off their sites. Best

Smart Tip

Discover dozens of banner exchanges with a visit to: http://dir.yahoo.com/Computers_and_Internet/ Internet/World_Wide_Web/Announcement_Services/ Banner_Exchanges. Find even more here: www.freecenter.com/ bannerx.html. Want to cut to the chase? Many experts point to Microsoft's Link Exchange (now incorporated into www.bcentral. com) as the premiere exchange for small businesses. A key advantage is that Link Exchange allows for fine-tuning where your banner shows, down to geographic preferences—and that's a big factor in determining a banner's effectiveness.

On The Trail? | Click

Page-view counts provided by a banner exchange may—and probably will—differ radically from the counts that show up in your logs (see Chapter 32 for the scoop on logs). Is the exchange cheating you? Could be, but the more probable answer is that your log is counting visits from search engine spiders, the robots sent out by the big search engines to prowl for new Web content. In a few cases, however, maybe the banner exchange just didn't count properly when a visitor dropped into your Web site. Balky servers and Net traffic jams are why that happens, and they are inevitable. But if it happens a lot, complain to the link exchange. If that does no good, sign up with a different exchange.

advice, though, is to seek to exchange banners only with other businesses in roughly the same market sector as you. Right there, you up the chances that people who see your banner will be interested in having a look at your site.

LINKING UP

Way back in the Web's infancy, the first tool sites used to build traffic was simple: They swapped links, with the deal being that if A put up a link to B, B reciprocated, and both just might see traffic gains. The link could be swapped banners or simply hyperlinked text.

Microsoft's Link Exchange extends that concept, but the downside is you have no precise control over what banners run on your site or where your banners run. Want that control? It's easy: Create your own informal link exchange, the traditional way, by asking sites that complement yours (but don't compete) to put your link on their pages and you'll do likewise. It may be old-fashioned, but it's still powerful. Amazon, for instance, sparingly doles out links to some of its partners on its front page, and being in front of that many eyeballs is a big plus for any Web site.

How to get in on this? Simple: As you surf the Web, note sites you like and that attract visitors who might be interested in your site, too. A PR agency, for instance, might profitably exchange links with an advertising agency, but probably neither would gain from an exchange with a pet groomer.

Keep links appropriate, and guess what—you've created your own mini-Yahoo, a human-edited selection of relevant sites that probably will interest your visitors. Might you lose visitors who click away to your linked sites? You bet, but odds are for every visitor you lose, you'll gain another. And if your links page is good enough, visitors may even bookmark it because you've done them the favor of compiling info they want.

But remember, fair is fair. Give links the same kind of exposure on your pages that you get on theirs, and if a partner isn't living up to the arrangement (or the site's quality dramatically drops off), don't hesitate to pull out of the deal.

Will everybody you approach say yes? Best guesses are that only a small percentage will, mainly because most people are busy pursuing other things in their lives and don't want to put in the time to keep modifying and updating their Web site. So don't get discouraged by rejection. Keep asking and, over time, you just may build up a tidy assortment of linked sites.

RING AROUND THE WEB

Link and banner exchanges aren't the only way to go. A variation is Web rings, which loosely link together dozens, sometimes hundreds, of related sites. Here's how it works: At the bottom of a page, there's a brief squib about the Web ring ("This ring is for sellers of handfed cockatoos"), and a visitor need only click the ring to go onto another site in the chain. Web rings are used by mainly hobbyists and enthusiasts (there are plenty on the HMS Titanic, vampires, and religions, for instance), but small businesses (sometimes all of a downtown shopping district) could also create their own rings to the profit of all.

Want more info on Web rings? Surf into Ring Surf, where there are hundreds to join and starting your own is free (www. ringsurf.com).

CHAPTER 24

e-Chat

$$\begin{bmatrix} \text{Drugstore.com} \\ \text{Peter Neupert, CEO} \\ \textit{Location: } \text{Bellevue, Washington} \\ \textit{Year Started: } 1999 \end{bmatrix}$$

What would it take to lure a high-powered Microsoft millionaire to quit Gates & Co. and join a brand-new Net start-up? Money clearly won't do it. Listen up as Peter Neupert—onetime vice president of online services at Microsoft—explains what prompted him to plunge into the role of CEO of Drugstore.com and what he believes it will take to succeed in the crowded online drugstore niche.

Robert McGarvey: *Why did you quit Microsoft to join a start-up?*

Peter Neupert: John Doerr [a legendary venture capitalist with Kleiner, Perkins] called and said, "I have a great opportunity." I told him, "I'm not interested." He kept calling, and it took about a month, but I became convinced and I took the position. The opportunity to run my own show in a big category of e-commerce was too good to pass up.

McGarvey: *How big will the drugstore category be?*

Neupert: This market is huge, around $150 billion in annual sales. But the Web can really change how people shop by empowering them with information. This literally is a way to revolutionize how people purchase healthcare products.

McGarvey: *This is a crowded niche, with PlanetRx, CVS, and many others seeking market share. What's your major competition?*

Opportunity Knocks

Closely scan your product sales reports—and don't be surprised to discover the unexpected. Somehow, on the Web, audiences we never expect find us. However, when you see unanticipated sales trends, react fast—that's a key edge of the Web over other kinds of retailing. Adjust product mix to meet customer needs and redo pages to point to what customers are looking for.

Neupert: Customer inertia. There are hundreds of thousands of places that buy what we sell—drugstores, grocers, Wal-Mart. People get into patterns. We want people to understand that shopping with us will save them both time and money. Our value proposition is this: Shop with us, and I will give you 20 minutes back a week because you no longer have to do this chore. It's much easier to click a mouse and get this merchandise delivered to your door.

McGarvey: *Hasn't the online drugstore space taken off more slowly than many expected?*

Neupert: Here we are talking about products people put on their skin and into their bodies—you have to believe the market will take off gradually. People really care about this stuff, and it will take more communication on our part to explain the benefits of buying online.

McGarvey: *How will you beat competitors?*

Neupert: Our focus is on the customer experience. Our product assortment is better than competitors', and we've made it easier for customers to buy. We provide deep, detailed product information. We believe those will be the most important factors to users.

McGarvey: *Where will your profits come from—prescription drugs or other merchandise?*

Neupert: Our revenue mix won't be dissimilar from traditional retail drugstores, about 50-50 prescription drugs and other merchandise. We see more profits coming from the nonprescription side. The profitability of prescriptions has been squeezed, but I do think there are profits to be made there as well.

McGarvey: *Have there been surprises in your mix of products sold?*

Neupert: We have found that anonymity—the ability to buy without embarrassment—is an appealing aspect of shopping at our site. We sell a lot of K-Y Jelly [a lubricant], and initially I couldn't figure out why. We also sell a lot more condoms than we expected.

McGarvey: *Critics say online drugstores will sell drugs to kids—is this a worry?*

Smart Tip

How do you persuade wary consumers to buy? For Drugstore.com's Peter Neupert, the answer is information—and that's an area where the Net can excel. Pick up a bottle of vitamins in a drugstore, for instance, and what do you know about it? Only what is printed—usually in microscopic type—on the bottle. On the Web, an e-tailer can offer detailed information at very little cost, and this is the fast track to gaining a leg up on traditional retailers.

Whenever you encounter customer resistance, try informing them into making a purchase. It just may be the key that opens sales.

Neupert: If I were a kid and I wanted Valium, I'd take a prescription pad from a doctor's office, and then pay cash at a local pharmacy. To do it on the Internet, you need a credit card and also a shipping address. If you were going to break the law, why would you leave that trail? That said, we spend a lot of time, money and effort ensuring that prescriptions are legitimate.

McGarvey: *What will this category look like in a few years?*

Neupert: E-commerce will look very different 10 years from now than it does today—and it will be fun to be a part of that.

CHAPTER 25

Cheap Tricks

eHolster.com
Tom Traeger, founder and CEO
Location: St. Augustine, Florida
Year Started: 1999

Who hasn't lost a PalmPilot or a cell phone? There's never any place to comfortably tuck them, and that's why they're so easy to leave behind in restaurants, airplane seats and such. But that also meant a big business opportunity for Tom Traeger, founder of eHolster.com (www.eholster. com), where the product is a shoulder holster for our personal electronics gadgets (priced at $59.95 or $99.95 for a leather version). Traeger designed the product, arranged for its manufacture, and built out his Web site—all on a thin budget. Here he tells how:

Robert McGarvey: *What were your start-up costs?*

Tom Traeger: Total costs to date have been less than $25,000 to develop the e-Holster product, create the electronic storefront, and complete the trademark searches and the LLC, etc.

McGarvey: *How long did it take you to build the site?*

Traeger: First I had to fully design the product, which has taken me nine months. Then it was on to the Web site, which has taken a solid six months.

McGarvey: *Other than the conventional steps, are you doing anything new to bring in site visitors?*

Traeger: Every e-Holster has a "branding label" on the back,

Beware

The good news about using the Web to launch an innovative product is that there aren't dozens of other sites all selling essentially the same product. The bad news is that it takes work, time, money and even luck to build public awareness that this new gizmo exists. It can be done, for sure, but don't think it's enough simply to come up with a clever product idea. That's just the first step on what will be a long, rough journey.

with the URL e-Holster.com, so every customer is a walking billboard.

Another cool thing I am doing is, I sent a sample to the costume designer for HBO's "The Sopranos," suggesting that an actor wear an e-Holster to symbolize the transition from wearing a shoulder holster for old-fashioned weapons to wearing an e-Holster for cell phones/PDAs, the new weapons of today. I'm always trying to get e-Holster in the movies or on TV.

CHAPTER 26

Extra Credit: [Accepting] Credit Cards

The number-one question on the minds of new Web site builders is, How do I arrange to accept credit cards for payment? Once upon a time (which means last year, in Internet time), getting merchant account status for an online storefront was tough because credit card companies were suspicious about vendors who lacked bricks-and-mortar storefronts. No more.

Even bankers have awakened to the reality that the Net is creating a dramatic revolution in how commercial transactions get done, and an upshot is that credit card issuers nowadays have truly "gotten it"—they understand that the Net is a legitimate retail channel, and they are rushing to set up merchant accounts with online stores.

But that doesn't mean it's suddenly easy. Issuers still want proof that yours is a real business and not a fly-by-night con game. Patiently answer all their questions and show the requested documents, and, likely, you'll get the status you crave.

TAKING CREDIT

A good first place to start your search for merchant status is your own bank. Most issue credit cards, and if you have a long-term relationship, that's a big plus. Your bank says no? Try a few other local banks—offering to move *all* your accounts—and you just may be rewarded with merchant status.

You may also try other companies that specialize in issuing accounts to online merchants, including:

○ *Cardservice International:* www.cardservice.com

○ *VeriSign:* www.verisign.com

○ *Credit Card Processing Services:* www.mcvisa.com

○ *The Processing Network:* www.processing.net

○ *21st Century Resources:* www.merchant-account-4u.com

Or log onto Yahoo and search for credit card processing. You'll find many dozens of outfits, large and small, that are on the prowl for start-ups seeking merchant accounts.

Credit cards aren't processed cheaply, however, at least not for a start-up. A typical fee schedule for a small-volume account (fewer than 1,000 transactions monthly) would include start-up fees amounting to around $200 and monthly processing fees of around $20.

Is that money you need to spend? Absolutely. It simply is impossible to run a real electronic storefront without credit card processing capabilities. In very special cases, yes, you can go online and ask customers to mail in checks, but when your aim is to build a volume storefront, you have to take credit cards—customers expect it, and it will make transactions easier for everyone involved.

SECURE HORIZONS

The one must-have for online credit card processing: secure, encrypted connections. You've seen this many times yourself. Go to virtually any major e-tailer, commence a purchase, and you are put into a "secure server" environment

Beware! Plenty of shady outfits are bent on getting rich offering bogus merchant accounts to gullible online beginners. Before shelling out any cash, make sure that you're setting up an account that will handle industry-standard cards (such as MasterCard and Visa, not "Big Bob's Lollapalooza Credit Card" or some specialty card). A stop at the Better Business Bureau—www.bbbonline. com—would be good policy before inking any costly deal with an unknown vendor.

You'd Better Shop Around   Click

My hunt for online credit card processing services revealed wide discrepancies in fees and pricing menus. Start-up fees ranged from $100 to more than $500, with monthly fees ranging from free to more than $100. Volume is a key factor—sites anticipating fewer than 1,000 transactions monthly often can arrange very low-cost credit card deals—but a lot of this seems simply to be Wild West pricing.

Should you go with the lowest price? Not necessarily. My advice is to go with companies you trust. If there's a premium involved, pay it if you can. Always do business with your local bank, if it will accept you as a customer, even if the rate schedules are higher than those charged by online credit card processing specialists. There have been many, many crooked operators, and caution can pay off big time.

where transaction data is scrambled to provide a measure of safety against hackers. Truth is, these worries are generally unfounded—the odds of a hacker grabbing an unencrypted credit card number from a nonsecure Web site are pretty slender—but buyers by now feel reassured when they see they're entering a secure site, and that means you need to provide it.

Is this a technical hassle for you? It shouldn't be. Whatever vendor sells you credit card processing should also, as part of the package, provide a secure transaction environment. If they don't, look elsewhere.

It may sound daunting to arrange for online credit card processing, a secure server, and the rest, but nowadays, you can have it in place in a matter of minutes. Sign up for a Yahoo Store, for instance, and it's simple to tack on an application for credit card processing through Bank One (which charges a $175 setup fee, a $45 monthly fee, and 30 cents per transaction). That's not necessarily the best deal—cheaper packages are readily available—but doing this as part of creating a Yahoo Store adds mere minutes to the process (and you are promised approval or disapproval of your merchant account within three days).

Opportunity Knocks

Had problems setting up a merchant account? Look into shifting your storefront to an established mall such as Yahoo's. Generally, credit card processors are more flexible about approving start-ups that are part of a mall. Why? Mall owners exert a bit of control over the business practices of their tenants, and the credit card processors seem to believe (probably correctly) that blatant abuses won't be long tolerated. So word is that they are quicker to say yes to tenants.

Once approved, you're set to take Visa, MasterCard, American Express and Diner's Club—nothing more has to happen. You may hear how hard and time-consuming setting up an online merchant account is, but that was yesteryear. Now it's one of the easiest parts of setting up your dotcom.

CHAPTER 27

e-Chat

StarMedia Network
Fernando Espuelas, co-founder and CEO
Location: New York City
Year Started: 1996

Uruguay-born Fernando Espuelas had just snatched a prestigious promotion to managing director of marketing communications for AT&T in Latin America, and to celebrate, he was on a trek in Nepal when a remarkable thing happened. He was lying on the ground, exhausted, when he saw that all around him Nepalese women were climbing the Himalayas with big logs on their backs and seemed to have no complaints at all. Espuelas first thought was that he was a whiner, but in his second thought he realized he could do "whatever I wanted to do! It was exhilarating," he says. With that, he ran up the mountain—and it hit him that what he really wanted to do was something with the Net.

Good thought, but when he came down off the mountaintop, he got nowhere with his AT&T bosses. Eventually, that led to him quitting to launch his own company, StarMedia Network, an Internet portal aimed at Latinos. Flash-forward a couple years, and StarMedia is now approaching leadership in Latin America. After raising nearly $100 million in venture funding over a few years, StarMedia went public in 1999 and currently has a market capitalization of more than $1 billion. In a recent filing, Espuelas reported ownership of more than 4.5 million shares with a market value of roughly $75 million.

Here, Espuelas tells more about walking away from a great job to take the Net plunge.

Robert McGarvey: *Why did you decide on the Net as you stood on the mountain?*

Fernando Espuelas: I asked myself, What's the most interesting thing I could do? The answer was the Internet. I thought about what the Net could mean on a continent of 500 million people—and I saw that the Net will be the most revolutionary thing to happen in Latin America since Simon Bolivar kicked out the Spaniards!

McGarvey: *Have U.S. businesses largely ignored South America?*

Espuelas: A lot of perfectly intelligent U.S. business executives would rather do business in Asia. There are many misconceptions regarding South America. It is very weird. One magazine asked me to pose for a photograph wearing a sombrero! A venture capitalist said to me as we sought funding, "Isn't Latin America that big blob south of Texas?" To many people, Latin America is defined by a Chihuahua!

Opportunity Knocks

A strange idea for a Web site hits you? Don't be too quick to scoff at the idea. Fernando Espuelas was a high-achieving AT&T executive when he walked away from that to live his dream of building a site for Latinos. Sure, doubtless there were many at AT&T who laughed at this—but with a personal wealth approaching $100 million, Espuelas is the one who can now afford a chuckle. Live your dream.

McGarvey: *When did you start StarMedia?*

Espuelas: In September 1996. I started it with my best friend from high school, Jack Chen. Between us, we put in seven figures in start-up cash. And before I left AT&T, I applied for 12 credit cards with very large limits and got them. That proved smart. We sought venture funding, but we were getting nowhere. By July '97, all we had were my credit cards. I remember taking an $18,000 cash advance, and that was literally the last dollar we could access. Two weeks later, we got a check for $3.6 million from Chase [a venture fund].

McGarvey: *What attracted venture cash to StarMedia?*

Espuelas: A confluence of two trends: a) the Internet and the modernization of Latin America; and b) the brand we are building in Latin America. We are very aggressively building our brand, our name recognition, and that's giving us an edge. We also were the first to really go after this market.

McGarvey: *How active have you personally been in building the StarMedia brand?*

Espuelas: At the beginning, when our traffic was low, I hung out in our chat rooms just to help build user enthusiasm. For me this has been a very, very hands-on business experience.

CHAPTER 28

Cheap Tricks

$$\left[\begin{array}{l}\text{Bowlingconnection.com}\\\text{Gary Forrester, owner}\\\textit{Location:}\text{ Tucson, Arizona}\\\textit{Year Started:}\text{ 1999}\end{array}\right]$$

Turned on by pink, retro bowling shirts? How about bowling jackets and T-shirts? If bowling is a passion of yours, you want to know about Bowling Connection, where pretty much everything a bowler craves is on sale.

Site owner Gary Forrester pegs his start-up costs at "just about zero," but still he's mounted a handsome, fast-moving site with plenty of functionality, including secure online ordering. How? He built the site using GoBizGo (www.gobizgo.com), a one-stop, nearly no-brainer solution offered by NetObjects (www. netobjects.com), a software and solutions provider to small businesses that want a Web presence. GoBizGo is offered both directly by NetObjects and also as a private-label product marketed by telephone companies under their own brand (in Forrester's case, he used US West's Sitematic, which is GoBizGo under a different name).

Yes, you could do all this yourself—and maybe you should, at least in some cases—but listen to how easy this proved for Forrester, who found GoBizGo so simple that after Bowling Connection, he promptly launched two more sites, www.southwest-gifts. com and www.usatiles.com

Robert McGarvey: *What were your start-up costs?*

Gary Forrester: My start-up costs were almost zero. I already owned the computer, and US West Sitematic made it so easy to build the Web site, I didn't have to employ any outside sources at all. One of my Web sites costs $49.95 per month, and the other two sites are $79.95 per month because the catalogs are bigger. I look at that cost as my "rent" payment. Where can you have a store that is open to the world 24 hours a day, and you don't even have to pay employees to take care of your customers? You actually make money while you sleep.

"Where can you have a **store** that is **open** to the world **24 hours** a day, and you don't even have to **pay employees** to take care of your **customers**?"

McGarvey: *How long did it take you to build the site?*

Forrester: The initial site only took a few minutes to get up. I knew nothing (and I stress nothing) about building a Web site. Sitematic has many templates to choose from. You fill in your company information and then choose how your site will be presented to the world. You just keep clicking on the templates to view your site in many different formats and then select the one you like best. I am constantly making changes to make the sites better, and I'm always adding new products to my catalogs.

McGarvey: *What is your monthly revenue?*

Forrester: The monthly revenue varies. After starting the first Web site, www.bowlingconnection.com, I started my second one, www.southwest-gifts.com, and then the third one, www. usatiles.com. Revenue increases almost weekly. This is all I do. I don't have a "real job." I'd rather not disclose the figures, but I will say that is has been very profitable.

McGarvey: *What's been the biggest surprise?*

Forrester: The [1999] Christmas season was our biggest surprise. I expected business to pick up a little more than usual. I didn't expect it to get crazy. We worked day, night and weekends to fill the orders. It was a challenge, but we did it—all our customers received their orders by Christmas.

Building Blocks

Click

J. Peterman built a hugely successful business starting from one item—a duster-type raincoat that he happened to discover in the West. It was a cool coat, different, and he began running little ads selling it. Orders came in and he expanded—and yes, he eventually filed for bankruptcy, but that doesn't mean there wasn't a good business in that duster, or in Forrester's retro bowling shirts. Think about it. It cost Peterman big bucks to buy even little ads in places like *The New York Times*. A Web site's cost is mere pennies by comparison. What cool products can you build a site around? Think unusual, easy to ship, good profit margins. In every product you think of, there's a thriving Web business that is waiting to happen.

McGarvey: *How do you promote the site?*

Forrester: There is a helpful site called www.selfpromotion.com that makes it easy to list your site with all the search engines. We promoted our Bowling Connection Web site by passing out fliers at bowling tournaments. We promoted our other two Web sites by opening a temporary gift store in Las Vegas. We passed out a lot of fliers and business cards to tourists from all over the world.

Another way we promote on an ongoing basis is by putting items up for auction on eBay. It's not only another source of income; it drives people right to your Web site to order more of your products. And it's only 25 cents to list each item. This has probably been the most cost-effective advertising I have ever seen.

McGarvey: *How do you handle online purchasing?*

Forrester: Online purchasing is made easy thanks again to US West Sitematic. When you set up your catalog, your secure ordering feature is ready. It's that easy! Most of our customers (98 percent) use the secure online server. A few of our customers elect to call or mail their orders in.

CHAPTER 29

Hello, World: [Tapping] International Markets

One of the lures of the Web is that once your site is up, you are open for business around the world, 24 hours a day. But don't be too quick to take the hype at face value. Yep, you're open 24/7, but international sales may prove elusive, and even when you land orders from abroad, you may wonder if they are worth the bother. Shocked?

There are excellent reasons for many e-tailers to aggressively pursue global business, but before you let yourself get dazzled by the upside, chew on the negatives. Then, once you've seen that foreign customers represent their own hassles but you still want them, you'll find the information you need to grab plenty of international sales.

FOREIGN AFFAIRS

Here's the root of the problem with selling internationally: Whenever you ship abroad, you enter into a complicated maze of the other country's laws. Let's assume you are in the United States (although you could be in Canada, Mexico, the UK, Ireland or wherever). You know Uncle Sam's laws, and you know that a neat thing about doing business in the United States is that barriers against interstate commerce are few. For a Nevada e-tailer to ship to California is no more complicated than putting the gizmo in a box and dropping it off at the post office. That's all the truer because, with some exceptions, few e-tailers collect sales tax on interstate sales.

Beware!
Know that e-tailers must collect sales tax on in-state purchases when their home state imposes a tax. Educate yourself about how and when to collect state sales taxes by visiting several key Web sites, including: Sales Tax Institute (www.salestaxinstitute.com) and Sales Tax Clearinghouse (http://thestc.com). State tax collectors don't forgive or forget—they just want the money from you.

Sell abroad, however, and it's a quick step into a maze of complexities, including customs, for instance. Generally, it's up to the buyer (not you) to pay any customs owed, but make sure your buyers know that additional charges—imposed by their home countries and payable directly to them—may be owed. You can pick up the forms you'll need from any U.S. post office.

Some countries will also charge national sales tax, or a value-added tax (around 20 percent on many items in many European countries). Again, as a small, foreign retailer, you can pretty safely not worry about collecting these monies, but your buyers may (and probably will, in many countries) be asked to pay, and they have got to understand this is not a charge at your end.

Mailing costs, too, escalate for foreign shipments. Airmail is the best way to go for just about any package, and that gets pricey. A 1-pound parcel post shipment to Europe costs more than $10, for instance. Insurance, too, is a must for most shipments abroad, mainly because the more miles a package travels, the more that can go wrong. Costs are low (insuring a $100 item costs $2.50 via the U.S. Postal Service), but they still add to the charges you have to pass on to the customer. Add up the many fees—

Beware!
It's tempting: Declare that an item is an unsolicited gift, and the recipient often doesn't have to pay any customs charges. The amount that can be exempted varies from country to country; usually it's $50 to $100. But do not make that declaration, even when a buyer asks (and savvy ones frequently will)—they are asking you to break the law.

Opportunity Knocks

When is a foreign customer not a foreign customer? When he or she wants you to ship to a U.S. address (perhaps an Edinburgh father sending a birthday gift to his daughter at a Boston college) or when the customer is an American in the military or diplomatic corps (shipping to their addresses is no different from mailing to any domestic address). Don't judge an e-mail address by its domain. The address may end in "it" (Italy) or "de" (Germany), but it could still be a U.S. order.

customs, postage, value-added taxes, insurance—and what might initially seem a bargain price can easily be nudged into the stratosphere.

Getting authorization on foreign credit cards can also be time-consuming. Although many major U.S. cards are well entrenched abroad (especially American Express and Diner's Club) and validating them frequently is no harder for a foreign cardholder, as a rule, this process is fraught with risks for the merchant, so be very cautious.

ALL ABOARD

If you're still not discouraged, do one more reality check to make sure international sales make sense for you. Is what you are selling readily available outside your country? Will what you sell ship reasonably easily and at a favorable price? Even with the costs of shipping factored in, will buying from you rather than from domestic sellers be a benefit to your customers? If you pass these tests, you're ready to get down to business.

Step one in getting more global business is to make your site as friendly as possible to foreign customers. Does this mean you need to offer the site in multiple languages? For very large companies, yes (American Express, for instance, puts up its site, www.americanexpress.com, in a half dozen languages). But the costs of doing a good translation are steep, and worse, whenever you modify pages—which ought to be regularly—you'll need to get the new material translated, too.

Small sites, however, can usually get away with English only and still prosper abroad. Consider this: Search for homes for sale on Greek islands, and you will find as many sites in English as in Greek. Why English? Because it's emerged as an international language. A merchant in Athens will probably know English because it lets him talk with French, German, Dutch, Turkish and Italian customers. An English-only Web site will find fluent readers in many nations. (But keep the English on your site as simple and as traditional as possible. The latest slang may not have made its way to English-speakers in Istanbul or Tokyo.)

Budget Watcher

Want a no-cost translation of your site? Offer a link to Alta-vista's Babel Fish, an automatic, online, and free translation service (http://babelfish.altavista.com). Before putting this up, however, ask friends—or pay an expert—to take a look at the translation. Babel Fish's translations are often very good, but you do not want to be the exception.

To make your site more friendly to foreign customers, put up a page—clearly marked—filled with tips especially for them. If you have the budget, get this one page translated into various key languages. (A local college student might do a one-page translation for around $20.) Use this space to explain the complexities involved in buying abroad. Cover many of the hassles we just discussed, but rephrase the material so that it looks at matters through the buyer's eyes. By all means, include the benefits, too, but don't leave anything out because the more accurate a customer's thinking before pressing the "Buy" button, the more likely he is to go through with the transaction.

Meantime, routinely scan your log files in a hunt for any patterns of international activity. If you notice that, say, Norway is producing a stream of visitors and no orders, that may prompt you to search for ways to coax Norwegians into buying. Try any one of many tactics, including a daily special for "Norwegian mailing addresses only" or perhaps running a poll directed only at Norwegians.

Clues about foreign visitors will also help in selecting places to advertise your site. While an ad campaign on Yahoo may be beyond your budget, it's entirely realistic to explore, say, ads on Yahoo Sweden. Start noticing visitors (or buyers!) from a specific country, and good policy is to explore costs involved in mounting a marketing campaign that explicitly targets them.

At the end of the day, whether you can expect to see substantial foreign orders is entirely your call. If you want them, they can be grabbed, because the promise of the Web is true in the sense that it definitely wipes out time zones, borders, and other barriers to commerce. That doesn't mean that these transactions are easy—they can be challenging, as you've seen—but for the e-tailer determined to sell globally, there is no better tool than the Web.

CHAPTER 30

e-Chat

> Send.com
> Michael Lannon, founder and CEO
> *Location:* Waltham, Massachusetts
> *Year Started:* 1997

When Mike Lannon was an employee, every night he would go home, dream a little bit about starting his own business, and maybe sip some wine. Then it hit him. He loved wine, and there had to be a business opportunity in the grape.

So he started up a little mail order operation—this was in '97—but promptly realized that the smarter place to be doing business was the Web, so he migrated there. Thus was born Sendwine.com, financed with $150,000 of his own saved cash. His idea expanded when he realized that while many people might want to send wine as gifts, others might prefer to send cigars, premium alcoholic beverages such as single malt Scotch, and maybe even exotic car rentals. So, with a gift-giving infrastructure in place, he gradually broadened the product line to meet the needs of more gift givers in a site now called Send.com.

Where is he going next? Here, Lannon talks about the company's start and his ambitions.

Robert McGarvey: *When you started, there already was a category leader in place on the Web, Virtual Vineyards (now Wine.com). Why did you think there was room for another player?*

Michael Lannon: Because what we offer is fundamentally

different. Virtual Vineyards sells wine over the Net, directly to consumers, who usually are buying for their own consumption. Ours is a very different business model. We are based on the FTD model [of the floral industry], where you place an order with us and we arrange with a local retailer to make the delivery. A big advantage is that we can sell in all states. [Because it cuts out local retailers, Wine.com faces restrictions on sales into many states.] And we are selling gifts. When a recipient gets one of our gifts, it is nicely packaged in a gift box.

McGarvey: *So you're not shutting out retailers?*

Lannon: Retailers are crucial to what we do. We buy our gifts from them, they package them, and in most cases they deliver them to the recipient. This gives us more immediate local reach, with same-day delivery available in many places.

McGarvey: *How do you ensure good customer service, which is essential with gifts?*

Lannon: Customer service is my passion. We work very hard to select the right retailers, to train them, and to give them the tools they need. We provide Send.com packaging, for instance, that's used with every order that goes out. This lets us control the recipient's experience.

McGarvey: *What about when a retailer drops the ball? You don't necessarily have control there.*

Lannon: Not long after we opened for business, we received a $35 order that, somehow, hadn't gotten

Smart Tip

There's already an established competitor in your desired niche? Do what Michael Lannon did, and look for other angles where you can compete. By sidestepping the wine enthusiast market, Lannon stepped into what could well be the more lucrative gift market. And impressively, he started the business with his own cash that later was supplemented with around $500,000 in angel money. Only after he had a business going did he approach VC firms, and he managed to make deals with leaders, including Benchmark (which has also funded eBay and WebVan). It adds up to a solid start for what could grow into a major brand.

filled. As soon as we discovered that, we spent $160 to get that order into the recipient's hands as soon as possible. This was at a time when we did not have substantial financial backing, but we had to do it because my belief is that to succeed in this business long term, you have to invest in customer service. For us, that was a sizable investment, but it pleased the giver and the recipient and it also let us see how we could improve our systems.

CHAPTER 31

Cheap Tricks

$$\begin{bmatrix} \text{LuLu \& Syd's} \\ \text{Leslie Paul and Pat Ramsay, co-owners} \\ \textit{Location: } \text{Pittsford, Vermont} \\ \textit{Year Started: } 1999 \end{bmatrix}$$

LuLu & Syd's
Leslie Paul and Pat Ramsay, co-owners
Location: Pittsford, Vermont
Year Started: 1999

Click onto www.vermontdogs.com, and you are greeted with LuLu & Syd's Gourmet Dog Cookies. These culinary treats—including "pizza slices" and a "maple moose" for pooches—sell for a couple of dollars per bag (a sampler with six different cookies is $2). Who are LuLu and Syd? I had to know, so I tracked them down in their home base, Pittsford, Vermont.

Guess what? LuLu and Syd are dogs, not Netpreneurs. But their owners—Leslie Paul and Pat Ramsay—offered up the scoop on LuLu & Syd's.

Robert McGarvey: *What were your start-up costs?*

Leslie Paul and Pat Ramsay: Approximately $750.

McGarvey: *Is this do-it-yourself, or did you hire a programmer?*

Paul and Ramsay: To reduce costs, Leslie took a Web design class so that we could create our own site. As it was her project in class, it took about four weeks to complete the Web site and get it uploaded to the Web. The cost of the class was $75, which was considerably less than if we had hired someone to build the site. Other associated costs were Internet fees (i.e., domain name registration and Web hosting fees).

McGarvey: *What are your monthly revenues?*

Paul and Ramsay: Our monthly revenues vary, but we had a

great holiday season! We are very pleased that we are seeing repeat customers on the Web. We are also supplying a number of stores that are carrying our products. Our goal this year is to increase the number of stores locally and across the United States.

McGarvey: *What are your monthly page counts, unique visitor counts?*

Paul and Ramsay: We are averaging 600 to 700 unique visitor counts per month with an average of 2,600 to 2,700 monthly page counts.

McGarvey: *What other work do you do?*

Paul and Ramsay: We both maintain part-time jobs in addition to running LuLu & Syd's. Pat is a registered nurse, and Leslie does some bookkeeping and bartending when we are not busy baking cookies!

McGarvey: *Where did you get the idea for the site?*

Paul and Ramsay: We were both extremely interested in e-commerce, and being dog lovers, LuLu & Syd's just fell into place. We felt confident there would be a market for a Vermont-made, all-natural pet product such as ours.

McGarvey: *How do you attract visitors?*

Paul and Ramsay: We have attended many New England-based dog shows and events and handed out product samples and discount coupons for Web orders. We have several

Budget Watcher
Do you make something unique, special? Put up a Web site, submit the URL to all the main search engines, and see if traffic comes in. Leslie Paul and Pat Ramsay tell you to build traffic on the cheap. Theirs isn't the kind of site that's likely to become a gazillion-dollar business, but it is a site that can easily generate a nice, steady cash flow, month in and month out.

Opportunity Knocks
Web site registration service Network Solutions offers free listings in its directory—sort of an online Yellow Pages—to businesses that register their domains through Network Solutions. Find out more at www.dotcomdirectory.com.

links on pet-related and Vermont products Web sites and do ongoing submissions to search engines. We also offer seasonal/ holiday items and do mailings to our customers. When we entered Network Solutions' "dotcom directory" last fall, we were featured in their ad campaign. We were very pleased with the results, and we'll look into other forms of advertising this year.

CHAPTER 32

Who's Knocking At The Door? [Really] Knowing Your Customers

Know thy customer. If there's a first commandment of business, that's it. Run a bricks-and-mortar store, and knowing customers is easy. Talk to them, size up their clothing, hear how they form sentences, and in a matter of seconds, a traditional storefront owner knows a lot about who's stopping in. But the question for companies doing business on the Web is, How do we know customers when all they amount to is a wispy cybervisitor?

This is a key issue because knowing who visitors are can help you more precisely target a Web site. Suddenly notice a flood of visitors from, say, Hawaii or Japan or Texas, and that could lead to a decision to edit certain sections of a Web site to make them more friendly for those users. See that you're a hit on a particular college campus or in a government agency, and you can post a special deal for just those people. Observe that you're getting a lot of traffic from Puerto Rico, and that's a clear signal to market there. Not knowing your customers makes no more sense than golfing in the dark.

LOG ROLLING

The good news: Every Web site visitor leaves a trail that, properly analyzed, will tell you country of origin, browser and platform used (Win '98 or '95 or Mac or Unix), the Internet service provider, and more. These data ordinarily are collected by Web hosting services in a "Log" file, but only hardcore techies could ever have the patience to scroll through a log because it contains a mind-numbing avalanche of details.

Want a peek at a log file? Here's a sample of the sort of information available:

we-24-130-40-120.we.mediaone.net - - [08/Feb/2000:16:08:47 -0700] "GET / HTTP/1.1" 200 5867 "-" "Mozilla/4.0 (compatible; MSIE 4.01; Windows 98; Compaq)"

we-24-130-40-120.we.mediaone.net - - [08/Feb/2000:16:08:47 -0700] "GET /indtextb.jpg HTTP/1.1" 200 959 "http://www.mcgarvey.net/" "Mozilla/4.0 (compatible; MSIE 4.01; Windows 98; Compaq)"

we-24-130-40-120.we.mediaone.net - - [08/Feb/2000:16:08:48 -0700] "GET /banner.gif HTTP/1.1" 200 27782 "http://www.mcgarvey.net/" "Mozilla/4.0 (compatible; MSIE 4.01; Windows 98; Compaq)"

Weird stuff? You bet—and that's only about 5 percent of the report on a single visitor who on February 8, 2000, dropped in for a look at just a couple of Web pages. Some interesting tidbits are that the user was running a Compaq computer with Windows 98 and he has high-speed cable access ("Media One"). But mainly this log is cluttered with details you don't need, or want, to know. There are smarter ways to measure traffic.

ANALYZE THIS

If you're curious about your logs, go to your Web hosting service and look for a directory called "Logs." Download the most recent file and have a look (any text editor should open the file). Your Web hosting service probably provides—free of charge—a basic analysis of those logs. The log is run through interpretive software, and the output is tucked in a folder that's usually called "Stats." Open that folder and have a look at recent files.

What will you see? Here's that same visitor's trail, as reported in the stats folder. The first column is the date, followed by the time of day, amount of time spent on the Web page, and the Web page (or other Web element, such as Java buttons) viewed.

we-24-130-40-120.we.mediaone.net
08 Feb—16:08:47—00:09—/

08 Feb—16:08:56—00:01—/UAButton.class

08 Feb—16:08:57—00:01—/UleadEffectBase.class

08 Feb—16:08:58—00:20—/UleadNeon.class

http://mcgarvey.net

08 Feb—16:09:18—00:09—/mcgarvey.htm

Here you see the visitor (with the Internet address we-24-130-40-120.we.mediaone.net) looked at two pages (www.mcgarvey.net and www.mcgarvey.net/mcgarvey.htm), spent under a minute, then split. How did he get there? What browser was he using? Other files in the stats folder provide those details, and sometimes they are worth a look. But ordinarily just the basics—who and how long?—are what you need to know.

The free stats file reports are good, but still better analysis is easy to come by when you use third-party software tools designed to dissect log reports and automatically produce spiffy, usable reports that will tell you not only which countries are producing visitors, but also their ISPs and more.

I See You   Click

Most stats folders include a file that details the search phrases used by visitors in finding your site. Check it out regularly. In analyzing McGarvey.net traffic, I found the most common search phrase was "cosmopolitan cocktail" (there's a recipe on the site). Other cosmo-related stuff also rated high as, for instance, seen in the number of visitors who come in via AltaVista:

- 40 cosmopolitan cocktail
- 14 cosmopolitan martini
- 14 Robert McGarvey
- 14 cosmopolitan drink

So the cosmopolitan information moved to the front of the site and a second cosmopolitan recipe was added, with big traffic increases resulting. Know what visitors want to find and give them more of it.

Just The Stats

Click

The building block for site analysis is the log file—but what if you don't have one? Users of free Web space (on AOL, Tripod, and such) often don't. But don't despair. Sign up with StatsView (www.statsview.com), a free, Web-based service that lets you track many facts about visitors including referrer stats, unique hits, browsers used, and more. Just register with StatsView, paste some HTML code (provided by StatsView) into your pages, and you're in business.

The downside? You have to put StatsView buttons on your pages, and that means not only more clutter, but the buttons can slow page loading. But when a log file isn't readily had, this is the way to go. And a twist provided by this service is that it also lets visitors vote on your pages, giving user ratings for design, speed and content. Painful as these votes can be to read, they're invaluable when it comes to modifying a site to maximize user-friendliness.

Top choices among traffic-analysis tools include:

O *Web Trends Log Analyzer:* This program offers dozens of reporting options, plus powerful tools that measure time spent by users on particular pages, "referrer analysis" (what external sites refer visitors to you? What key words lead search engine visitors to you?), and path analysis (how do visitors navigate through your site?). You can also get a spiffy "geographical profiling" tool that allows for tracking visitors back to specific cities of origin. Get a trial download from www.webtrends.com. Cost: $399.

Budget Watcher
Find plenty more free analysis tools and hit counters at "Web Site Counters and Trackers," a page devoted to linking with almost every tool around (www.adbility.com/ba_counter.htm). Most of these tools are free.

O *HitList Professional:* Some 40

reports are provided with a few mouse clicks. It's a full-featured, fast, and easy-to-use tool. Get a trial download at www.accrue.com. Cost: $395.

Which should you use? Download a trial version of both programs. Put them through their paces and see what you prefer. Also, before deciding to buy, ask yourself if you really need this level of analysis. Many low-traffic sites don't, and, for them, the free stats files provided by the server may be sufficient. When traffic increases to the point where you need more fine-tuned analysis, buy a more sophisticated tool—but certainly wait until the traffic increases to more than 100 visitors daily.

GETTING TO KNOW YOU

Logs provide a step toward knowing your customer, but more can be done. Here, the big guys can clue you in on strategies you can use. Such as?

SURVEY SAYS

In this morning's e-mail came a discount coupon from Amazon, with a string attached. If I answered a half-dozen multiple-choice questions, I would earn a $15 credit, good on any electronics item sold by Amazon. Through highly specific questions about competitors and Amazon's own product offerings, prices, and service, Amazon picks up valuable insight into the thinking of a customer and its competition. Wow!

Why aren't you doing likewise? Don't kick yourself too hard, because Amazon is as good as they get in e-tailing. But it amazes me: I recall getting an Amazon survey every couple months, always with a discount coupon that's activated when I answer the survey, but I cannot remember getting anything similar from any other e-tailer, and I shop at lots.

Strip this down, and what Amazon is doing is taking its customers' e-mail addresses, firing off a survey, and, to sweeten the pot and up the percentage of responders, offering a discount if you answer the survey—but the discount isn't so hefty that it would obliterate margins; it's exactly what it seems to be, a small thank-you.

Don't wait: Do a survey right now. Keep it short, and offer a tangible reward. You don't have Amazon's many millions of people to survey, so randomly choose, say, 10 or 100 customers. Then, and this is crucial, read every answer that comes in. Trust me: Jeff Bezos isn't doing this surveying to fill slow days. The CEO of Amazon honestly wants to know what's on his customers' minds, and, for sure, every response is logged. Odds are, Bezos—a notoriously hands-on boss—personally puts in time eyeballing survey data because he knows what every CEO needs to know: If you want to find out ways to do your business better, look at it as customers do.

> ### Smart Tip
>
> A must in Web site customer service is to include a phone number on your Web site. Different folks like different channels. Some thrive on e-mail, but others still need the reassurance of a human voice before placing a large order. I've done it myself. On the L.L. Bean Web site (www.llbean.com), I found $3,000 in furniture that I liked—but rather than click the "Buy" button, I called the 800 number, and the friendly voice that answered the Bean phone helped win a big order. The Web changes many, many things—but it won't soon eliminate the need to pick up the phone.

Surveys also are sweeping the Web, though more commonly as "pop-ups"—screens that jump up when you surf onto a site. Pop-up windows may be popular (I have seen maybe 10 in the past week), but I don't recommend them. Surfers don't like them—complaints about pop-ups are epidemic because pop-ups often cause system crashes. They also are technically tricky to put into place—probably beyond your budget and technical know-how. And the data they produce is highly suspect, at least in my mind—I cannot recall ever completing a pop-up questionnaire, mainly because the things are so annoying. Don't feel left out just because your site lacks pop-ups. Rejoice instead!

GOING TO THE POLLS

What tools should you use besides e-mail? Online polls can be tailored to serve many ends, and you'll find many variations, all free:

○ *PollsWhatiz.Com:* http://polls.whatiz.com

○ *Pollit:* www.pollit.com

○ *Pollwizard:* www.pollwizard.com

○ *Visitor Poll:* www.visitorpoll.com

These tools may cost you nothing, but, used intelligently, they are powerful. "You Are Five Minutes From Taking Live, Interactive Polls At Your Web Site," shouts Pollwizard on its front page, and these resources live up to that promise. How good will the data you collect be? As good as the polls you create and as good as the tools you use for analyzing your responses.

Don't just put up a poll as a plaything for visitors. Oh, sometimes that's useful—polls are fun and we all like completing them, at least when they are short (never go over 10 questions in a poll—five or fewer questions is ideal). But the real payoffs come when you carefully construct polls to target highly specific concerns. Do customers like your Web site's speed? Your product selection? Pricing? Ask them, and watch out, they'll love telling you their answers. Big corporations pay megabucks to marketing wizards who poke into customers and their motivations, but, the truth is, you can get most of the payoffs from this work, free of charge, simply by using the tools that are readily at hand.

And one last thing: Read and respond to as much customer e-mail as possible because it, too, opens a real window on customers and their motivations. Strangely, many small businesses, when asked, will mumble and admit that they don't read e-mail and certainly do not respond to it, but there is no faster way to make yourself obsolete than to stay aloof from customers. Sure, nine customers will write with complaints for every one who has good things to say about you, but read it, absorb it…and stay alert to trends. If one person complains about your packaging materials, big deal. If 10 do and you only sent out 12 orders last week, you have a problem—and the great thing is that now you also have the opportunity to fix it.

Opportunity Knocks

Want to wow your customers? Respond to all e-mail the same day—and offer answers that are truly responsive to what the customers are writing about. One sure way for a small business to excel is with a personal touch, and e-mail gives you a powerful weapon. Use it.

PRIVATE EYES

Now that you're excited about gathering information on your customers, know this: It all has to be done gently, respectfully, and cautiously. That's because a sensitive topic these days is Web site snooping. And odds are, sensitivities will increase as more users realize how detailed a trail they leave behind when visiting Web sites.

But there is a remedy, one that will let you gather information you need while also reassuring your visitors. It's simple: Develop a privacy policy. If you don't, this lack may cost you big bucks.

How big? Jupiter Communications, a Net-oriented research firm, recently found that 68 percent of European Web businesses collected information on their visitors—but only 10 percent bother to post any kind of formal privacy policy. And another Jupiter survey found that 60 percent of European users who do not buy online said they might if there were better security for personal and credit card information.

Add those two surveys together, and a stark conclusion is that these Web businesses may well be shooting themselves in their own feet. By not winning trust—and by not safeguarding visitor privacy—these e-tailers just may be inadvertently pushing would-be customers toward the exits before the cash registers ring.

TOO CLOSE FOR COMFORT

In America, proof of consumers' sensitivity to this issue are the PR nightmares suffered by RealPlayer, Alexa, and numerous other Net companies that were found to surreptitiously collect information on users. The companies claimed no harm was done—that the information (mainly pertaining to a user's viewing habits) was collected so that user needs might better be served—but for a time, dark clouds hung over many Net companies as users fretted about invasion of privacy.

Privacy isn't a concern only for the paranoid, either. For a demonstration of just how much information is easily collected from Web surfers without their knowledge or participation, go to http://privacy.net. In a minute or so, you will probably see a long—and spooky—report on exactly how much information you surrender at every Web site. Everything from your Internet address to your computer's name is readily known by sites you visit. Also knowable—although not included in Privacy.net's demonstration—is your e-mail address, so this can get very personal, very quickly.

Why do Web sites want this information in the first place? Mainly because it's a marketer's dream. In an era when "knowing thy customer" is seen as a path to riches, it's hard to resist collecting the vast stores of customer data that tumble into your lap, just by creating a Web site. Know where a visitor has been before—what sites he's visited earlier in this Internet session, for instance—and an alert marketc⁻ can use that insight into the surfer's interests to tweak offerings so they more closely match this surfer's wants.

Smart Tip

See your visitors giving out e-mail addresses at Hotmail, Excite, and Yahoo, and, guess what, you're probably getting their secondary addresses. Sure, some employees at big corporations use such addresses for personal e-mail, but, mainly, folks set up these accounts to help dodge spam. What can you do better to earn their trust—and their primary addresses?

That's so tempting that some sites dramatically up the ante by overtly collecting more detailed and personal information from visitors. Usually that occurs in tandem with an offer the visitor accepts. Before you create a free e-mail account at ProntoMail (www.prontomail. com), for instance, you have to provide a name, geographic location, age, and a few more details. This is common, and experienced Web surfers have come to expect a trade-off of personal information for freebies…except the savviest surfers long ago stopped giving out accurate information. Many maintain a separate e-mail box just for use in connection with freebies and simply lie when filling out the forms.

Another dose of bad news is that, in some cases, information collected in "cookies" has been transmitted to third-party sites—and that strikes fear in just about everybody. A cookie, theoretically, is a bit of information about you that is written to your hard drive while visiting a Web site that will in the future let that Web site identify you as a repeat visitor. This is how some sites greet you with "Welcome Back, Fragonard" (or whatever your name is) when you return for an encore visit. Cookies, their architects argue, save users time and make the surfing process more efficient. Who could complain? Well, Consumer.net has found instances where those cookies have been visible to other sites—and that's a scary thought indeed.

A last privacy breach is that, wherever you go on the Net, you leave a trail. Very good hackers can hide their trails, but 99.9 percent of us leave tracks that are easy to follow. That is no big deal to most of us. But it means that your feeling of anonymity on the Net is a false one: Your movements can be cataloged and associated with you.

Added up, the situation is this: Experienced surfers do their best to mock the system, while comparative newcomers—fearing privacy violations—avoid making purchases to protect their

---

DSL Dangers   Click

Are you using high-speed Net access via a cable modem or always-on DSL? If you are, you're enjoying the best Web access around, but you also are exposing yourself to invasion by hackers. The threats are real.

Theoretically, a hacker could penetrate your system when you're connected to the Net with a dial-up connection, but the likelihood is not high. Why? Usually when you're connected you are sitting at the computer. If, suddenly, you see that you're opening Quicken financial files—and in fact you're not—you would know a hacker was there, and poof, you shut down. End of threat.

"Always on" connections raise different worries. Maybe 20 hours a day your computer is sitting there, open to invasion. But antidotes are plentiful. I use Norton Internet Security (www.symantec.com/sabu/nis/nis_ pe). It costs less than $100, and, in minutes, it installs and protects your system against intruders. Plenty of other packages are available. Whatever you use, if you have high-speed access, get software to protect the privacy of your computer. It's an ounce of prevention that can save many pounds of tears.

---

identities. This is not good for you, and it's not good for Web users, either, because it limits their use of the medium.

CONFIDENCE BOOSTERS

What do you need to do to reassure visitors? As a rule, mainline Web sites fairly openly explain their privacy policy. At the Entrepreneur.com site, for instance, at the bottom of the front page is a link that says "Privacy Policy." Click it, and you are delivered to a clear, concise statement of what information is collected from visitors, what's done with it, and if it's made available to other companies. (The answer in this case is no—"Any information collected about you will never be sold or rented to any third party for any purpose," says the Entrepreneur.com privacy statement.)

Beware!
Get another eyeful at BrowserSpy—www.gemal.dk/browserspy/spy.html. Exactly how much this Web site knows about you, instantly, is frightening. Check it out!

Most other leading U.S. sites you'll visit will, somewhere, explain their privacy policy in much the same way. They may vary in how easy it is to find the link and how clear the statement is, but poke around, and you will find a policy.

Another trend: privacy promises made by third parties, such as by the Better Business Bureau Privacy Program (www.bbbonline. org/businesses/privacy/index.html) and TRUSTe (www.truste.com). Program mechanics vary a bit, but the essence is that a business site meets certain basic privacy requirements, pays a fee, and then gets to display a button on the Web site touting that it fulfills the program's requirements. Some users grumble that these programs don't truly guarantee privacy so much as they promise disclosure of what happens to information surfers reveal, but pretty much everybody agrees that such programs are a step in the right direction.

Should you join? Since the cheapest TRUSTe membership was $299 annually at a recent look, it may not be the shrewdest use of sparse cash in a start-up. My advice: Keep the money in your pocket and look for do-it-yourself tactics to up visitor security.

Detailed guidance on the how-to of raising visitor confidence

Get Lost | Click

Never, ever assume your online activities are private. With court orders in hand, law enforcement can track virtually all surfers in a matter of minutes. That may be no big deal to most of us, but if you're doing stuff you want kept private, think about it. One way to avoid the scrutiny is to head to a public Internet cafe and pay cash for a surfing session. You might do that simply to keep competitors from knowing you are checking out their sites.

Another option: Go to Anonymizer—www.anonymizer.com—which allows anonymous surfing. A bare-bones model is free, while heavy users will opt for the subscription version ($49.99 per year).

AOL users, incidentally, can breathe easily. Many ISPs give users a fixed Internet address—like a street address, it uniquely identifies the user—but AOL owns many fewer addresses than it has members, so it dynamically and randomly assigns addresses, which means no AOL address can be seen as identifying a particular user. When presented with a court order, AOL has opened its records and pinpointed which user had a specific address at a specific time—but only serious lawbreakers need fret about that. For most people, an AOL address actually gives all the privacy they are likely to need.

can be found in groundbreaking research—conducted by AT&T Labs and several universities, including Harvard and MIT—that pinpoints exactly what Internet users fear regarding the Net and privacy and what steps reassure them. A key finding: When an explicit privacy policy is combined with a third-party seal of approval, surfer confidence soars.

Users are especially sensitive when their data is shared with other sites or businesses. Most seem to feel that if they are interested enough in a site to want to hang around, revealing a bit about themselves is OK—but they do not want that information passed on. A third finding: Users are very, very unwilling to reveal any information about their children. Why? Who knows—just accept that as fact and don't ask. (Get your free copy of the full report at: www.research.att.com/projects/privacystudy.)

To sum up, the steps you should take are to post, in a prominent place, a link to your site's privacy policy. In that policy, be clear, simple, direct. Good strategy is to say: "We sell no information that we collect about you. Never. To nobody." Don't ask questions about visitors' kids—unless there's a compelling and obvious reason to do so. And if you offer visitors free sign-up to e-mail newsletters or sales notices, be quick to remove anybody who asks—preferably on the very day you receive the request. Users grumble a lot about spam, and an easy way to win visitor confidence is to promptly remove anybody from any list upon request.

Winning—and keeping—visitor trust really isn't and shouldn't be rocket science. Lots of the same hurdles were overcome years ago by direct mail and catalog sellers. In the case of the Net, plenty of credit card issuers (American Express, Citibank, etc.) are working overtime to encourage their cardholders to make online purchases with the full assurance that the card will protect them from fraud. And in probably the broadest, most objective look at Net privacy issues, the Federal Trade Commission—a lead government agency in the e-commerce arena—has argued that there is no need for government intervention to offer more assurances of privacy and that, on balance, the industry is doing a satisfactory job. For most site operators, this means don't screw up, and you'll be able to develop trust on the part of visitors. And once they trust you, they will buy.

Beware!
In some states—among them, Washington—sending spam is illegal. Granted, enforcement of anti-spam laws has been uneven, but the fact is plain: Smart retailers don't spam away the good will of customers.

CHAPTER 33

At Your Service: Customer Service For [Success]

E-tailers used to be innocents who thought that with Web-based retailing, all customer service would be a thing of the past with the entire sales and service process becoming neatly (and oh, so inexpensively) automated. Hah! If there's a mantra for e-commerce players, it's this: Customers may be virtual, but their dollars are real.

"They expect and need the same level of service in-person customers get," says Cynthia Hollen, president of Knowledge Strategies Group (www.kstrat.com), a New York City-based Internet consulting firm that's worked with Bloomingdale's, among others, in creating online stores. "When you don't understand that, you lose sales. Consumers now expect high levels of service from online retailers, and the better ones see it as a competitive edge and are delivering." How? Just follow the leaders:

○ *Anticipate questions.* At OfficeDepot.com, anticipation is the watchword, says Keith Butler, a vice president. "We anticipate many questions and answer them in our FAQs," says Butler, who adds that many questions are asked because "people don't read. They ask questions we've already answered on the site." But Butler doesn't grumble about this, because he realizes customer e-mail and calls are research vehicles. "They tell us what's working and what we need to work on," he says.

Get lots of e-mail complaining about a certain feature that the customer has simply misunderstood or bemoaning the lack of a particular product that you know is in fact in stock, and you are learning important things about how your site is failing to communicate to visitors. As e-mail comes in, do not ever look for how the e-mailers are wrong. Look for ways to reshape your site to eliminate user problems (even the ones they only imagine they have).

Smart Tip

Do it now: Create a place for FAQs—frequently asked questions—on your site ASAP. View your FAQs as a work in progress. You will continually update and expand them as more customer concerns and needs come to light.

○ *Stay in touch.* At Hewlett Packard's Shopping Village (www.hpshopping.com), every customer is asked if he would recommend Shopping Village to friends, and 97 percent say they would, according to director of marketing and operations David Deasy. But the 3 percent who say "no" aren't forgotten. "We contact them via e-mail or phone and ask how we can satisfy them," says Deasy, who adds that it's usually not hard to do: "Just contacting them alone is often enough to win them back."

○ *Respond quickly.* The Web is an instant medium—except when it comes to getting responses from many businesses that seem to route incoming e-mail into a folder labeled "Ignore Forever." Smart e-tailers know better, however. "Our goal is to respond to every inquiry within 24 hours," says HP's Deasy. Others raise the bar higher still, with responses within four hours emerging as the new goal of many. What's right for you? With a smaller staff (and probably no staff during night hours), you might find a 24-hour standard to be enough of a challenge. But monitor customers. If they demand faster response, somehow you have to find a way to meet their needs.

○ *Hold their hands.* "Online, not every customer knows how to shop, and you have to be ready to help them buy," says Anne Marie Blaire, brand marketing manager for Victoria Secret's online store. No B&M retailer has to teach customers how to buy, but online, that remains a thorny problem. Every day thousands of shoppers log on for the first time, and these new-

Opportunity Knocks

You'll blow customers away when you send instant responses. Maybe that's not a realistic goal for you to set, but if you happen to be online when an e-mail comes in, try answering it right then—and know you are really impressing the customer who gets an instant and personalized response.

bies genuinely crave handholding as they make purchases. Understand that and be ready to help. Be patient, too. Only a very stupid e-tailer complains about how stupid his newbie customers are. They can, in fact, become your best customers, because they will shop only where they feel comfortable—and if your site makes it on that short list, watch the orders tumble in.

○ *Use cut and paste.* Canned responses—cut-and-paste scripts—are used by all the leading sites, which track questions, hunt for the most asked, and produce templates for their representatives. You can do likewise. As you answer customer questions, file away your responses. Odds are, you'll be asked the same question within the week, and it's a great labor saver to have an answer ready.

○ *Stay sensitive.* A worry with e-mail: It's easy to seem cold and unresponsive in the formality of the written word. Read and re-read your responses before they go out. You want to be—and appear—interested in the customer's issues and eager to find solutions.

○ *Aim higher.* In the online space,

Smart Tip

Hewlett Packard's way is cheap. Why aren't you doing likewise? A week or two after any order is filled, e-mail the customer and ask if they would recommend your shop. "No" answers will hurt, but follow up on every one because these are the people who will tell you what you need to do to build a winner of a Web site. Given how awesomely powerful this simple tool is, it's stunning that more e-tailers haven't jumped on it. Don't make the same mistake!

the service bar is being lifted ever higher. E-mail alone will no longer cut it, and neither will FAQs, though most sites should keep such tools in place. "Real-time chat is where service is heading," says Ken Young, a vice president with 1-800-flowers (1800flowers.com). "It's not good enough to answer e-mail questions the same day, or even within two hours, not when that customer might not log on again until tomorrow. Customers want answers now." To meet that need, 1-800-flowers has introduced online tools for immediate, real-time chatting—by voice or via text—which let buyers stay connected to the Web but still get the help they need.

Opportunity Knocks

Take a tactic used by the slick catalog companies, and when you haven't heard from a customer in a while, drop him or her an e-mail: "Have we disappointed you in any way? We would really value your feedback." Maybe the customer indeed is irked with you; maybe not. Either way, this e-mail will remind the customer that you are a store that cares.

Can you rise to that level of service? Free, easy-to-use, off-the-shelf software, such as AOL's Instant Messenger (from www.aol.com), lets you come very close to matching these cutting-edge abilities. If at all feasible, make yourself available to customers via Instant Messenger, and know that the more accessible you are, the more sales you are likely to log.

○ *Offer choices.* "You cannot force the customer to contact you your way. Offer a choice, e-mail or the phone," says Mitch Reed, a vice president at CVS.com, the Seattle-based e-commerce arm of the giant drugstore chain. "You need to make the online shopping experience easy."

These steps will get you started delivering better customer service, but they are not enough. "The only way to do online service right is to have the right attitude," says Reed. "For us, that attitude is not that the customer is right. That doesn't go far enough. We believe the customer is king, and every customer service rep knows it. Have that attitude, and service gets easy to provide. It's that simple."

Many fail on this score, but when you've made customer service your top and continuing priority, success is within reach.

Don't get seduced by the notion that the Web sites with the best technology will inevitably win. Usable, reliable technology is a must, but where the real e-tailing battlefield will be is service. That's the irony about e-tailing: At the end of the day, what prevails online is what prevails off—and that's consistent, respectful, considerate service.

e-Chat

Priceline.com
Rick Braddock, chairman
Location: Stamford, Connecticut
Year Started: 1998

Priceline is a phenomenon, a major Web business that when launched mainly met with snorts of contempt by experts but has gone on to show that its unique approach to putting discounted merchandise into consumers' hands is both smart and profitable. Probably the only other Web business about which all the same could be said is eBay—which also met with much derision when it launched, but it, too, has shown itself to be cleverly lucrative.

As for Priceline, personally I have been on the wrong side, too. In 1999, I wrote an article for *UPSIDE* magazine that basically said the online name-your-price auction company was a turkey. Was I wrong! Here, Rick Braddock, a onetime top executive at Citibank, gives the scoop on what it's like to be steering one of the mightiest vessels on the Net.

Robert McGarvey: *How did you get involved with Priceline?*

Rick Braddock: I was an early investor in the company. I was investing in early-stage companies and helping them in whatever fashion I could. I worked with Jay [Walker, Priceline's founder] and, eventually, in August I joined the company as CEO. Jay didn't see his proper role as managing the company in what he thought would be a fast-growth phase.

McGarvey: *Why did you join Priceline?*

Braddock: I think we're building a new financial model that lets customers transact with large companies in a way that gives them a lot more control. The model empowers customers and gives them more control than they historically had. In so doing, we're also generating for sellers a type of buyer they had never been able to locate and on whom they can make a lot of money because of where the transaction is in the food chain.

McGarvey: *Critics say that Priceline has goosed its revenue by selling products to consumers below cost. Is that true?*

Braddock: When we actually introduce new products, we sell a substantial percentage below cost. We view that as a promotional allowance. We can look at each piece of demand and decide to apply a promotional allowance in a very specific way. We start there; then as the business matures—in terms of number of customers and amount of inventory—we dial toward margin maximization.

> "We **create** a customer who is **price-oriented**. A Priceline **customer** is not brand **loyal**."

With airline products, starting in April '98, we wrote almost all our business at a loss. Our gross margin was a negative 13.9 percent. We were doing 2,500 tickets a week. Now we're writing 50,000 tickets a week and we're running a 9 percent gross positive margin. We still subsidize a modest percentage of our airline business—the logic is we're attracting new customers.

McGarvey: *Isn't that a much higher margin than traditional travel agents earn?*

Braddock: That's right. Our proposition is different. We create a customer who is price-oriented. A Priceline customer is not brand loyal. He'll fly on any carrier at his price. The airline proposition is that revenue equals profit on an incremental seat.

McGarvey: *Why has Priceline expanded into groceries—a move that's attracted much attention and a significant degree of criticism?*

Braddock: WebHouse [Priceline's grocery partner] is one of many initiatives we have to build out our business model, which we think will apply over a wide range. Eventually, we'll probably have 50 or 60 categories, compared to four or so today. As for

Opportunity Knocks

The essence of Priceline is both very simple and very complex. Its founder, Jay Walker, realized that the Web is the perfect tool for economically collecting demand for airfares from price-sensitive customers without brand loyalties. Tomorrow's new billionaires are likely to come from the ranks of creative thinkers who get out of the box and see new ways to put the Web to use. What new ways can you think of?

grocery shopping in particular, it is heavy frequency; the average person shops 75 times a year. It creates a frequency product for us. Margins are terrible in the grocery business, but our thought is that by bringing in brand-neutral customers, manufacturers will give us something off their prices. The margin isn't created out of the grocery P&L [profit and loss statement], which is hideous, but is in effect created out of the manufacturers' P&L.

McGarvey: *How will Priceline beat competitors?*

Braddock: I don't think we have direct competitors. Our proposition is pitched to the consumer in a relatively unique way.

McGarvey: *Don't you run the risk that your suppliers can disintermediate you and simply set up their own auction sites?*

Braddock: Take airplane tickets, for instance. An individual airline cannot really offer this product. How could it say to its passengers "Name your own price"? It would alienate customers who paid the higher price. We offer airlines another channel, and by giving them anonymity, we provide pricing latitude they couldn't have on their own. And at Priceline, our growth is happening before your eyes. We are growing very, very fast.

CHAPTER 35

Cheap Tricks

Frugalfun.com
Shel Horowitz, founder and owner
Location: Northampton, Massachusetts
Year Started: 1996

Want to see a simple site that also makes money? Check out Frugal Fun. For sure, it's frugal—really cheap, in fact—but its developer and owner, Shel Horowitz, says the site brings in a steady stream of income, mainly from sales of his books (which include *Marketing Without Megabucks* (Megabucks). To keep the traffic flowing, Horowitz serves up generous portions of freebies—tip sheets on frugal living, reams of low-cost marketing tips, even travel tips for the frugal. Read on to find out more about why this site is a success.

Robert McGarvey: *What were your start-up costs?*

Shel Horowitz: I went online in 1994 with an AOL account. When I set up my own site in 1996, I registered a domain name ($70/two years). In the past six years, I've spent $60 on ads hawking the site. I have paid nothing for content or site design (for which I bartered)—though I have promised to pay $45 to someone who is redesigning my order form and is almost done. I'll probably pay her $60 because she's worked really hard on it.

Oh, yes, and I had to renew my domain name when the time was up. I started with a $45-per-month account covering e-mail, Web hosting, Web surfing, and site updating. I switched to an $18-per-month provider about two years ago. Now I'm looking to switch again and will probably pay about $30 a month. I'm currently also paying $56 a year for third-party secure ordering through BookZone, www.bookzone.com ($28 per title).

McGarvey: *Where did you get the idea for the site?*

Horowitz: People started telling me in early 1995 that I needed a Web site. In my field, marketing, I was shooting myself in the foot not having one. I thought for several months about what the site would contain, did a lot of preplanning, and found an intern who wanted to learn HTML. She coded the first 40 pages, which went up in April 1996. She also taught me what she'd learned. A year later, I bartered with a Web site designer for the template I now use. That design, dating from 1997, is now somewhat tired. I have a designer willing to do a template for me on barter, so I'll see what she comes up with.

McGarvey: *How do you attract visitors and market the site?*

Horowitz: I have done very little to formally market the site. I participate actively in many discussion lists, and my sig [e-mail signature] draws people to the site (I use some 20 different sigs, depending on what I want to emphasize). I do radio talk shows (as a guest) about 30 to 50 times a year, and I always mention the URL (and a reason to visit—for example, "On my site at www.frugalfun.com, you can find out how to have a wedding for $300," or "One of my tip sheets has a really good article on trade shows. You will find the back issues archived on the marketing page at www.frugalfun.com.").

Also, I actively solicit book reviews and editorial coverage, and most mention the URL. Search engines draw a fair amount of visitors, but they're mostly in to see a particular page of the rather diverse content. They'll

Opportunity Knocks

Listen up when Shel Horowitz tells you how he markets his site on the cheap. Maybe you don't have books that will win reviews, but you do have e-mail. Are you using your "sig" (signature) for maximum impact? You should keep it short—two lines are twice as powerful as four. Then, as Horowitz says, get busy scouting out Internet chat groups and online forums where visitors who might find your site useful hang out. Put up your posts, sig included, and watch the traffic come in.

find one article that interests them, and then they move on. If they're looking for marketing info, they stay a while. I've been averaging 20,000 visitors a month lately—not huge, but it's the quality I want, not the numbers.

McGarvey: *What's your look-to-buy ratio?*

Horowitz: Low—one of the reasons I want a redesign. I'd like to get a higher percentage of people buying a book or at least signing up for the free tip sheets.

McGarvey: *How big is the average purchase?*

Horowitz: I have two kinds of buyers: those who buy books, who spend $20 to $35, and those who buy marketing services, who spend between $75 and (over time) several

"**Pretty** much **anyone** could duplicate my **success**."

thousand dollars. Because of the integrated nature of my business, it's hard to separate revenues. It's not an uncommon pattern, for instance, to have someone visit the site to order my marketing book, and then some weeks or months later they come back to look over the pages about my marketing services—and then they buy.

McGarvey: *Is your site profitable?*

Horowitz: This site, while not bringing in megabucks, achieves a very high return on investment in my estimation. I sell a fair number of books directly from the site, and I also secure a number of lucrative marketing clients from the site. I also now have more than 6,000 subscribers to my two tip sheets, so I have a way of marketing to my visitors.

How's that for a cheap, effective Web site? Of course, I've written three books on cheap marketing and one on cheap fun, so I am a very good shopper—but pretty much anyone could duplicate my success.

CHAPTER 36

The Web's Dark Side: Security Holes, Fraud, And More [Bad] Stuff

I t seems too simple: Put up a Web site, and you're on the road to riches. Guess what? There are plenty of potholes in that road. Experts are eager to point out the dark side of the Web, the many ways it is easy to go wrong often before you even suspect there's a problem.

"I'd say 75 percent of Web sites are inadequate; they won't succeed," says Janet Asteroff, an analyst with e-business consulting firm The Concours Group.

E-commerce consultant Wally Bock shares her pessimism. "At least 70 percent of Web sites are just up there and don't do much at all," he says. "The problem with a bad Web site is that you're making a fool out of yourself in public." Keep talking to experts, and the general guesstimate is that *at minimum* two in three e-businesses are doomed.

Swallow hard on that glum prediction, then inhale this sobering reality: "It's easier to lose $1 million overnight with a Web site than to make it," says Stephan Moen, a vice president at e-business consulting firm Aspen Consulting.

"It is hard to do a Web site right," adds Phil Terry, CEO of Creative Good, a Web strategy consulting firm. "And there are so many ways to do one wrong." From visitors who look but never buy to wholesale theft of your most sensitive information, fledgling Web e-tailers need to know the problems this industry faces. Keep reading, and you'll discover the obstacles e-businesses face on the way to the top.

○ *Security:* "Security remains a key issue, maybe the critical issue, and it's where many e-businesses fall down," says Jeff Johnson, president of Meta Security Group, a tech security consulting firm. How can that be when most Web browsers and e-business server computers use encryption technology that scrambles a customer's credit card information when it's moving through the Internet? Says Johnson, "That is not the problem. That is rarely an issue."

Beware! What is your vulnerability to hackers? Do a vulnerability scorecard to pinpoint exactly where your weaknesses are. One common solution: Keep credit card and customer databases on a separate computer from the one connected to the Internet. This isn't the only security issue, however, so ask yourself what you would do if you were a hacker—then find ways to thwart that line of attack.

The possibilities are much worse, says Johnson: "Hackers break into the Web site's computers and steal the whole credit card database. It happens much, much more often than you'll ever read about." Johnson puts the odds of any server getting hacked into at 1 in 10. When he tells that to clients, many scoff, but then, he says, "we look through their access records and show them when and how hackers already have broken into their system. Maybe they haven't accessed the credit card database, but they've been inside and looked around. Probably they'll be back, too. There are lots of hackers out there—usually amateurs who do it for fun—and they are always searching for sites they can penetrate." The cure: "Work with security experts. Usually inexpensive solutions can be implemented that will safeguard your data."

Need convincing that security is a worry? Chew on this: In March 2000, two teenagers in Wales were arrested on charges that they stole upwards of 26,000 credit card numbers from various Web sites. Even security experts were amazed by this case because the teens, far from being seasoned hackers, were amateur enough to leave a clear trail from the hacks back to their personal computers. They used none of the tactics of slick hackers, yet, seemingly with ease, the kids broke into a number of business Web sites and waltzed out with credit-card numbers—some 6,500 of which they re-posted on various hacker Web sites. And that has become a disaster for the sites that were cracked, mainly small businesses that thought they could go unnoticed by hackers.

Don't delay: Start today improving security features at your site.

○ *No buyers:* The startling news is that 75 percent of online customers who fill shopping carts bail out before clicking the "Buy" button, according to research from e-commerce marketplace BizRate (www.bizrate.com) and research firm NPD Group (www.npd.com). The news gets worse, according to Creative Good's Phil Terry, who helps clients calculate what he calls "the conversion rate," meaning the percentage of visitors who actually buy something. "For most sites it's less than 1 percent," says Terry.

Fight hard to get traffic, in other words, and that might not matter at all. A site can be jammed, but the cash register may never ring. "Most sites focus on the wrong thing—they seek traffic, not conversion into customers," says Terry, who adds that the remedy is to build an e-tailing site, from the ground up, with the goal of enhancing and simplifying the shopping experience. "But you don't see many sites that do it."

○ *Outages:* EBay has had them, and so have many of the online stock brokerages. The inevitable result is a flood of bad publicity as daily newspapers rush to slam a falter-

Opportunity Knocks

How can you make your site one where people buy, not just look? Experts heatedly debate all aspects of site design, but the one area where there is clear agreement is that visitors will shop when the site is created with a firm intention to make it easy to shop. A role model is Amazon—everything is there to enhance and simplify the buying experience. You don't want your site to be a carbon copy, but if you are an e-tailer, ask yourself about every site feature, Does this simplify buying? When the answer is no, cut out that feature. It's that simple.

ing Web business. Sometimes outages are flukes—bugs that surface in software or during a site upgrade—but "often the problem is implementation of a poor plan at the beginning," says Moen.

More troubling still is the fact that outages often happen exactly when a Web site begins to catch on. "Many sites simply don't scale," says Moen, and that means a site that works fine when there are 100 visitors a day may show strains at 1,000—"you'll see many sites slowing down and becoming unresponsive to users," says Moen—and they go into meltdown at 10,000 visitors. "You need to build a site that readily scales as traffic increases," advises Moen, and, frankly, doing that requires nothing more than planning. Always ask, If traffic goes up tenfold, how will we handle it? If you don't know the answer, make sure your technical consultants do. And if you can, address the issue before launch—because when a Web site catches fire, it often becomes a wildfire.

○ *Fraud:* A dirty secret about the Web is that crooks love it. What better place to use stolen credit cards than under the relative anonymity afforded by the Internet? Jonas Lee, founder and CEO of GiftCertificates.com (www.giftcertificates.com), knows something about this. "From day one, we've had problems with fraud, but every e-tailer does," he says. "Fraud is part of selling on the Internet. We're lucky we started slow. As we grew—as public awareness of us grew—we also grew more expert at detecting fraud. Every e-tailer has to do the same."

Most e-tailers flatly refuse to talk on the record

Budget Watcher
Well-funded e-tailers install systemwide redundancy—if the whole Amazon setup were to collapse, for example, a carbon copy is ready to stand in and do the job. You probably don't want to incur those expenses, but you need to back up all your files. No need to get fancy here. Backups on Zip disks that are kept off-site will do. Why off-site? Losing your backup files as well as your originals in a fire, flood or hurricane is a nightmare you'll want to avoid. If off-site storage is too much of a hassle, use a fireproof and waterproof safe.

about their losses from fraud, but know that every site has had to do battle with crooks. Just ask retired librarian Cherie Magnus. As owner of www.viveladifference.com (a Hollywood, California, site devoted to selling condoms and promoting safe sex), Magnus had just launched her e-tailing operation when her first orders came in, a number of small purchases from Romania. Magnus decided she'd seen the "world" in World Wide Web, and after she got authorizations from credit card providers, she sent off her products.

Then she got a big order from the same Eastern bloc customer. "It totaled around $5,000," recalls Magnus. She was dancing with excitement over how easy this making money on the Web was—until, a few weeks later, she got a fax from her bank saying the charges had been disallowed because the card had been used fraudulently. She was stunned—she'd followed the rules and gotten authorizations. "I didn't know I needed to look into the discrepancy between the 'bill to' address and the 'ship to' address," says Magnus.

She's since learned a lot by becoming an active participant in online discussions of fraud against entrepreneurs. "Crooks are out there looking for newly launched sites," says Magnus. "They know you'll be delighted with an order. They place a couple small ones, then put in a big one." There's no easy cure—except "you have to be aware there are people looking to rob you."

○ *Fighting off the big dogs:* Larry Cuneo, the 48-year-old CEO of Minneapolis-based CarSoup, knew he had big problems from the day he launched in 1998. The space he coveted—selling cars on the Net—had

> **Beware!** Nobody knows how much is lost to credit card fraud on the Internet, but conservative estimates are that the tab long ago reached the $100 million mark. The e-tailer conundrum is that you don't want to lose a sale to a valid customer due to cumbersome security clearances, but you also cannot afford to get ripped off. But think about it. It's better to lose a sale than it is to become a victim. Always look for ways to improve your security as well as the customer's shopping experience, but keep an eye firmly on the till at all times.

Opportunity Knocks

Thinking local remains a smart route to Web wealth. Knocking heads with Amazon, Drugstore.com, or 1-800-flowers.com isn't smart—the war will be expensive and painful. But stake out a well-defined local turf, offer more in-depth local knowledge than any national site could hope to provide, and you just may be on to something.

already been staked out by very big dogs, including Microsoft (with CarPoint) and Autobytel.com. But Cuneo thought he had a unique twist—his site wouldn't be national; it would be local, pegged strictly at nearby dealers and car buyers. Sounds good—"but we had considerable difficulty gaining credibility," says Cuneo. "That's lowered our recognition—and our revenues—from advertisers and e-commerce partners."

Small might sometimes be beautiful, but on the Web, it's rarely a distinct advantage. Cuneo didn't quit, though. For one thing, he budgeted "about 50 percent of gross revenues for marketing and promotion," he says. He also invested substantial time in coming up with local promotions the big boys couldn't rival. "We'll sponsor cars in parades and little local events," says Cuneo. The upshot: Today, his site, www.carsoup.com, holds a genuine lead in its market over the national rivals. "Seventy of 132 local car dealers are signed up with us—but we've had to work hard to get here, and we'll have to work to hold this spot."

Is this dark side of the Web so gloomy that you should rethink your enthusiasm for this business venue? Nope, because the upside is the potential of fantastic wealth—the payoffs scored by the founders of, say, Amazon, Yahoo and eBay. Another take is offered by eHome's CEO Andy Oldham, who is still a distance from his payoff. His site is prospering and eHome is expanding into new markets, but, so far, this is not an overnight billion-dollar success. Still, he says, "although I never would have imagined how much energy and anxiety go into building a dotcom business, this *is* a great way to pursue business success. There's a lot of tension—but it also is a lot of fun."

CHAPTER 37

A Site To See:
A [Tour] Of The Web

S am Walton, the legendary founder of Wal-Mart, loved to shop—especially in competitors' stores. He did not necessarily buy anything, but he delighted in roaming the aisles, noting prices and observing unique, eye-catching ways to display merchandise. Why? Every shopping trip turned into an exercise in competitive intelligence, and whenever Walton caught a competitor doing something right, he looked for ways to do it still better in his Wal-Mart stores.

You would be wise to do the same, and that means routinely surfing the Web, visiting pace-setting e-tailers, and learning everything you can about what people are doing right. Don't think of surfing as goofing off. When you are doing it so that you can become a better e-tailer, it's some of the best work you can do. It's said that Jeff Bezos, founder of Amazon, keeps his Tuesdays and Thursdays open whenever possible to give himself time to surf the Web in search of cool ideas.

Here's a yardstick: You are doing valuable work when, after every surfing session, you have specific, concrete ideas for improving your site. If you're not getting ideas, you're surfing the wrong sites or not thinking hard enough. And neither will get you ahead in the competitive world of e-commerce.

Want to know how to look at Web sites? In the following pages, many name-brand Web sites are critiqued. Some win generous praise, but throughout, the emphasis is on what we can learn from these sites. And next time you put in a surfing session, ask yourself the kinds of questions you'll see in these site critiques.

RIVER OF DREAMS

$$\left[\begin{array}{c} \text{Amazon.com} \\ \text{www.amazon.com} \end{array}\right]$$

Amazon founder Jeff Bezos named his Web site "Amazon" because that river is exponentially bigger than any other river on earth, or so the story goes. And Bezos' aim from the get-go was to build the Web's biggest store.

Bezos came up with the idea when, as an employee of a New York financial firm, he was asked to run numbers on various possible Web businesses. When he hit upon books, all the lights went on—Bezos knew he had a winner. Just a couple distributors stock pretty much every book in print, and it seemed simple to set up a business that amounted to a Web site with no inventory. As orders came in, books could be bought from distributors, and whoosh, profits would roll in. Bezos took the numbers to his bosses, asking them to join in funding a start-up, but the verdict was no way. So Bezos quit, moved to Seattle, and got busy building out what just may rank as the Web's crowning e-tailing achievement.

The **emphasis** is on making it **easy** for the buyer to **make** a **purchase**.

In Internet research firm Media Metrix's May 2000 tally of Web site visitors, only one e-tailing site placed in the top 10 sites: Amazon, which ranked ninth. Why is Amazon so successful? Its pages and tools are brilliantly executed, and, throughout, the emphasis is on making it easy for the buyer to make a purchase.

Case in point: "1-Click" buying. Like a book? A registered Amazon user can, with a single mouse click, buy it. It's that fast and that simple (so much so that tests showed users didn't believe it could be so easy—so afterward a screen pops up that says the deal has been done). It doesn't work only on books, however. Anything Amazon sells can be bought with a single click, and nowadays that includes TV sets, videos, CDs, power saws, toys, and more. Doesn't Bezos risk diluting Amazon's message by expanding into so many diverse product lines? Remember the company's name—from the start Bezos envisioned expanding into other product lines.

What else is cool about Amazon.com? Notice how fast the page loads. The look is fresh and clean but is primarily text-based, with plentiful use of white space to make the page easy on the eyes. With its treasury, Amazon could well afford to put up the glitziest tech tools imaginable, but it doesn't. Cool tools—Java applets, sound effects, and so on—gobble up bandwidth and really bloat page-loading times. And Bezos, from the start, has put a primacy on making it easy for a customer to buy what he or she needs, fast.

Keep looking at the page, and you'll notice that if you've bought from Amazon in the past, the page is personalized in keeping with your prior purchases. Books, music and video are recommended in line with an educated guess about what you'll like. Although personalization is hard for a low-budget site builder to incorporate, any site builder can insert a "Deals of the Day" button or a "Gift Ideas" button, just as Amazon does. Amazon also offers a freebie on its front page—"Free E-Cards," says the button. Again, any site builder ought to find a useful freebie to give away.

One exceptionally clever feature: "Help a Charity," where you put a link to Amazon on your page, and for every purchase, a charity of your choice gets a contribution from Amazon. A variation on the usual affiliate program, this charity tool is geared to bringing in computer users who might not

Beware!

Amazon has filed patents on various bits of its site operation, and although nobody is clear about what Amazon intends to do to assert its rights, wary site designers are treading softly when it comes to closely imitating Amazon. This will not likely be a worry for you, both because your operation will be small and your technology not nearly as robust as Amazon's, but if you find yourself exactly duplicating the "1-Click" purchase tool, back up a few steps and try another approach.

want to bother trying to earn a few dollars for themselves but will feel good helping the American Indian College Fund or the World Wildlife Fund raise money.

Smart e-tailers know to bookmark Amazon, whether they shop there or not, and at least monthly check in just to look at the site. This is as good as e-commerce gets, and there are always tools, techniques and tactics to learn.

IN FULL BLOOM

$$\left[\begin{array}{c} \text{1-800-flowers} \\ \text{www.1800flowers.com} \end{array} \right]$$

Wall Street hates this company. Its stock (Nasdaq: FLWS) sells for well under half the IPO price and, after plummeting almost immediately after the IPO, has never gone anywhere. Why? 1-800-flowers now operates at a loss (for the six months ending 12/27/99, it lost more than $34.7 million) as it spends heavily on advertising and promotion. Probably a bigger problem as far as the Street is concerned is that the company's business model (booking orders via a toll-free telephone number) is under attack by Web-based competitors who undercut the prices charged by 1-800-flowers, sometimes by up to 50 percent.

This is a company that **truly** understands and **embraces** Net-based **selling**.

But 1-800-flowers has advantages, and one of them is that this is a company that truly understands and embraces Net-based selling. It also was a pioneer: Its first electronic storefront opened on CompuServe in 1992, followed by an AOL store in '94. Its Web site went up in 1995, which is so early in Internet time that 1-800-flowers accomplished that by serving as a beta tester for what became Netscape's Commerce Server. While other leading businesses often stumbled when it came to jumping into the online world, 1-800-flowers got it right from the start.

Does its site still work? Absolutely. And keep this in mind:

Flowers are easier to sell on the visual Web than they are by phone. Do you know what a "Fields of Europe" arrangement looks like? Of course not. And even if you're told it has miniature sunflowers, daisies and button poms, you may be clueless about its looks. But at the Web site you see the arrangement, which can usually be magnified.

A fast-loading site that's primarily text-based (but with enough imagery to capture the visuals of the floral business), 1-800-flowers aims to make the shopping experience as easy as possible. Flowers appropriate for an upcoming holiday are noted. Tabs offer gift suggestions for common events— birthday, get well, love and romance. A "Best Sellers" tab tells a visitor what others are buying so it's easy to follow the pack.

Smart Tip

Always compare your site to competitors', and do this ruthlessly and without an iota of favoritism. What do your competitors do better? If you cannot list a dozen things, go back and look at their sites more closely until you come up with a dozen. The only way to make your site the best it can be is to study competitors, see what they are doing well, and then do it better yourself.

The most impressive thing about 1-800-flowers is it offers up lots of information on a page that nonetheless doesn't seem cluttered or overwhelming. That is exceptional page design, and it is a goal every site designer ought to aspire to.

Another plus: If you are truly clueless about flowers, or reach a roadblock in trying to make a purchase, a real-time, live chat with a customer service person can be had at http://eshare.1800flowers.com. This is a well thought-out strategy that looks at several issues from the customer's point of view, such as the slow speed of e-mail (by the time the user gets a return e-mail, he has probably already purchased elsewhere) and the inconvenience of making a telephone call (many home users have only one line, and to use it, they have to disconnect the computer from the Net).

Can you implement a real-time feature? Probably not. The service is offered by a third party, eShare (www.eshare.com), but odds are, it's beyond your ambitions and budget. Even so, what any site builder can take from this is the focus on anticipating and solving customer needs before the customer even knows he has a problem.

Is there anything that doesn't work with the 1-800-flowers site? To my eyes, the cookies on prime, midpage real estate confuse the message. But 1-800-flowers insists its customers wanted more gift choices, and perhaps the company is right.

For comparison, take a look at a competitor—Proflowers (www.proflowers.com). Prices are terrific: One dozen Ecuadorian roses cost $39.95. But the page is cluttered and unhelpful to the shopper. Who needs a list of every possible flower ("Shop by Flower Type") on the opening page? Maybe it would work on an inside page, but on the front page it's an unnecessary detail.

Note, too, that "Shop by Flower Type" is above "Shop by Occasion" on the page. The reason for that is a puzzle because you don't know anybody who ever said, "Today's a day I need to buy a dozen freesia," but you do know lots of people who have said, "Today's my wife's birthday, and I need a dozen roses." Only a thorough lack of focus on the customer could have prompted the placement of flower type above occasion. Too bad for Proflowers, too, because I have bought their flowers, and the price-value relationship is high. But the Web site isn't constructed in a way that makes it easy for customers to shop.

PUSHING THE ENVELOPES

[
Staples, Office Depot and OfficeMax
www.staples.com
www.officedepot.com
www.officemax.com
]

The big three office supplies chains—Staples, Office Depot and OfficeMax—slug it out online every bit as vigorously as they do in the bricks-and-mortar world. And think of the barriers to building a good office supplies site: The products are nonvisual (who wants to look at a ream of paper?) and inherently unexciting. Nobody gets a tingle thinking about buying the month's toner, paper clips and envelopes. This is boring stuff, and, as consumers, we want to get in and out as quickly as possible.

But that's good news for office supplies site designers. With some kinds of retail, shoppers actually enjoy the physical shops (fine jewelers, for instance), but with office supplies, if we never have to step into a B&M store again, likely we'll all toast our good fortune. The trick for a site designer is making it all work on the Web so that it's easy to make the purchases we need.

Unsurprisingly, all three of the office supplies giants take essentially the same route. In fact, Staples and Office Depot erect pages that are stunningly similar—heavily text-oriented, scant use of graphics, with an organization that revolves around imitating the aisles in a physical store (the paper aisle, say).

Smart Tip

How can you make your customers' shopping easier? Are there "ready-made lists" you can create? How about lists of the most ordered items? Face it: No matter what any tech head says, Web shopping lacks the buzz and fun of a mall (although it has other strong advantages). Build in tools that make shopping go fast, and your customers will thank you by spending more money in your store.

OfficeMax follows the same organizing concept but is much more generous in the use of graphics (a chair, a box of paper, a scanner). You've got to wonder exactly why OfficeMax's designers use so many graphical elements because again, if you've seen one box of 500 #10 envelopes, you've seen all you ever need to see. Granted, the images have very low resolution and don't add appreciably to load time (a shot of a scanner, for instance, is a trace more than 1 KB), but this also means they have so little detail (the scanner could be a photocopier or a printer) that their inclusion adds nothing positive to the page.

Which site comes out on top? For my money, it's Staples, but only by a nose—all three of these Web sites seem closer to first-generation pages than mature e-tailing vehicles. Staples wins because it builds in numerous useful shopping tools— "Personalized Lists," "Ready-made Lists" (for instance: supplies for a new employee), "Past Purchase History," and more. The others have similar tools, but finding them on those sites is tough. Staples puts them right in your face, and for that the designers deserve congratulations. By making it easy to replenish supplies with just a couple mouse clicks, Staples takes some of the drudgery out of this chore.

IT'S IN THE MAIL

[Stamps.com
www.stamps.com]

The biggest challenge in selling is convincing somebody to do something new, something they have never done before. Witness escargot. You have seen them on menus. Have you ever eaten snails? If you have, you either like them or don't like them, and you know without further ado if you will order them again. But if you have never ordered them—never tasted a snail—it's very difficult to be persuaded to order one at a restaurant. A freebie may help, but probably not. What would tempt you to try? Tough question, with no easy answer.

Its **highest goal** isn't to sell you; it's to **tempt** you to **try** the service.

What do snails have to do with the Web? A lot, actually. Just look at Stamps.com, a site where you can do things you have never done before. Of course you understand postage, but the way it has always worked is that you've gone to the post office with money and walked out either with a sheet of paper stamps or with credits entered into a postage meter. Stamps.com wants to change all that.

Its aim is to entice you to buy postage on the Internet, from a company you have never heard of and—somehow—to affix this postage to your outgoing mail in ways you do not understand. How could you ever be enticed into taking this deal? Simple: Sign up with Stamps.com, and you get $20 in free postage. Because it's free, you just might try it out.

Look closely at Stamps.com's front page. Its highest goal isn't to sell you; it's to tempt you to try out the service by clicking either "Learn About Stamps.com" or "Special Offer." Is that

Free For All
Click

What can you give away? Stamps.com gives away $20 in postage—which is something visitors know the value of and will use. But if you use this tactic, keep close tabs on both your visitor counts and the numbers that take advantage of any freebies you are offering. If the visitor count dramatically exceeds the number of folks who go for the freebie, maybe you are trying to give away escargot—meaning visitors don't know if they actually want what you are offering. The remedy? Think hard about finding a way to position what you are offering as both valuable and desirable, and keep tinkering with this value proposition until a healthy percentage of visitors are jumping on your freebie.

putting priorities in the wrong place? No, because you won't be sold into buying Stamps.com's service until you try it, and the smartest, fastest, best way to induce you to try it is to give it away.

Everything about this front page aims at achieving that goal, and that makes this a well-designed site. It's a lesson many Web site designers should absorb. Sometimes the Web merely offers new ways to do old things (as, for instance, Amazon adds a cyber-twist to book buying), but in other cases the Web is about wholly new things to do, which is the case with Stamps.com. And the only way to get customers to plunge into uncharted waters is to tempt them with freebies.

Once you're tempted, the "Learn About Stamps.com" kicks into action. In four quick steps, a visitor is guided through the how-to of the Stamps.com process, offered multiple sign-up bonuses, shown clear pricing, then prompted to do the deed and sign up.

The jury is out on the near-term viability of Stamps.com or any of its competitors, but for now the site wins applause for doing all the right things to persuade us to at the very least give this newfangled way of buying and affixing postage a whirl.

THE RIGHT DOSE

[**Drugstore.com**
www.drugstore.com]

Who likes shopping for aspirin, soap, razor blades, prescription medicines, and the rest of the stuff that brings us to drugstores? Almost nobody, and that's why an early niche targeted by trailblazing e-tailers was the drugstore category. Imagine if you could save yourself a half-hour—maybe more—weekly by eliminating those shopping trips and instead clicking a mouse a few times.

That's the value proposition put forth by Drugstore.com, a leader in this tightly fought category (where prime competitors include CVS.com—formerly Soma.com, a Washington start-up bought outright by bricks-and-mortar chain CVS in '99—and PlanetRx.com). And Drugstore.com so far has managed to stay ahead of the pack. Ranked No. 1 by e-commerce analysts Gómez Advisors (www.gomez.com) in the drugstore category, Drugstore also has won the top spot in Forrester Research's Power Rankings (www.forrester.com). Said Forrester in its review: "Reasonable prices, intuitive navigation, one-click shopping, and saved shopping list and billing information place Drugstore.com in the No. 1 spot for online health retailers."

Check **out** the Drugstore.com **home page, and it's shockingly** reminiscent of **Amazon's**.

Check out the Drugstore.com home page, and it's shockingly reminiscent of Amazon's, right down to the use of navigational tabs at the top of the page (home, health, beauty, etc.). That is actually unsurprising because Amazon owns a large slice of Drugstore.com's equity, and the two are strategic partners who do many cross-promotions. Buy from Drugstore, and when the box arrives, it might contain a discount coupon good at Amazon, or vice-versa.

Keep poking around the Drugstore.com site, and there's much to admire: pages that load very fast, a "Light Graphics" option that lets pages load faster still by killing most images, numerous tools for personalization ("My List"), and well-organized "Aisles" (health, beauty, and so forth) that make browsing reasonably easy. Sale items are highlighted on the front page, and a "Specials" button opens the door to many more discounted items.

Also eye-catching are deals Drugstore has cobbled together with bricks-and-mortar pharmacy Rite Aid (which enables Drugstore to fulfill prescriptions under most medical insurance plans) and vitamin seller GNC.

Hop over to the pages for PlanetRx.com and CVS.com, and they are remarkably similar, which perhaps ought to be unsurprising; bricks-and-mortar drugstores look much the same, too. Can you tell a Walgreens from a CVS? Certainly those companies would like to think so—and they spend big money trying to develop unique identities—but over-the-counter allergy pills look alike no matter whose shelf they are on.

So what puts Drugstore.com in the lead? Two things. One, Drugstore's page layout and design are strikingly close to Amazon's. That's a plus because as the most trafficked e-commerce site, Amazon is understood by millions of consumers who have acquired a comfort level in dealing with the bookseller. Drugstore can do this because of its financial intertwining with Amazon, but, again, other e-tailers must be careful not to copy too closely those patented features.

The other distinguishing feature about Drugstore.com is that it's leveraged upon joint marketing arrangements with well-known businesses—notably Rite Aid and GNC. Both those companies have spent many millions of dollars nurturing consumer awareness and comfort, and they

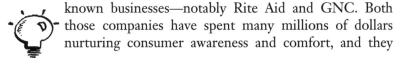

Smart Tip

With whom can you forge alliances? What companies will dress up your pages and build higher levels of visitor trust in your business? Make up a list, and start knocking on doors. For a dotcom start-up, these kinds of partnerships can spell the difference between a fast ramp up into success or a swift plunge into failure. A few partnerships are plenty; put up too many on your page, and you risk blurring your message and losing your identity.

rank high in their niches. Drugstore.com gets to parlay their investments into a powerful play for consumers' trust and shopping dollars.

That's a brilliant move because no matter how fast a cyberstorefront spends to drive traffic to its pages, it still has to wrestle with consumer distrust. Nobody's "seen" it, nobody's been inside, nobody's touched the merchandise on its shelves. Those are high hurdles, but not the only ones faced by Drugstore. Its products touch a customer's body, and that's a field where trust is paramount. Lack it, and selling is simply impossible. Drugstore wins cheers for its attempt to bridge the trust divide through strategic alliances. That simply is first-rate marketing smarts.

RIDING THE WAVE

[Yahoo
www.yahoo.com]

No Web site comes close to Yahoo in winning visitors. It was among the Net's first Web sites, but it's remained a powerhouse. In a recent count by research firm Media Metrix (www. mediametrix.com), Yahoo had more than 43 million visitors in one month. Second place went to Microsoft's MSN (www.msn.com), with 34 million—that's 9 million fewer. White-hot eBay (www. ebay.com) managed only 12 million visitors in the same period. Yahoo's performance is simply amazing, especially since this is month-in, month-out leadership that has lasted for years.

Yahoo is a monument to an **Internet** philosophy of less is **more**.

Surf into Yahoo, and what you find is a monument to an Internet philosophy of less is more. Graphical elements are so few as to be almost not used at all, and the page is heavily text-based—but somehow manages to remain both uncluttered and readable. This is as skilled as Web site programming gets: Yahoo programmers manage to make an extremely sophisticated site design somehow look simple.

Now notice how many services and options Yahoo offers, from personalized stock quotes to e-mail, auctions, even a customized "My Yahoo" page where registered users can select exactly what kind of information they want to see. It is a rich array of individualized information, and since it's free, smart users tap into it.

Smart Tip

Surf around and visit all the portal or gateway sites that, in the past five years, Yahoo has trounced: Excite.com, Infoseek.com, Snap.com, AltaVista.com. Keep asking, What does Yahoo do better and how can I adapt it to my site? Odds are you cannot duplicate the sophisticated programming or the high level of personalization offered by Yahoo. But keep surfing, and you'll soon be jotting down concrete ideas for your own site.

For insight into why Yahoo consistently tramples MSN in the ratings, head over to the MSN site. You will see a very different look, consisting of more visuals and, strangely, both less information and more irrelevant stuff. On a recent site visit, I found a question out of nowhere, "Did unisex bathrooms kill the ERA?" and an even dumber line, "Go fishing on your PC." Huh? Yahoo manages to be sober and useful, compared to a kind of frivolity at MSN. Most users want to dispense with the frivolous and get down to business.

Learn from Yahoo that less is definitely more, and information—useful, relevant information—is power. Give surfers facts, make the page load fast, and you are following in Yahoo's footsteps, which is an excellent path to take.

It Takes A Village

[iVillage.com
www.ivillage.com]

A site aimed at women, iVillage.com, recently ranked 28th in Media Metrix's tally—the highest showing for a special interest site—and attracted 6 million visitors in a month. With the intense competition that's out there, what moved iVillage to the top of the heap? Log into iVillage and see for yourself. It's evident that the site strives to be a portal for women, the kind of page it hopes users will set up as their start page. That's because the site offers a full-range of services, everything from horoscopes to joke of the day and free Web-based e-mail. There are recipes, beauty tips, pointers for parents, places to chat online, and many places to shop (from Petopia.com to PlanetRx.com). Whatever a person could want to find online is offered on this page somewhere.

Smart Tip
Have you defined your target audience? The more you know about your likely viewers, the more closely you can match your site to their interests and needs. Get to know your viewers—run surveys, solicit e-mail feedback, and routinely seek to find out what's on people's minds—and that will pay rich dividends in making it easier for you to gear site content to them.

One problem: The page is cluttered, and finding anything in particular isn't easy. But at the top of the front page there's a link for new visitors to iVillage. Click it, and you enter an orientation on the site's content. The tone is warm, woman to woman, with absolutely no techie blabbering. On many sites, you'll find a similar tool, but usually it is labeled "site navigation" or something similarly cold, and its content consists of a grid. At iVillage, the navigational aid is friendly and helpful.

The most impressive thing about iVillage is it knows its target audience and gears everything to those viewers. Many sites are unfocused, or try to be all things to all people, and that never works. What does work is knowing who your viewers are and gearing everything on the site to them. In this respect, iVillage excels. Looked at from a functional point of view, it is not fundamentally different from, say, the AOL start page (www.aol.com), with the major exception that iVillage has defined its audience and pursues it. And it pays off with those solid Media Metrix numbers.

In The Cards

[**Blue Mountain Arts**
www.bluemountain.com]

Stephen and Susan Schutz founded Blue Mountain Arts—a poetry and fine arts publishing house—back in 1971 when they were hippies. Visit their Web site, and, a few pages into it, you'll find old photographs of the Schutzes, including one from 1969 when they were on their way to Woodstock, driving a gaily painted "Freedom Car," a 1957 junker that had been transformed by this artistic couple into a moving political statement.

While Susan is a poet, Stephen is a Ph.D. physicist (with a degree from Princeton) who is fascinated by the use of computers in making art. In 1996, the couple combined their interests and launched their Web site with a novel idea: They would let you send a greeting card to anybody, for free. There's a catch, of course. To send the card, you have to visit the Blue Mountain Web site, and the recipient has to do likewise to see the card. That's textbook marketing. Every card means at least two visits, which provide ample selling opportunities, both for third-party advertisers and for Blue Mountain's own line of poetry books.

If it sounds good to you, you're not alone: In a recent Media Metrix traffic count, Blue Mountain Arts placed as the 12th most visited Web site, with more than 13 million visitors in one month.

Go to the Blue Mountain Arts Web site, and it—yet again—is extremely plain, simple and text-based. Upcoming holidays (including obscure celebrations like National Pig Day and Hoodie-Hoo Day) are displayed chronologically, and there's also a list of reasons to send cards (love, retirement, get well).

It's **functional**, with no **glitz** or **pizazz**, but it gets the job **done**.

It's functional, with no glitz or pizazz, but it gets the job done—exceptionally well, in fact, as shown by the flood of visitors to the site.

Arguably, the site design—which screams cheap and home-made—is something of a plus because it links with the hippie motif that's articulated throughout the site. If GM put up a site that looked like this, people would wonder why GM was insistent on being so stingy, but when some Colorado hippies do it, well, that certainly makes good sense. It makes all the more sense because the site's main function is to give stuff away, so who could possibly complain about an ultrasimple design (which, by the way, Stephen says he does himself)?

In the years since Blue Mountain launched, a flood of imita-tors hit the market, mainly because it is extremely easy and cheap to set up this kind of card site. But nobody has matched the suc-cess of Susan and Stephen Schutz, in part because they were there first (and first-mover advantage is powerful on the Web) and also because, better than anybody else, they have the knack for putting together this sort of site.

News flash: Blue Mountain Arts, in 2000, was bought by Excite for $780 million, who was no doubt lured by the more than 10 million visitors who come to the site in most months. Although now owned by Excite, the site's look and functionality remain much the same as when it was independent. Why mess with such a success? Still, worth pondering is whether a home-made look will work as well for Excite as it did for a pair of Colorado hippies.

Smart Tip

At Blue Mountain, the medium is the mes-sage, and the message is the medium. The simple design is in perfect sync with the site's mission of giving away free cards. Is your site design in sync with your core mission? Do you want to seem slick, homespun, technically savvy, or warm and friendly? Each is a very different atti-tude, and each will benefit from a different site design. Rules aren't hard and fast—there is no recipe for creating a homespun site, say—but your visitors will know it when they see it, so strive to create a design that reflects your underly-ing philosophy.

IT'S FREE!

[**Bonzi Software**
www.bonzi.com]

Reading over Media Metrix's listing of the top Web properties, my eyes stumbled over No. 34. Bonzi? I dimly recalled a

maker of a voice e-mail module for AOL, but how
could that little San Luis Obispo, California, company
have pushed its way into the elite group of most-visited
Web properties?

Sure enough, they were one
and the same. Visit the Web
site, and it's a delight: simple,
with an inexpensive, home-
brewed look and feel. But the
site has a powerful draw in free
downloads of Internet utility
programs, which no visitor can
fail to see because "Free"—still
among the most powerful words
any Internet marketer can use—
is highlighted and instantly in
your face. Other highlighted
words, "New" and "Updates,"
lead existing Bonzi software
users to the latest releases.

Smart Tip

Navigation
is key to a Web
site—can users
find what they're looking
for in a glance? Heavily
monied corporations actu-
ally test and time users as
they poke around rough-
draft Web sites. You can
do the same. Ask employ-
ees, or friends and neighbors, to navigate around
your site, and listen to
their feedback. It does no
good if you hide your
gems—they need to be
readily visible, even to
casual lookers.

Just a few software programs
were offered by Bonzi when I
visited, but each gets a neat
block of copy, with key words—
"Internet Alert," "Voice E-mail,"
"Internet Boost,"—highlighted. I give this site an "A" for being
so easy to navigate. It may not be pretty and certainly isn't glitzy,
but no visitors will have to waste time wondering what to click to
get where he wants to go.

How does Bonzi get so much traffic? Costs aren't released,
but the company has various advertising/marketing deals with
the AOL family of properties (namely, AOL and CompuServe),

and those ads doubtless are a key source of visitors. Advertising in other media by Bonzi is slim to none. Critics may express skepticism about the efficacy of online advertising, but in the right place, for the right products, it definitely gets results. Bonzi sells Internet software, so where better to advertise than on the Internet? Ask yourself where your customers will see your ads, and that's where you want to be. Bonzi's stunning success in the traffic wars proves the value of that proposition.

SHIPPING OUT

[MotherNature.com
www.mothernature.com]

MotherNature.com is yet another e-tailer that's struggling to win marketplace mind share in an ever more cluttered retailing environment. You can buy vitamins and minerals at your local supermarket or drugstore, via established mail order outlets, or from heavily funded e-tailers like Drugstore.com. Out of that stiff competition, MotherNature.com's challenge is to get you to click into it when you want to buy St. John's Wort, Echinacea or vitamin C. And it also has to make some money in the process.

 The stakes are high: MotherNature.com's is trying to reach an ideal Net customer, who uses

Budget Watcher

How can you give away shipping and not go broke? While FedEx and its competitors negotiate highly favorable rates with big shippers, they won't do the same with little businesses. But that doesn't mean only big-bucks options are left. Use UPS standard delivery or the post office. Both are cheap. A 1-pound package can be shipped cross-country via the post office for around $3.25, and that buys two-day, priority mail delivery. If that gets you a buyer who becomes a repeat customer, isn't it some of the smartest money you've ever spent? Don't be too quick to say you cannot afford to give away shipping.

the same stuff day in, day out. These are products that don't need to be seen and touched before purchasing and that are easy to ship—lightweight and with little sensitivity to temperatures. Sell a customer a month's supply of a cholesterol-cutting herbal formula today, and odds are he'll be back for another bottle next month. That's a great customer.

How does MotherNature.com hope to win consumers' patronage? For one thing, it uses most of the proven tricks and tactics that make online shopping easier, from stored shopping lists of favorite items to "hot lists" of popular products. MotherNature.com also goes farther than most e-tailers in meeting head-on a major obstacle to online buying: shipping charges. Survey after survey identifies shipping charges as a major customer peeve. It's hard to say why, because the customer who drives 10 miles to avoid paying an e-tailer shipping charges is probably spending as much in wear and tear of the car. Consumer behavior isn't always rational, but e-tailers need to understand it nonetheless.

MotherNature.com knows that, so, in bold print, it proclaims that its shipping is free. Smaller print adds the catch, which is that you've got to spend $50 to qualify for this, but it's still a good deal for customers—and a good deal for MotherNature.com because it eliminates that big source of buying resistance.

How can MotherNature.com afford to do this? A better question might be, How can other e-tailers afford not to do it? Sure, the company kisses off around $5 in shipping per sale, but think of how many sales it makes that it otherwise wouldn't. Giving away shipping might cause a bit of short-term pain, but it's a direct solution to a big e-tailing problem. And its long-run impact on sales and profits has to be favorable.

COME SAIL AWAY

[**World Explorer Cruises**
www.wecruise.com]

It's trendy to mock "brochureware"—Web sites that aren't e-commerce enabled and in effect offer nothing beyond a company's brochure—but that doesn't mean good brochureware isn't a smart move. Case in point: World Explorer Cruises' site sells nothing, but it provides all the information found in brochures—and saves money in the process. Have you ever calculated how much it costs you to send out brochures and what your rate of return is? Do it, and don't be surprised if the results are sickening. Many businesses are losing money on their fancy brochures but don't even know it because they have never instituted a tracking system.

Budget Watcher

The real draw of putting product literature up on a Web site is that it will save you money. Some customers and prospects still will want printed materials, but don't be surprised if many—maybe even most—are satisfied with Web-based brochures. The advantages: The customer always know where to find it (and how many printed brochures get misfiled and lost?), and in most cases, you can actually provide many more details than you'd likely print. Check it out, and you may see your printing bills tumble.

World Explorer is a smaller cruise line, operating just one ship and only during the few months of the year that cruising to Alaska is desirable and realistic. Compared to Carnival or Royal Caribbean—which operate dozens of ships, year-round—World Explorer is a speck of an operator, but that makes it all the more essential that it spend its money wisely. Mass-mailing expensive, full-color brochures is very expensive, but putting the content of a brochure on a Web site is cost-effective and can be downright cheap.

The mission World Explorer's site takes on is daunting—it aims to convey the flavor of a cruise into an untamed, unpredictable region. It also aims to help simplify a cruising complication: The amount you pay is dependent upon the cabin you book—the bigger the cabin and the better the view, the more you pay. And, of course, cruisers want to know what they're buying—"Is the more expensive B-class cabin worth the premium?"—and the more specific the details, the happier a cruiser is.

Check out the World Explorer site, and it's obvious this is not a big-budget production—there are no high-cost Java applets or Shockwave elements. But all you need to know to make an intelligent booking choice is right there, on the site.

Why isn't the site e-commerce enabled? Traditionally, travel agents have sold nearly all cruises. Some lines—notably Renaissance (www.renaissancecruises.com)—are eager to cut travel agents (and their commissions, which run upwards of 10 percent) out of the equation, but most lines are going slower in that regard. World Explorer clearly fits into the cautious camp. So it takes visitors up to the brink of online purchasing, but backs off.

That's fine, though, because it proves that "brochureware" can still work. Let the trendy scoffers mock it, but know that if it suits your business, putting up detailed product information may be your smartest use of the Web.

CHAPTER 38

Stop Right There: The [Must-Have] e-Commerce Bookmarks

H ere's the blunt truth about e-commerce: Most of what you want to know isn't in books or even in magazines and newspapers. This industry is exploding so fast that the only medium that is successfully tracking developments is the Web itself. When you want to know more, or need answers to questions, log onto the Web and go searching. The information you crave is rarely more than a few mouse clicks away. Here you'll find dozens of the sites that deserve tracking.

COMPETITIVE INTELLIGENCE

Get the goods on competitors, background-check new hires, and buy credit reports on your customers by using the Web to locate what you need. Not all of this info is free, but you may well need it to make sure you're paid, to grow your business, and to hire the right people.

○ *Company Sleuth (www.companysleuth.com):* Tell Company Sleuth the names of up to 10 public companies, and it will send you regular e-mail reports with breaking news about the targets. SEC filings, press releases, even rumors get covered in Company Sleuth's filings, and the price is free.

○ *CreditFYI (www.creditfyi.com):* $14.95 buys you a credit report on a business, delivered in seconds, and much of the data comes from Experian (see TRW Credit).

○ *Hoover's (www.hoovers.com):* The best content is available only for a fee, but there's ample free content to be found by anyone who surfs in. Research competitors, track stock market performance, and keep tabs on IPOs.

○ *KnowX (www.knowx.com):* The savvy engine ferrets through public records and—for costs of $1 to $5 in most cases—will report on bankruptcies, liens, judgments and such, against both individuals and businesses.

○ *Thomas Register (www.thomasregister.com):* The sourcebook on U.S. and Canadian companies. The print edition costs $149, but almost all the content is here to read for free.

CONSUMERS AND THE NET

From the beginning, there's been an avalanche of worry about fraud and the Net. Mainly problems have been grossly overblown, but these issues will continue to shape how customers view e-tailers. Find out how to make your site look good from a consumer advocate's point of view by checking out these sites.

○ *BBBOnLine (www.bbbonline.org):* The Better Business Bureau's entry into monitoring e-tailers

○ *BizRate (www.bizrating.com):* A leader in evaluating e-tailers

○ *E-commerce and the Internet (www.ftc.gov/bcp/menu-internet.htm):* Advice from the Federal Trade Commission that pinpoints common frauds

○ *How to Protect Yourself: Shopping on the Internet (http://legal. firn.edu/consumer/tips/internet.html):* Counsel from Florida's attorney general

○ *SafeShopping (www.safeshopping.org):* Created by the American Bar Association, which bills it as "the place to stop before you shop"

○ *WebAssured (www.webassured.com):* Another e-tailer evaluator

E-COMMERCE MISCELLANY

Here are the sites that make e-commerce easier to do right.

○ *!n Free Web Site Promotion (http://usa-www.hypermart.net/free. htm):* Submit your site to many leading search engines, free of charge

○ *All Domains (www.alldomains.com):* There's more to Web sites than "net," "com," and "gov" domains. Find out about (and buy) international domains here; countries from Afghanistan (af) to Zimbabwe (zw) have domains for sale.

○ *ClicksLink (www.clickslink.com):* Explore offbeat affiliate programs (astrology, watch stores, and more) at this Web site

○ *Compare Web Hosts (www.comparewebhosts.com):* They are not all the same, and this site helps you compare competing hosting services.

○ *eGroups (www.egroups.com):* Still the easiest and best way to set up an Internet mailing list. It's free.

○ *LinkExchange (www.linkexchange.com):* Now part of Microsoft's bCentral portal for small business, LinkExchange remains the Web's best banner exchange program.

○ *LinkShare (www.linkshare.com):* Put money in your pocket by signing up for affiliate status with L.L. Bean, Renaissance Cruises, Toys "R" Us, and more name-brand e-tailers at this site.

○ *NetMechanic (www.netmechanics.com):* Check your site for bad code and broken links, free of charge

○ *Network Solutions (www.networksolutions.com):* The primary marketplace for registering U.S. domains

○ *TopHosts (www.tophosts.com):* Useful articles and background material to digest before picking a host

GLOBAL COMMERCE

It's right in the name: *World* Wide Web. The Net is a global medium, and the smart players know to keep close tabs on what's happening abroad. How? Plentiful Web sites will help. Here are some of the best.

○ *Electronic Commerce and the European Union (www.ispo.cec.be/ecommerce):* Filled with facts and stats about e-commerce in Europe

○ *European E-Business Review (www.ft.com/ebr):* From the *Financial Times* newspaper

○ *Global Business Resources (www.cio.com/central/globalinks.html):* Compiled by *CIO* magazine, a publication for chief information officers at major corporations

○ *International Business Resources (http://ciber.bus.msu.edu/busres. htm):* A rich collection of links produced by Michigan State University faculty and staff

○ *Planet Business (www.planetbiz.com):* Business resources, arranged by country. A good place to look for foreign contacts, partners and information.

MONEY TALKS

Find out more about business financing, maybe even land venture or angel financing, at key Web sites.

○ *Benchmark (www.benchmark.com):* Said by some to be the top venture capital firm. Companies include eBay, WebVan, Art.com, PlanetRx.

○ *Business Angels (www.business-angels.com/us/index.html):* This group, founded in Europe, is now also looking at U.S.-based businesses in search of seed money.

○ *Garage (www.garage.com):* Don't know where to begin researching venture funding? No site is better than Garage.com.

○ *Kleiner Perkins Caufield & Byers (www.kpcb.com):* The other top VC firm. Companies include Amazon, Drugstore, Netscape, Healtheon, myCFO.com, and Realtor.com.

○ *MoneyHunt (www.moneyhunter.com):* The home page for the TV show that helps entrepreneurs link with VCs and angels

○ *Venture Capital Resource Library (www.vfinance.com):* A good site for getting info on who's who in the VC world and how deals get cut

MUST-AVOID SITE DESIGNS

It's surprisingly easy not to build a bad Web site—just follow the advice that's freely dispensed on the Web.

○ *How To Build Lame Web Sites (http://webdevelopersjournal.co.uk/ columns/perpend1.html):* Insightful (and sometimes funny) look at bad site design

○ *Jakob Nielsen (www.useit.com):* The guru of Web usability, Nielsen particularly revels in pinpointing the "must-nots" of Web site architecture. If Nielsen says don't do it, don't.

Net Traffic Reports And Ratings

Television has its Nielsen ratings, radio has Arbitron, and while Net ratings perhaps remain an emerging science, many companies have stepped forward to do their part. Check out their findings when you want to see what sites are triumphing.

○ *Forrester (www.forrester.com/ER/PowerRankings/0,2141,0,FF.html):* The PowerRankings compete with Gómez's write-ups.

○ *Gómez (www.gomez.com):* Many e-commerce sites are critiqued and ranked by Gómez Advisors.

○ *Internet Traffic Report (www.internettrafficreport.com):* This site measures router volume at various points around the world.

○ *Media Metrix (www.mediametrix.com):* Another take on Web site traffic

○ *NetRatings (www.netratings.com):* Sites are ranked by traffic volume

Search Engines

There's just so much stuff on the Web—how do you find what you need, now? Cut to the chase and use the best-of-breed finding tools on the Internet.

○ *Dogpile (www.dogpile.com):* A meta search tool, Dogpile simultaneously puts your query to more than 10 search engines (from InfoSeek to Google). It's slick, fast and thorough.

○ *Fast Search (www.fastsearch.com):* A first-place search engine; the aim of this Norwegian company is to capture all the Web.

○ *Google (www.google.com):* Tied for best search engine, Google's name is funny, but it's a serious hunting tool. Don't miss the "Cache" feature, where Google stores pages on its servers. If a site is down, the page may still be readable at Google.

○ *Northern Light (www.northernlight.com):* Some of the material is free, some will cost you, but this is fast, intelligent searching.

Shopping Bots

Bots do the work for you. Send a bot—a robot—out on a mission, and it automatically "pings" dozens of sites, meaning it asks for the information you request. For a merchant, bots are a joy because they take all the mystery out of product pricing. Want to know what competitors are charging? Send out a few bots, and they'll tell you.

○ *Bidder's Edge (www.biddersedge.com):* A bot that prowls auctions

○ *BidFind (www.vsn.net/af):* Another auction bot

○ *BotSpot (http://botspot.com/search/s-shop.htm):* An ambitious round-up of pretty much all the bots there are

○ *BottomDollar (www.bottomdollar.com):* An excellent, all-purpose shopping bot

○ *eSmarts (www.esmarts.com):* Another all-purpose shopping bot

○ *mySimon (www.mysimon.com):* A must-see shopping bot

Software For Builders

If you build it, they will come—and this software gets you started. FrontPage remains the industry leader, but it has competitors worth a look.

○ *Adobe PageMill (www.adobe.com/products/pagemill/main.html):* A solid software tool for putting a business on the Web

○ *FrontPage (www.microsoft.com/frontpage):* This is it—the best program for most businesses.

○ *Trellix (www.trellix.com):* Want low-budget? This is the answer. Trellix's software is free, and the resulting pages are top-grade. Templates designed for small business are especially good.

○ *WebExpress (www.mvd.com/webexpress/index.htm):* The David to Microsoft's Goliath. WebExpress is robust, powerful software, and a free trial is available.

○ *Zy (www.zy.com):* Free Web-based tools for creating your own site. Results can be first-rate.

Stats And More

How many computers are there in Greece? What are users' biggest gripes about the Net? Plenty of information is regularly compiled about Net practices; here's the cream of the crop for monitoring developments.

- *e-commerce Times (www.e-commercetimes.com):* More news from the e-tailing front lines
- *eMarketer (www.emarketer.com):* A great news source with an e-commerce focus. Lots of stats.
- *Internetstats (www.internetstats.com):* All kinds of Net-related statistics
- *Nua (www.nua.com):* Nua compiles all the Net-related stats it can find and puts them into a readable format.
- *Yahoo E-commerce (http://smallbusiness.yahoo.com/smallbusiness/ecommerce):* A roundup of key e-commerce links

WEB ART

Want graphical elements to dress up your pages? From bullets to banners, Web art is abundant and usually is free to snag. Look at these resources first.

- *A+ Art (www.aplusart.com):* Lots of freebies are yours here
- *About.com: Clip Art (http://webclipart.about.com/internet/web clipart):* More links than you'll ever need to click are found here
- *Clip Art Searcher (www.webplaces.com/search):* Looking for something specific? This meta search tool will scour the Web in your service.
- *Free Clip Art (www.free-clip-art.to):* Free art and links
- *Task Force Clip Art (www.nvtech.com/index.html):* Images especially aimed at businesses

WEB SITE BUILDING

You still want to know more about building out your e-tailing site? The good news is that you'll find lots of information online, and you'll also be able to easily keep in touch with developments.

- *Builder.com (www.builder.com):* From CNet, Builder.com aims to be a destination for Web site creators. Find news, tools and more here.
- *Web Developer (www.webdeveloper.com):* One-stop shopping for advice and tools for building better Web sites

○ *Webmonkey (http://hotwired.lycos.com/webmonkey/e-business)*: Originally from *Wired* magazine, now a product of Lycos, Webmonkey still does a good job.

○ *ZDNet (www.zdnet.com/ebusiness)*: From the leading publisher of tech magazines, a solid offering of cutting-edge tips and information

WEB SITE TOOLS

From guest books to counters, Web site tools abound, and many sites thrive on handing out freebies to Webmasters. Get your goodies here.

○ *Free Site Tools (www.freesitetools.com)*: A directory of cost-free tools

○ *1 2 3 Webmaster (www.123webmaster.com)*: Links to thousands of tools, from CGI scripts to free banner creation

○ *Webmaster Station (www.exeat.com)*: Sophisticated tools are yours here, including an automatic meta tag generator.

○ *Web Site Resource (www.wsresource.com)*: Still more links to more tools

○ *Yahoo's Credit Card Merchant Services (http://dir.yahoo.com/business_ and_economy/business_to_business/financial_services/transaction_ clearing/credit_card_merchant_services)*: Looking for a company to enable you to take credit cards? Here are hundreds. Hint: Just type "credit card merchant services" into Yahoo, instead of this long link.

WIRELESS WEB

This is it: the new frontier, the next horizon for e-commerce. Already you can buy stuff—books, stock, flowers—with a few clicks on your cell phone. Watch this space because the most exciting (read: profitable) Web innovations will be in the wireless arena.

○ *Hoiley (www.hoiley.com/dl.htm)*: A free tool for creating WAP-compliant sites

○ *The Independent WAP/WML FAQ (http://wap.colorline.no/ wap-faq)*: WML (wireless markup language) is the HTML of the wireless space, while WAP (wireless application protocol) is a set of specs for wireless programs. This FAQ covers the guts inside wireless.

○ *TagTag (www.inetis.com/english/solutions_tagtag.htm)*: Want to make your Web site wireless Web-ready? TagTag is a free tool that will help you do it.

○ *WAP Forum (www.wapforum.org)*: As WAP emerges as a wireless standard, this organization gains in clout.

○ *Waply (www.waply.com)*: A directory of wireless Web sites— see who's there first!

THE WORLD OF PRINT

The traditional business magazines mainly were caught flatfooted when the Web exploded and still are playing catch-up (and newspapers, really, have never quite awakened). Shrewder, more timely coverage mainly is found in newer magazines.

○ *Business 2.0 (www.business2.com)*: A monthly look at the forces and players shaping the new economy

○ *Entrepreneur (www.entrepreneur.com)*: From the folks who published this book. There's continuing coverage of, and opinions on, e-tailing.

○ *The Industry Standard (www.thestandard.com)*: The weekly news magazine for the new economy. A must-read.

○ *Red Herring (www.redherring.com)*: Business technology reporting with attitude

○ *Upside (www.upside.com)*: Lively reporting on the world of tech business. Lots of attitude.

CHAPTER 39

e-Commerce: A Look Into The [Future]

Where is e-commerce heading? Tough topic, but to get insights into the future, I asked Boston University e-commerce professor Bruce Weinberg for his thoughts. A writer and thinker about the Net—whose Web site, EcommerceAndMarketing.com, is a rich resource—Weinberg is both a tough critic of present-day e-tailing and a bona fide optimist about the role of e-commerce in tomorrow's retailing mix. You may not always agree with the opinionated Weinberg, but his thoughts are well worth pondering.

Robert McGarvey: *What's the best e-tailing site on the Web?*

Bruce Weinberg: It doesn't exist yet because no one has created it. The best online retail site will:

- ○ allow me to place an order via the Internet faster than I can via the telephone;

- ○ clearly describe a product so that I know exactly what I am considering (check out a camera review at www.steves-digicams. com, and you will see an example of a site that leaves little to the imagination in describing a camera);

- ○ really understand me through communications and sincere interest, not think it understands me based on my click streams [a record of a user's mouse clicks];

- ○ provide full and accurate information upfront about what is being offered (don't make me go through the checkout process to find out whether an item is in stock or to find out the full cost of my order including sales tax and shipping); and

○ deliver the next day when I pay for next-day service. Next-day service should mean the product will be in my hands the next day; it should not mean that the product will arrive on the next day after it is shipped.

McGarvey: *Do you have a personal favorite Web site?*

Weinberg: My favorite on-line retail site is Kozmo.com. It has many everyday items that I need (e.g., ruby earrings, milk, Palm Vs, sandwiches, magazines, candy bars, soda and diapers), and Kozmo delivers quickly. In some instances, the time that it takes Kozmo to get to my house with an order is less than the time it would take for me to go to a store and get the items myself. Kozmo performs a task better than the status quo, and its price for this service is reasonable, so that I judge it to have great value. By the way, I am delighted to see that its product prices are comparable to or perhaps a tad higher than those of similar items for sale in a convenience store, as it suggests that Kozmo wants to stick around for the long haul—which will benefit me as well.

> **Next-day** service should **mean** the product will be in my **hands** the **next** day; it should **not** mean that the product will **arrive** on the next day **after** it is shipped.

McGarvey: *What's wrong with all (or virtually all) e-commerce sites today?*

Weinberg: They are doing everything in their power to be loved without expecting enough love in return. That is not healthy, and it either shows insecurity or a lack of discipline and faith in customers. Offering products below cost on a regular basis, all else being equal, will certainly generate interest and happy customers. I believe history will show 1999-2000 to be one of the greatest times to be a consumer because so many items were available for sale either at or below wholesale cost. But doing business in this way will put a retailer out of business.

In the short run, from a consumer perspective, there is no problem with below-cost pricing. Well, guess what? Companies that are not profitable in the long run cease to exist. This could be a problem to consumers who have come to enjoy and value a particular service offering.

McGarvey: *Why are the B2C e-commerce sites dying?*

Weinberg: I am convinced that important B2C services will thrive; B2C is not dead. We have seen, however, a large number of people who wanted to make quick, easy money with little effort. The most popular techniques have been using smoke and mirrors or playing on people's dreams (akin to what some channelers do to those who want to speak to the spirits of their deceased ancestors). Some people have been able to cash out nicely and have played the game well. Alas, the results suggest that many of the firms created by these people have been found out in that their value proposition to customers is weak. As a result, many firms are in the middle of a death dance.

Another reason for B2C failures at this time is that many of the folks with good intentions did not adequately understand how to take a great idea and "make it happen." There is a long history of entrepreneurs developing greater mousetraps that did not result in everyone beating a path to their door.

McGarvey: *What niches have yet to be fully attacked by e-tailers?*

Weinberg: My understanding is that luxury goods are not selling well online. I have a solution that could increase the sale of luxury goods. Some consumers shop inside a luxury store for the perceived esteem and prestige associated with an exclusive brand. These consumers love to be seen inside these stores; they love being seen as they walk out of these stores; and they love being seen carrying a shopping bag from these stores. Shopping online does not allow for any of these beloved activities.

A successful solution would provide, at a minimum, the very same benefits derived from these consumer behaviors. How can this be done? My proposal is to deliver luxury goods to a household in a chauffeur-driven luxury car at a time when all of the neighbors can see the delivery occur. If desired, the customer can be taken on a 10-to-15-minute drive around the neighborhood or town as he/she inspects the purchase or asks questions about it.

Another major problem that is receiving little attention: In a number of situations, the major delivery providers (e.g., UPS, FedEx) will not leave a package in an unattended and potentially unsecured environment (e.g., an apartment vestibule) should a package recipient not be home at the time of delivery. In these situations, the delivery provider will either leave a notice that another delivery attempt will occur during the traditional workday hours, provide a release form so that the recipient can authorize the packages to be dropped on another day in the unattended environment, or invite the recipient to collect the package at a delivery center. The bottom line is that situations like this not only nullify the benefits of home delivery, but also create additional burdens for the online consumer.

Some consumers have partially solved this problem by requesting delivery to their work address, where someone will be able to receive a package. This works, but some firms are getting overwhelmed by this type of delivery and are requesting that employees cease this behavior.

Opportunity Knocks

Where does Kozmo excel? It's a master of "the last mile," as e-commerce gurus call it, and that's the path leading up to a customer's home or office. Big dollars will be made by anybody who can figure out low-cost ways to master the last mile, and Kozmo's solution won't be the only one. Do you see other ways to effectively get goods in consumers' hands?

An obvious solution comes to mind. A system for "after work" delivery would do the trick. I envision a local service provider who can take these packages on the "last mile." UPS, FedEx and USPS may not want to engage in this directly, though it may be critical that, for economic reasons, they partner with the provider of this service.

One firm positioned to potentially provide this service right now is Kozmo.com. As they could ostensibly leverage their competitive advantage of fast delivery, this could make perfect economic sense for Kozmo, major "daytime" delivery providers, online retailers, and consumers.

McGarvey: *What will the next-generation sites offer that today's sites don't?*

Weinberg: Speed, fidelity (e.g., speech recognition, the ability to feel items), and ease of use.

McGarvey: *Why haven't B&M retailers "gotten" the Web? Will they?*

Weinberg: The answer is pretty simple and age-old. They do not get it because they do not choose to use it or embrace it. I believe that most people realize success because they get immersed in their passions and work their tails off. If bricks-and-mortar retailers want to get it, then they need to get everyone in their company online, using the Internet and shopping online.

McGarvey: *What are two bad e-commerce sites? Why?*

Weinberg: Pick any two that make your blood boil or bring out frustration. The most common causes are grounded in content (e.g., limited product information, limited product availability) or functionality (e.g., navigation, checkout, customer service). A high-profile site that bothers me is Home Depot's (www.homedepot.com). I cannot buy anything online from the Home Depot. That ticks me off. Home Depot offers delivery from local stores, so why not coordinate this service with online ordering? Rumor has it that they are soon going to sell online. I hope so, as I need mass quantities of mulch, fertilizer and grass seed very soon.

McGarvey: *Does a business have to be on the Web in 2000? What kinds of businesses don't have to be?*

Weinberg: The Internet and the Web are about communicating with others and being part of a shared network. A business does not have to be on the Web in 2000 or in any other year. Similarly, people need not use the words "please" and "thank you."

McGarvey: *Why all the hype over B2B e-commerce sites?*

Weinberg: First, it was unmined terrain. Second, the revenue forecasts for commerce in this context are exhilarating for many. Third, the venture capitalists started pouring their money into it. Fourth, a number of high-profile firms announced intentions to transform industries through B2B ventures. Fifth, the collection of these points makes for interest from the media, and they report on these activities. Sixth, the "tipping point" is reached and a full-

Beware! Never count out B&M retailers. They may be dumb, but they aren't dead. And they do have money, domain experience and deep supplier relations. When a B&M decides to make a move into a space, it can cause real pain to other e-tailers, so always assume that tomorrow you will be competing against them. And know how you will prevail!

blown feeding frenzy is born. If you seek only one reason for the hype, then on your keyboard, press the shift key with one finger and the key with "4" on it with another finger; repeat this several times. Many firms have a love for money.

I foresee a better model evolving. Perhaps it has already raised its head in The Valley [Silicon Valley], Alley [Manhattan, aka Silicon Alley, where many Web sites are launching], or some other digital hot spot. Watch for B4C4B—my term to express a network that engages both businesses and consumers in an enterprise where each party is encouraged to participate and share in the power and benefit of collaboration.

Smart Tip

No, you don't have to be on the Web, but if you've read this far, odds are high that either you are or you soon will be. But if you still decide not to go online— well, good luck because you will need it to compete in an age where more consumers routinely look to the Net for the shopping information they need.

McGarvey: *What's fundamentally ailed the prevailing B2C Web site business models?*

Weinberg: I see a few thousand problems. Here are two:

○ Great ideas are wonderful things. They stimulate other great ideas. A great idea, however, is not enough for building a sustainable enterprise.

○ Web sites lack personality; they can be sterile. Let's see some faces or caricatures on these sites. Provide cues that bring out human affect—we humans like emotion.

McGarvey: *Is Kozmo a look into a Web future?*

Weinberg: The concept acted out by Kozmo is brilliant. I loved it the second I became aware of it, and I used Kozmo soon after they launched in Boston. Here is what got my juices flowing about Kozmo. So many consumers were complaining about the time delay between placing an online order and receiving the products from an order. Kozmo not only removes that objection to online shopping, as they typically deliver an order within 90 minutes after it has been placed, but also provides a process that is superior to bricks shopping in many cases.

Kozmo is going to own that "last mile" and develop a per-

Wireless Wonders   Click

In "The Graduate", the future revolved around plastics, or so the young grad was told. Today, the future definitely revolves around wireless technologies. Find your niche in wireless, and you are on a very fast track to success. "The opportunities today in wireless are much, much bigger than what I saw in the computer business back in 1983," says Phillipe Kahn, CEO of Lightsurf, a Santa Cruz, California, company focused on image products for the wireless Web. "Today's opportunities are 10-fold greater."

When Kahn says this, it's a meaningful mouthful. Back in '83, Kahn was a pioneering software developer who quickly created a couple of hits—SideKick and TurboPascal—and thereby snagged an enduring place in tech history. But, he says, the possibilities in front of the rugged pioneers who are today defining the wireless information landscape are vastly richer than what he saw in 1983, for a very simple reason: "The numbers were so much smaller back then," says Kahn, who recently sold his TrueSynch technology—for synching data between devices such as a cell phone and a computer—to cell phone giant Motorola (for an undisclosed amount). In the early '80s, PC users were sparse, and that meant the market upside was fundamentally tiny. But nowadays, explains Kahn, the potential audience for wireless Web products and services is already in the tens of millions of users. "Today's landscape is explosive," he adds.

Again, the numbers have it: The wireless Web soon will be in more hands than the conventional Web is. That seems incredible? In 2003, shipment of wireless-Web-ready smart phones will hit a stunning 350 million units, predicts Datacomm Research, a consulting firm. Factor in access via different kinds of devices—Internet appliances, wireless computers, and more—and the numbers of potential wireless Web users just

Continued on next page

Continued from previous page

> keep mushrooming. You can tap into this. Don't stop thinking until you've found six ways—then get busy implementing the best. Wireless is a wave that hasn't crested yet, but when it hits, early in the 21st century, it will be a monster.

sonal relationship with its customers; they will be physically face to face with customers on a regular basis and will be able to "speak with and listen to" them. Perhaps this will prove to be more powerful than analyzing click streams. I see many online retailers partnering with or using Kozmo to improve their service and, ultimately, customer value. Why do you suppose that Amazon.com invested $60 million in Kozmo? To me, it's not that hard to figure out.

McGarvey: *Is Jeff Bezos the smartest e-tailer around? Why or why not?*

Weinberg: This appears to be the consensus. He is on every top e-list in existence. You can fool some of the people some of the time, but you can't fool all of the people all of the time. I've never met him, so my perceptions are based on my understanding of him through the media. Amazon continues to be miles ahead of all other online retailers. I believe that he is extremely passionate about his life pursuits, and as long as he keeps at it, he will remain a step ahead of everyone else.

McGarvey: *Is anybody safe from Amazon as Bezos extends his retailing empire into more new categories?*

Opportunity Knocks

Remember: Amazon offers many ways for you to gain success by helping it get more successful. There are auctions, the low-cost zShops—instant storefronts with fixed pricing—and, of course, the slick Amazon affiliates program. By all means, Jeff Bezos wants to be the top dog on the Net, but he is shrewd enough to see that your success can forward his goals. So do as Bruce Weinberg suggests, and find ways to help yourself while helping Amazon.

Weinberg: Amazon can flow on and on. I love its model of involving everyone and helping them get a piece of the pie (e.g., zShops, affiliates). The Internet is partly about creating connections, sharing information, helping people identify their passion, helping people realize their dreams, getting people involved and using their brainpower and voice, and being fair. I believe that Amazon does most of this reasonably well. Ask not what Amazon.com can do for you, but what you can do for Amazon.

Smart Tip

Sine qua non— without which none. It's Latin, but for many Web e-tailers, trust has been Greek to them. They don't understand it and don't understand that, without trust, customers won't shop at their sites. Earn your customers' trust, and you will do fine.

McGarvey: *If e-commerce is different in 2001, how will it be? How will it be the same?*

Weinberg: Here are the highlights:

- ○ Fulfillment will still be highly labor-intensive.
- ○ Consumers will develop loyalties, and trust will emerge as the *sine qua non* for success in e-commerce.
- ○ There will be instantaneity.
- ○ Advocates will play a major role in helping consumers band together, leverage their power and maintain their privacy.
- ○ Think back to the 1969 movie "The Graduate," and say the word "Wireless (see "Wireless Wonders" on page 263)."

GLOSSARY

Angel: someone who invests his or her own money in a start-up

Banner: a graphic image used on a Web site as an advertisement; the information superhighway's version of billboards

Beta site: a test site, usually erected in the authoring phase of a Web site

Bot: a robot, or program, that automatically does specified tasks

Bricks and mortar (B&M): a term describing traditional businesses made of bricks and mortar rather than the bytes of cyber businesses

Business to business (B2B): companies that seek business, not consumers, as customers

Business to consumer (B2C): companies that market to consumers

Common Gateway Interface (CGI) script: a simple program that runs on the Net; guest books, for instance, often are CGI scripts

Clip art: off-the-shelf images anyone can use; Web site authoring programs usually include lots of clip art

Cookie: data created by a Web server that's stored on a user's computer to identify that user on return visits to the Web site

Domain: domain is what comes before the "com" or "net" or "edu," all of which are known as top-level domains; for example, McGarvey.net is the name of the author's Internet domain

File transfer protocol (FTP): the system used to transfer files over the Net; you FTP files to your Web host

First-mover advantage: the built-in advantage of being the first business in a particular category

Host: a company that provides space for storing ("hosting") a Web site

Hyperlink: a connection between one object and another; also known as a link. On a Web page, the line "www.mcgarvey. net" is a hyperlink that takes users to the author's Web page.

Hypertext markup language (HTML): a code that creates Web pages

Internet service provider (ISP): the company that provides a telephone connection that lets a user connect to the Net. AOL is the leading ISP.

Link: also known as a *Hyperlink*

Log: a record of all visits to a Web site; a log usually gives a click-by-click report on a visitor

Look-to-buy ratio: a common metric (or measurement) used in analyzing the effectiveness of an e-tailer. Ideal would be 1 to 1—one looker produces one buyer. Most e-tailers are happy with look-to-buy ratios well under 10 to 1.

Meta tag: an HTML expression that defines a Web site's content, to be read by search engines and crawlers

Mind share: consumer awareness and loyalty

Newsgroup: an Internet message board, or bulletin board

Ping (Packet Internet Groper): a Net utility that tests Web sites

Portal: a Web "supersite" that offers links to substantial amounts of information and often to other sites; Yahoo is the premiere portal

Search engine: Web sites that exist to help users find other Web sites; Google (www.google.com) is one of the best search engines

Spam: unwanted, unsolicited commercial e-mail

Spider: spiders (also known as crawlers) search the Web for information; search engines use spiders to find Web pages

Template: a predesigned document; a Web page template, for instance, requires the user simply to fill in some blanks to produce a publishable document

Term sheet commitment: a written offer from a venture capitalist that sets out how much money the firm will put into a start-up in return for what percentage of ownership

URL: universal resource locator, or, more simply, a Web page's address

Venture capitalist (VC): a professional lender of money—often raised from university endowment funds—who seeks out high-potential tech start-ups to fund

Webmaster: a person skilled in creating and maintaining Web pages

Wireless application protocol (WAP): the standard underlying programs that run on cell phones

Wireless markup language (WML): the underlying computer code that produces pages that display on the wireless Web

Wizard: a help tool (usually in step-by-step format) that steers the user through to completion of a task

WYSIWYG (What you see is what you get): when the computer screen reproduces what the final output will be (for a printed page or a Web page)

INDEX

I

J

K

L

M

N

About The Author

Robert McGarvey has covered the Web since 1994—just about forever in Internet years. He first went online in 1987 with Genie, then migrated through CompuServe and Prodigy before hitting on AOL, where he stayed.

McGarvey traces his involvement with computers back to 1983 when an insolvent client offered to satisfy a debt by giving him a personal computer. At the time, he would have preferred the money, but he quickly fell in love with PCs and has been using them and writing about them much ever since.

Perhaps unsurprisingly, he remembers his first e-commerce purchase—an online buy of Mother's Day flowers in 1994. It was so fast, so easy, he knew he had seen the start of something.

When he isn't playing with computers, Robert has kept busy writing magazine articles—he has no idea how many, but it's more than 1,000—for dozens of magazines, from *Reader's Digest* and *American Legion* to *Playboy*, *Selling Power*, and *Islands*. His columns appear in *Entrepreneur* magazine, HomeOfficeMag.com, Entrepreneur's *Start-Ups*, Corel's *Office Community*, and FreeAgent.com.

Find out more by visiting his Web site, www.mcgarvey.net.

Current titles from Entrepreneur Press:

Benjamin Franklin's 12 Rules Of Management:
The Founding Father of American Business Solves Your Toughest Problems

Business Plans Made Easy:
It's Not as Hard as You Think

Creative Selling:
Boost Your B2B Sales

Extreme Investor:
Intelligent Information From The Edge

Financial Fitness in 45 Days:
The Complete Guide to Shaping Up Your Finances

Gen E:
Generation Entrepreneur is Rewriting the Rules of Business—And You Can, Too!

Get Smart:
365 Tips to Boost Your Entrepreneurial IQ

How to be a Teenage Millionaire:
Start Your Own Business, Make Your Own Money and Run Your Own Life

Knock-Out Marketing:
Powerful Strategies to Punch Up Your Sales

Radicals & Visionaries:
Entrepreneurs Who Revolutionized the 20th Century

Start Your Own Business:
The Only Start-up Book You'll Ever Need

Success for Less:
100 Low-Cost Businesses You Can Start Today

303 Marketing Tips
Guaranteed to Boost Your Business

Where's The Money?
Sure-Fire Financial Solutions for Your Small Business

Young Millionaires:
Inspiring Stories to Ignite Your Entrepreneurial Dreams

Help ensure your success with this easy-to-understand guide.

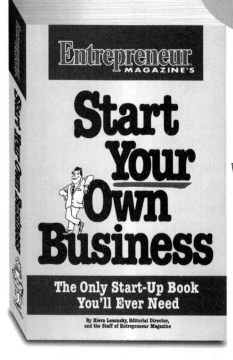

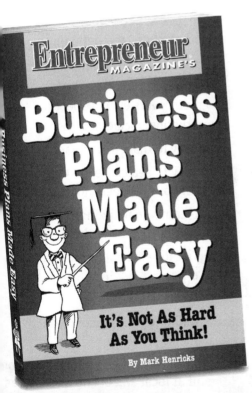

Discover the Secrets of Today's Brightest Entrepreneurs

Proven techniques, tips and advice from such innovative entrepreneurs as...

Dan Dye, 39
Mark Beckloff, 34
THREE DOG BAKERY
Upscale Bakery for Dogs
Founded: 1990

Dave Kapell, 36
MAGNETIC POETRY
Make Your Own Poetry Kits
Founded: 1993

Dineh Mohajer, 26
HARD CANDY
Cosmetics With an Attitude
Founded: 1995

Entrepreneur MAGAZINE'S

Young Millionaires

*Inspiring Stories To Ignite
Your Entrepreneurial Dreams*

By Rieva Lesonsky,
Editorial Director, Entrepreneur Magazine,
and Gayle Sato Stodder

Learn How Nearly 100 Young Entrepreneurs Started Their Own Million-Dollar Businesses... and How You Can Too!

In this entertaining collection of profiles, nearly 100 of today's brightest entrepreneurs share with you the secrets of their success.

Through the inspirational stories of their extraordinary achievements, you'll find out how they got started, how much it cost and what challenges they had to overcome. You'll also learn winning strategies, insider tips and proven techniques you can use to start your own million-dollar business.

But most important, you'll discover that even if you make a million mistakes, or are not entirely prepared, with hard work and determination you, too, can become a young millionaire!